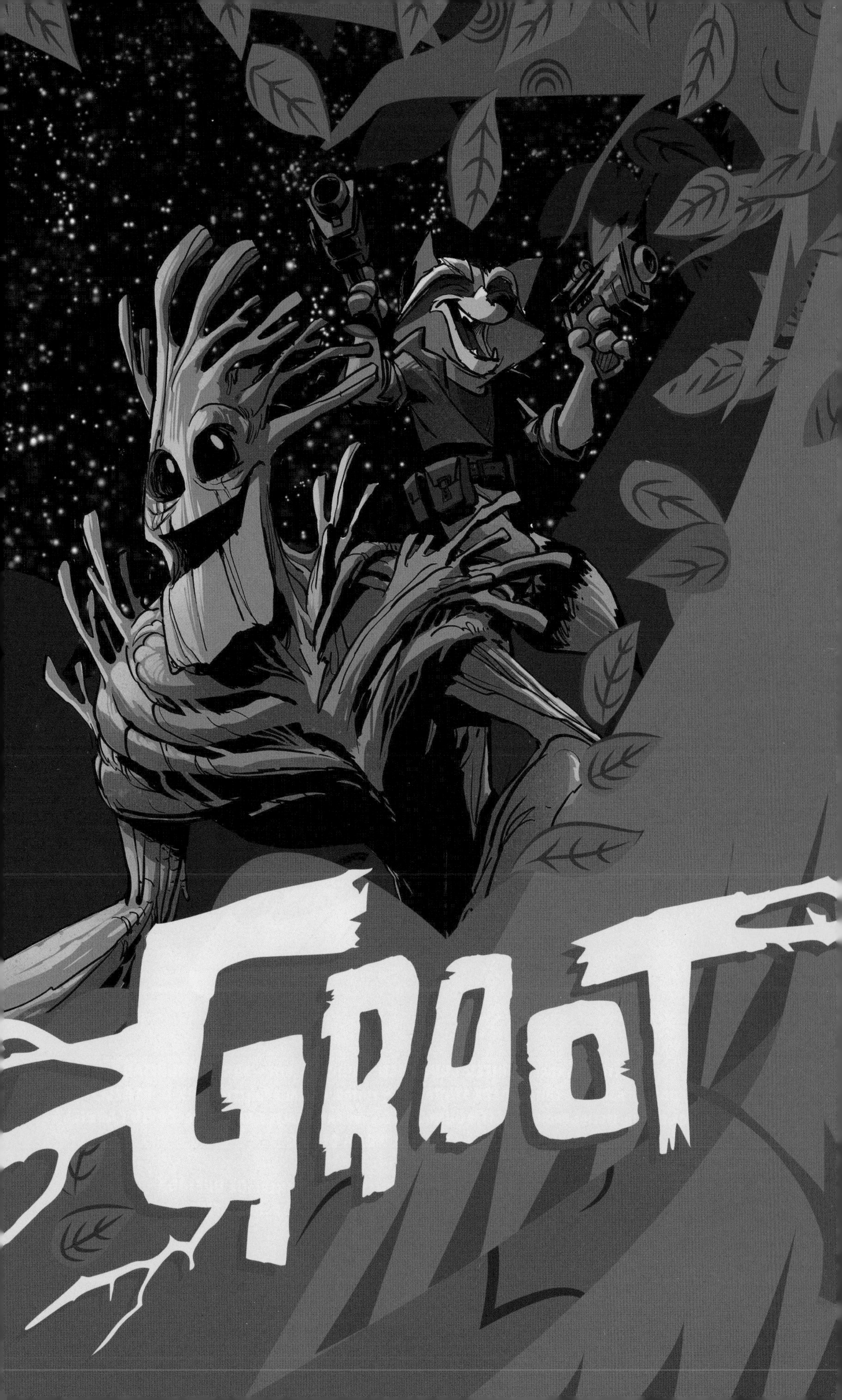
GROOT

COLLECTION EDITOR: **JENNIFER GRÜNWALD** • ASSISTANT EDITOR: **SARAH BRUNSTAD**
ASSOCIATE MANAGING EDITOR: **ALEX STARBUCK** • EDITOR, SPECIAL PROJECTS: **MARK D. BEAZLEY**
SENIOR EDITOR, SPECIAL PROJECTS: **JEFF YOUNGQUIST** • SVP PRINT, SALES & MARKETING: **DAVID GABRIEL**
BOOK DESIGNER: **ADAM DEL RE**

EDITOR IN CHIEF: **AXEL ALONSO** • CHIEF CREATIVE OFFICER: **JOE QUESADA**
PUBLISHER: **DAN BUCKLEY** • EXECUTIVE PRODUCER: **ALAN FINE**

GROOT. Contains material originally published in magazine form as GROOT #1-6. First printing 2016. ISBN# 978-0-7851-9552-8. Published by MARVEL WORLDWIDE, INC., a subsidiary of MARVEL ENTERTAINMENT, LLC. OFFICE OF PUBLICATION: 135 West 50th Street, New York, NY 10020. Copyright © 2016 MARVEL No similarity between any of the names, characters, persons, and/or institutions in this magazine with those of any living or dead person or institution is intended, and any such similarity which may exist is purely coincidental. **Printed in the U.S.A.** ALAN FINE, President, Marvel Entertainment; DAN BUCKLEY, President, TV, Publishing and Brand Management; JOE QUESADA, Chief Creative Officer; TOM BREVOORT, SVP of Publishing; DAVID BOGART, SVP of Operations & Procurement, Publishing; C.B. CEBULSKI, VP of International Development & Brand Management; DAVID GABRIEL, SVP Print, Sales & Marketing; JIM O'KEEFE, VP of Operations & Logistics; DAN CARR, Executive Director of Publishing Technology; SUSAN CRESPI, Editorial Operations Manager; ALEX MORALES, Publishing Operations Manager; STAN LEE, Chairman Emeritus. For information regarding advertising in Marvel Comics or on Marvel.com, please contact Jonathan Rheingold. VP of Custom Solutions & Ad Sales, at jrheingold@marvel.com. For Marvel subscription inquiries, please call 800-217-9158. **Manufactured between 12/4/2015 and 1/11/2016 by R.R. DONNELLEY, INC., SALEM, VA, USA.**

10 9 8 7 6 5 4 3 2 1

GROOT

JEFF LOVENESS
WRITER

BRIAN KESINGER
ARTIST

BRIAN KESINGER (#1-2, #4 & #6) &
VERO GANDINI (#3 & #5)
COLOR ARTISTS

JEFF ECKLEBERRY
LETTERER

DECLAN SHALVEY & JORDIE BELLAIRE
COVER ART

DEVIN LEWIS
EDITOR

SANA AMANAT
SUPERVISING EDITOR

NICK LOWE
SENIOR EDITOR

GROOT CREATED BY STAN LEE, LARRY LIEBER & JACK KIRBY

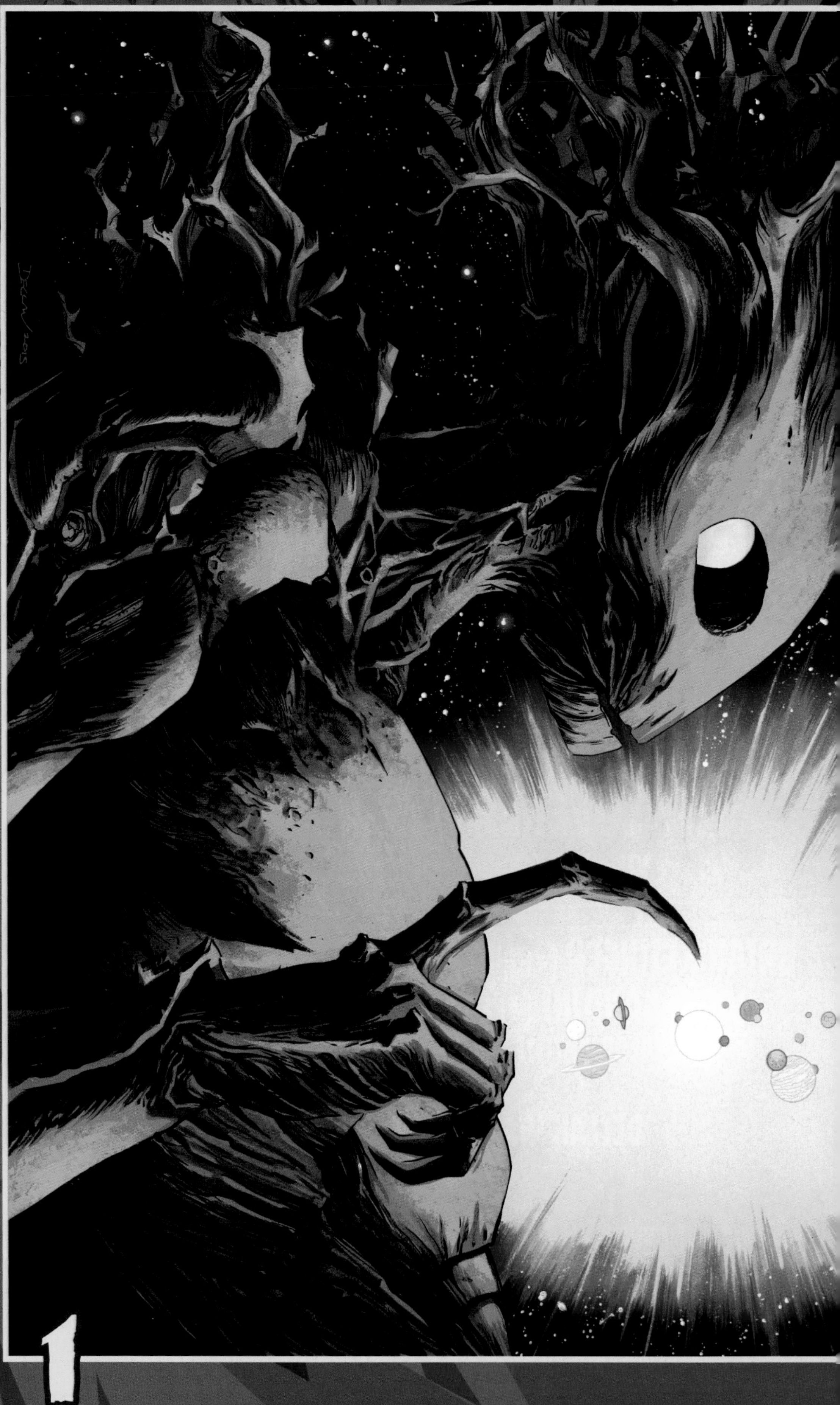

1

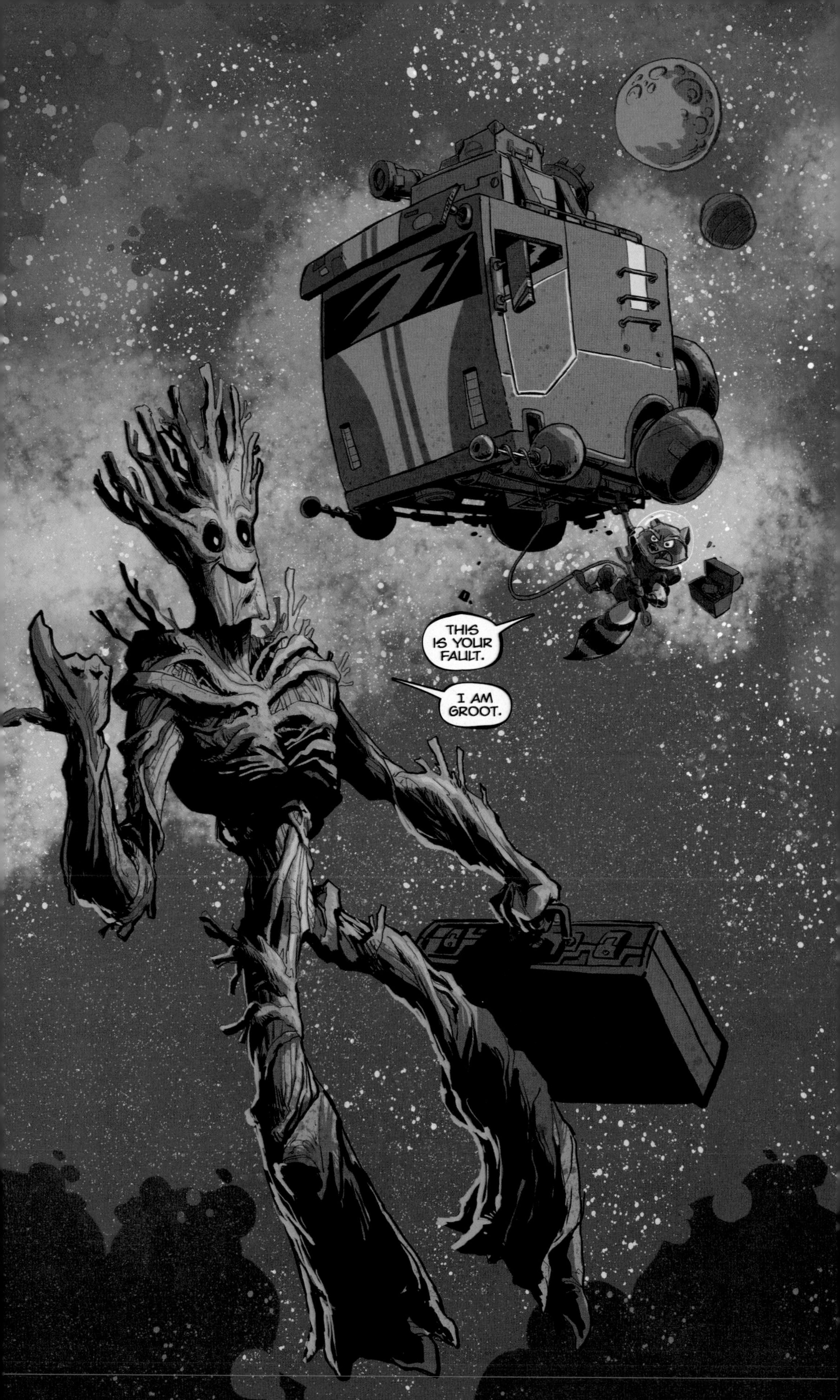
THIS IS YOUR FAULT.
I AM GROOT.

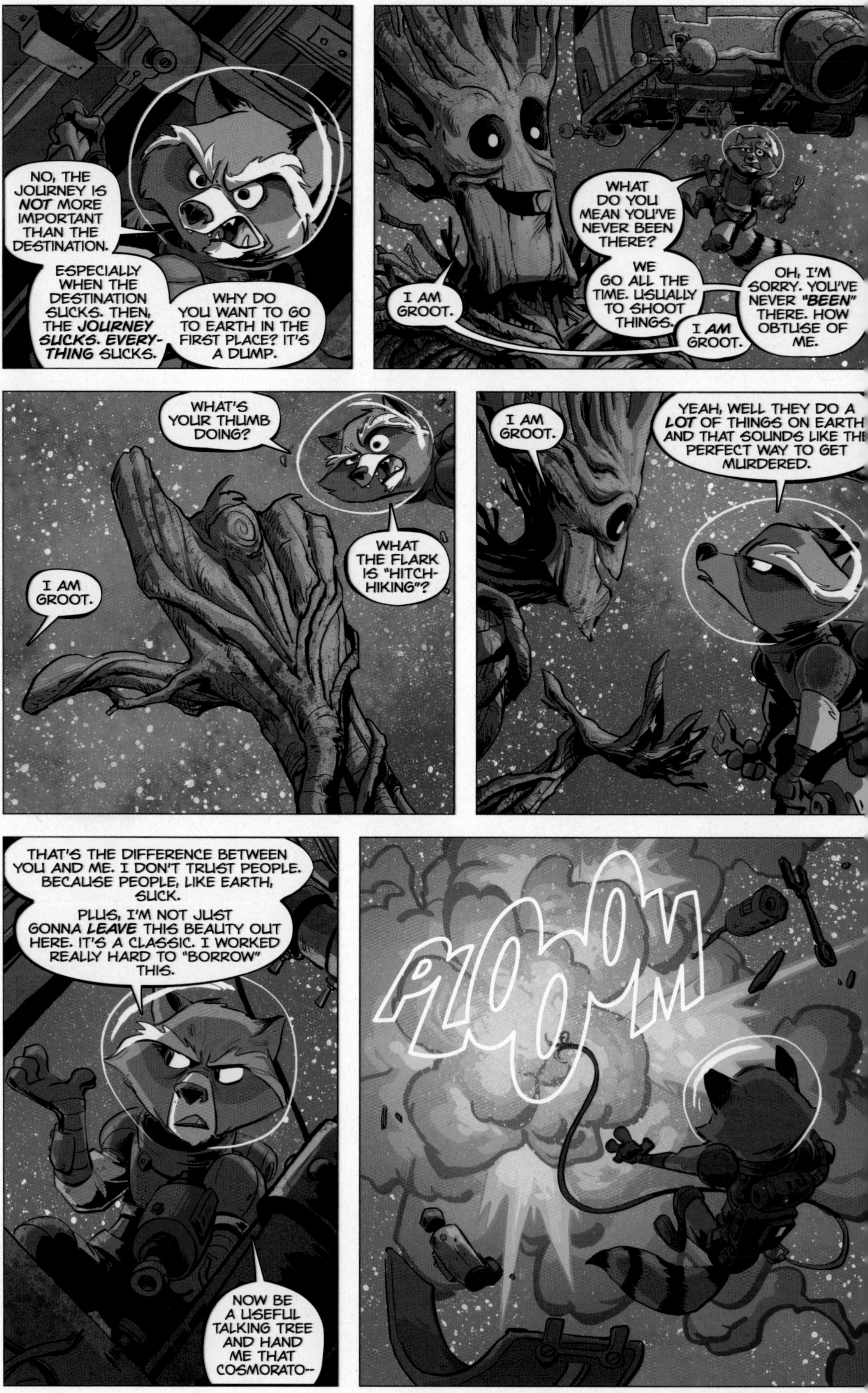
NO, THE JOURNEY IS NOT MORE IMPORTANT THAN THE DESTINATION.
ESPECIALLY WHEN THE DESTINATION SUCKS. THEN, THE JOURNEY SUCKS. EVERYTHING SUCKS.
WHY DO YOU WANT TO GO TO EARTH IN THE FIRST PLACE? IT'S A DUMP.
I AM GROOT.
WHAT DO YOU MEAN YOU'VE NEVER BEEN THERE?
WE GO ALL THE TIME. USUALLY TO SHOOT THINGS.
I AM GROOT.
OH, I'M SORRY. YOU'VE NEVER "BEEN" THERE. HOW OBTUSE OF ME.
WHAT'S YOUR THUMB DOING?
I AM GROOT.
WHAT THE FLARK IS "HITCH-HIKING"?
I AM GROOT.
YEAH, WELL THEY DO A LOT OF THINGS ON EARTH AND THAT SOUNDS LIKE THE PERFECT WAY TO GET MURDERED.
THAT'S THE DIFFERENCE BETWEEN YOU AND ME. I DON'T TRUST PEOPLE. BECAUSE PEOPLE, LIKE EARTH, SUCK.
PLUS, I'M NOT JUST GONNA LEAVE THIS BEAUTY OUT HERE. IT'S A CLASSIC. I WORKED REALLY HARD TO "BORROW" THIS.
NOW BE A USEFUL TALKING TREE AND HAND ME THAT COSMORATO--
PLOOOOM

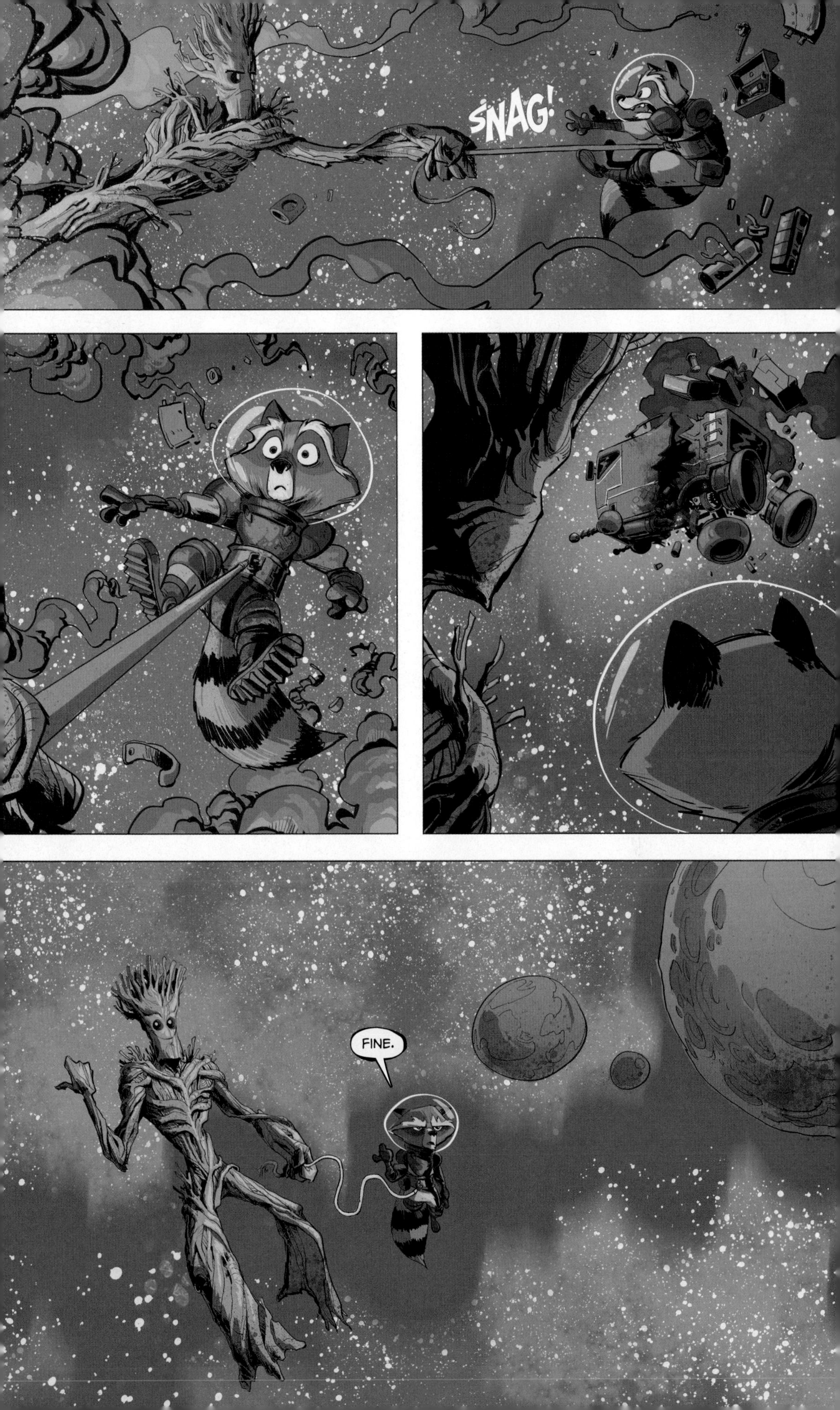
SNAG!
FINE.

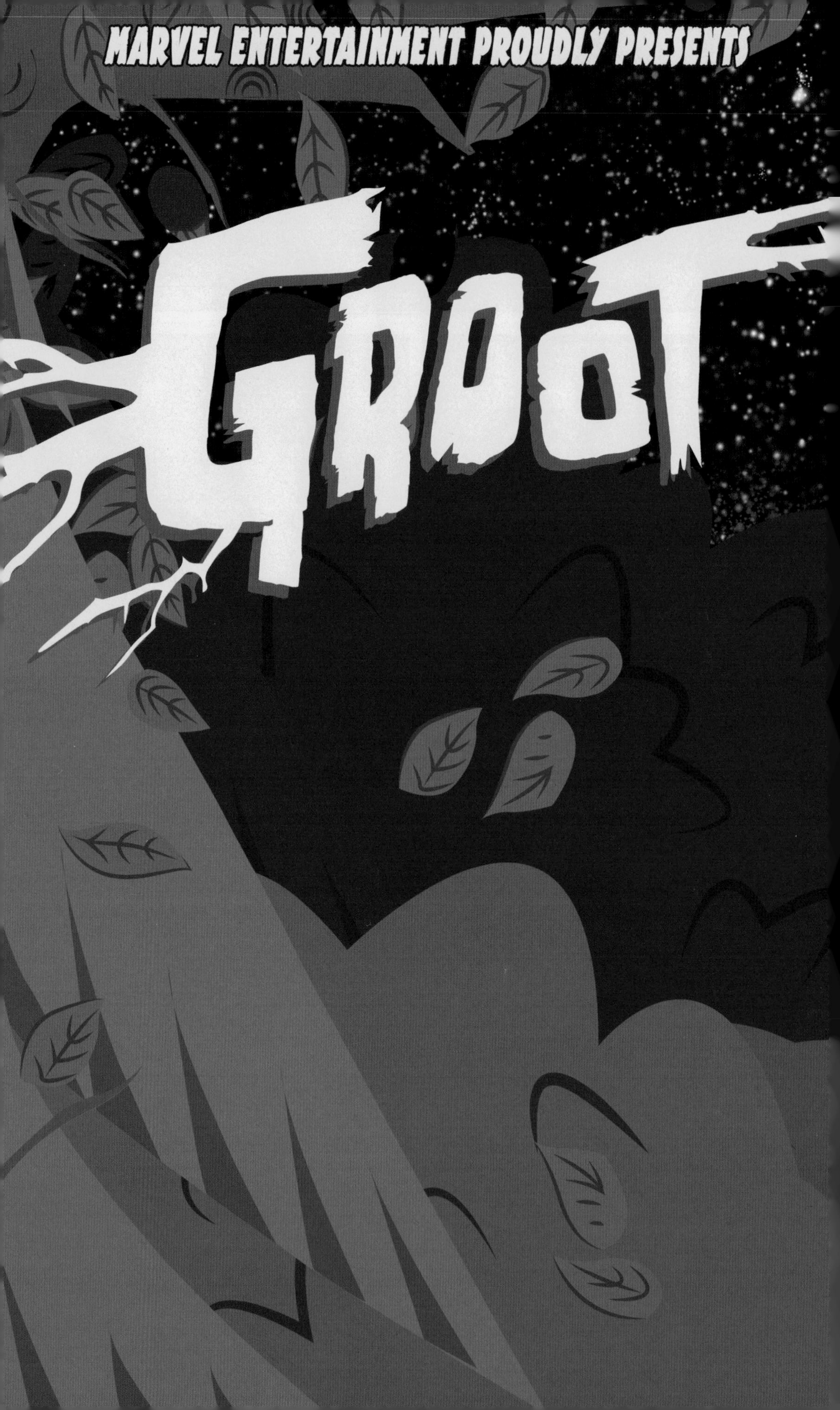
MARVEL ENTERTAINMENT PROUDLY PRESENTS
GROOT

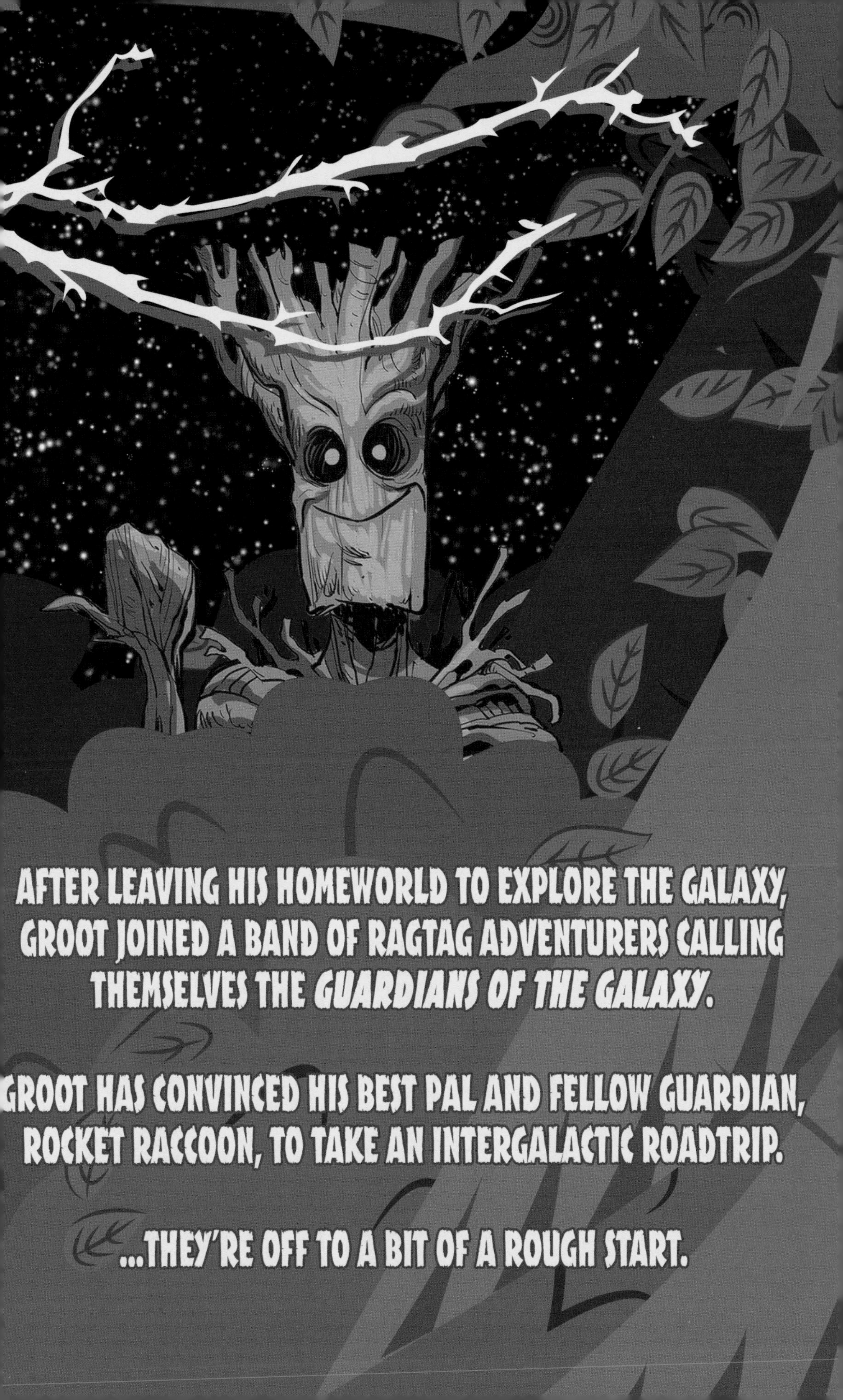
AFTER LEAVING HIS HOMEWORLD TO EXPLORE THE GALAXY, GROOT JOINED A BAND OF RAGTAG ADVENTURERS CALLING THEMSELVES THE *GUARDIANS OF THE GALAXY*.
GROOT HAS CONVINCED HIS BEST PAL AND FELLOW GUARDIAN, ROCKET RACCOON, TO TAKE AN INTERGALACTIC ROADTRIP.
...THEY'RE OFF TO A BIT OF A ROUGH START.

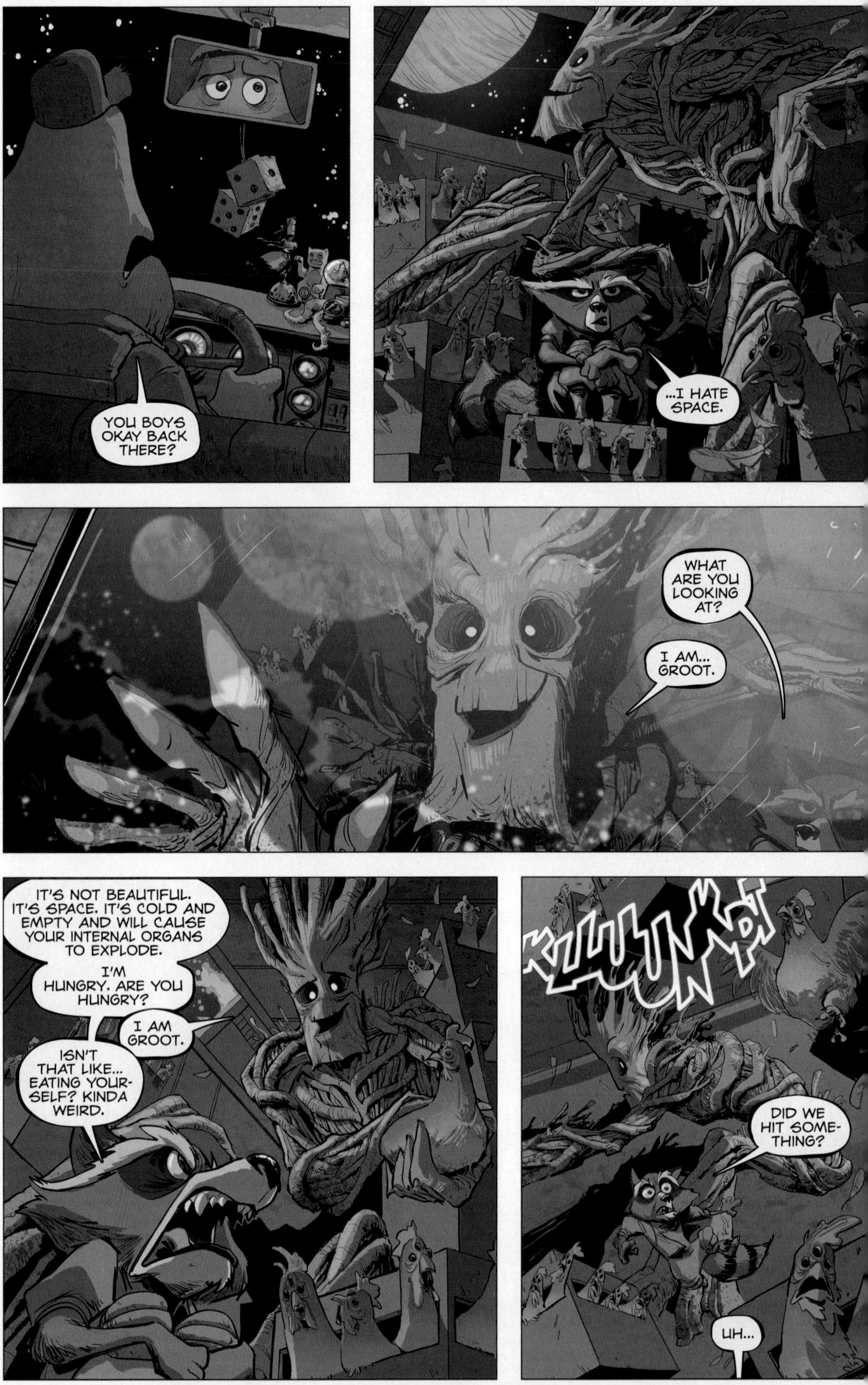
YOU BOYS OKAY BACK THERE?
...I HATE SPACE.
WHAT ARE YOU LOOKING AT?
I AM... GROOT.
IT'S NOT BEAUTIFUL. IT'S SPACE. IT'S COLD AND EMPTY AND WILL CAUSE YOUR INTERNAL ORGANS TO EXPLODE.
I'M HUNGRY. ARE YOU HUNGRY?
I AM GROOT.
ISN'T THAT LIKE... EATING YOURSELF? KINDA WEIRD.
KUUUNKD!
DID WE HIT SOMETHING?
UH...

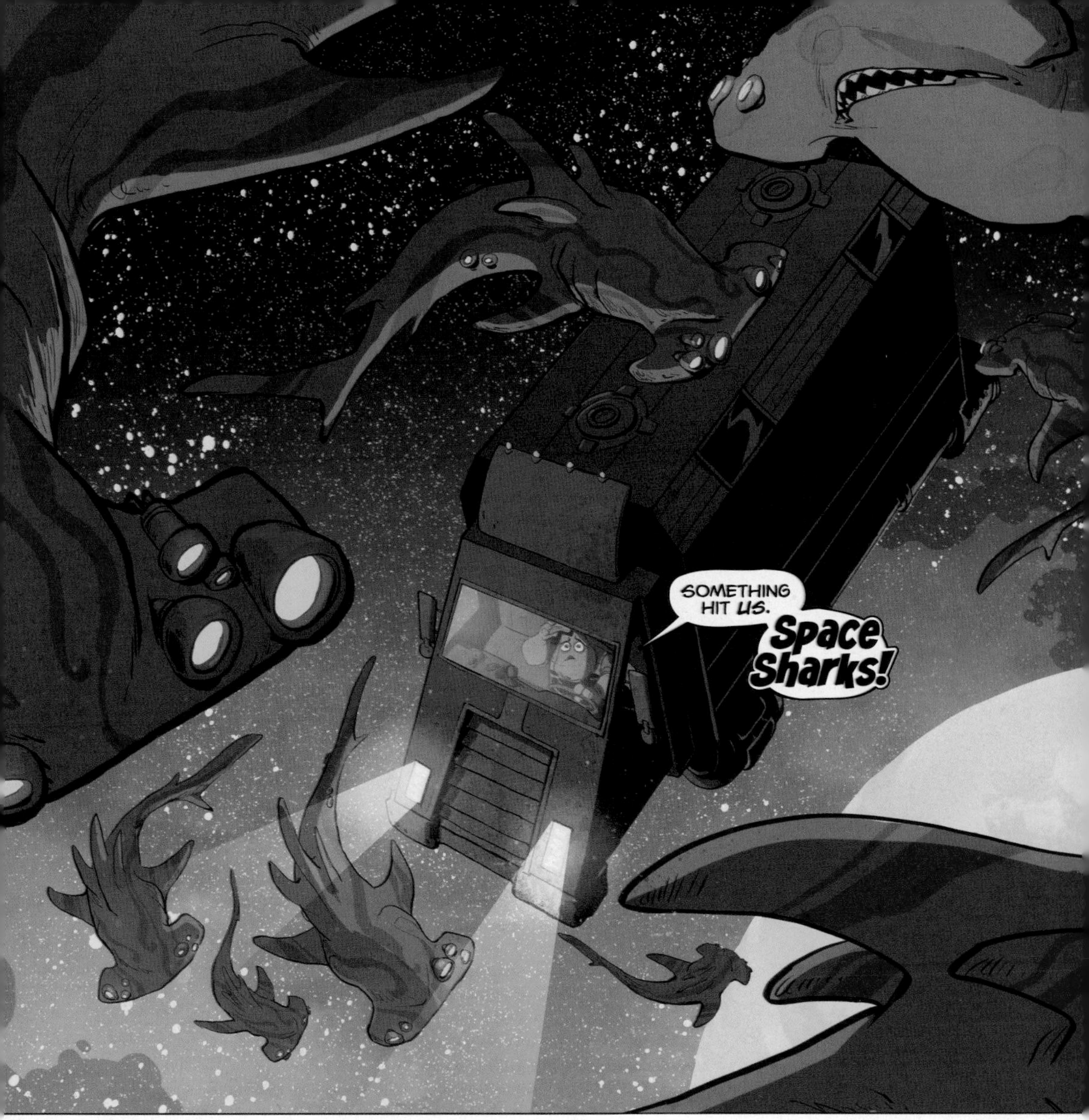
SOMETHING HIT US.
Space Sharks!

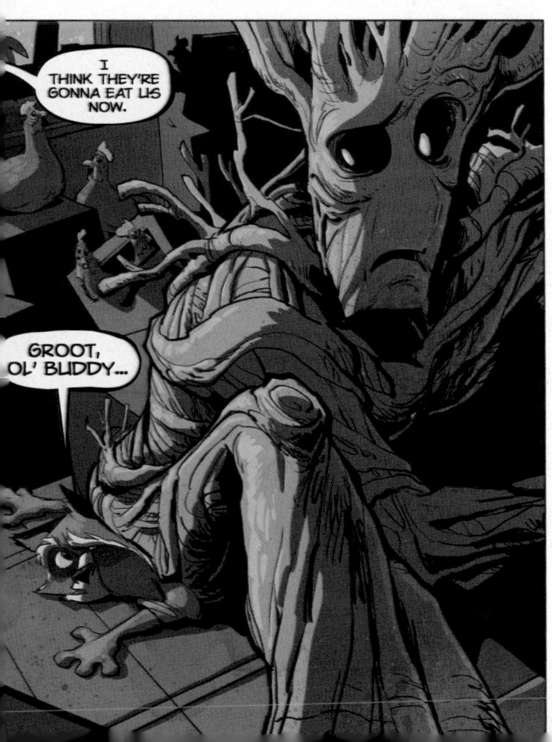
I THINK THEY'RE GONNA EAT US NOW.
GROOT, OL' BUDDY...

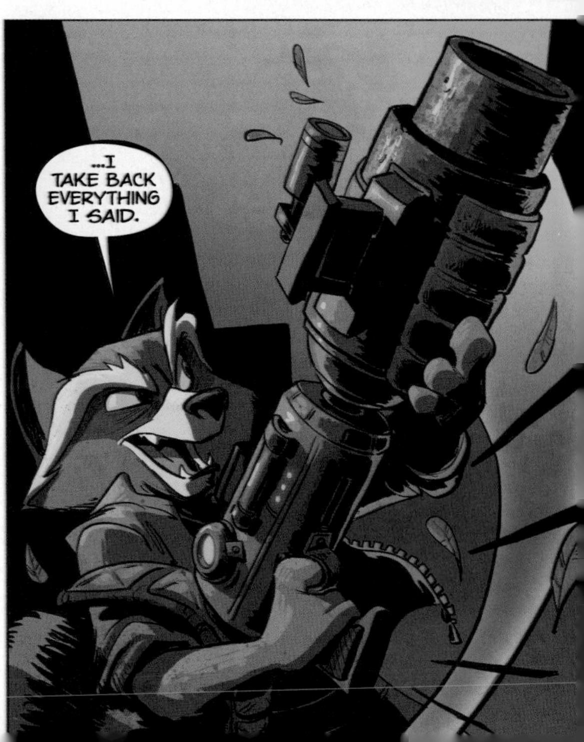
...I TAKE BACK EVERYTHING I SAID.

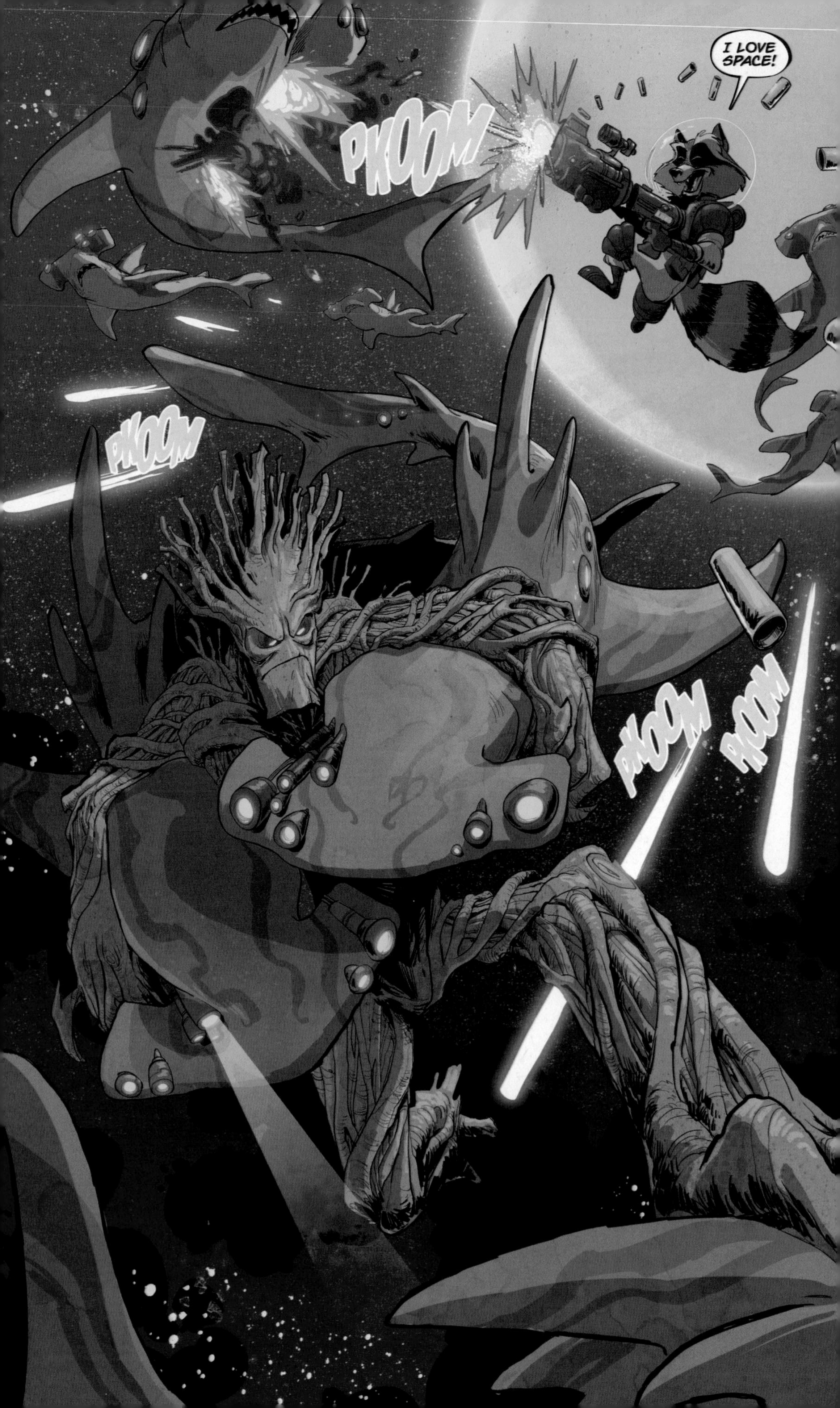
I LOVE SPACE!
PKOOM
PKOOM
PKOOM
PKOOM

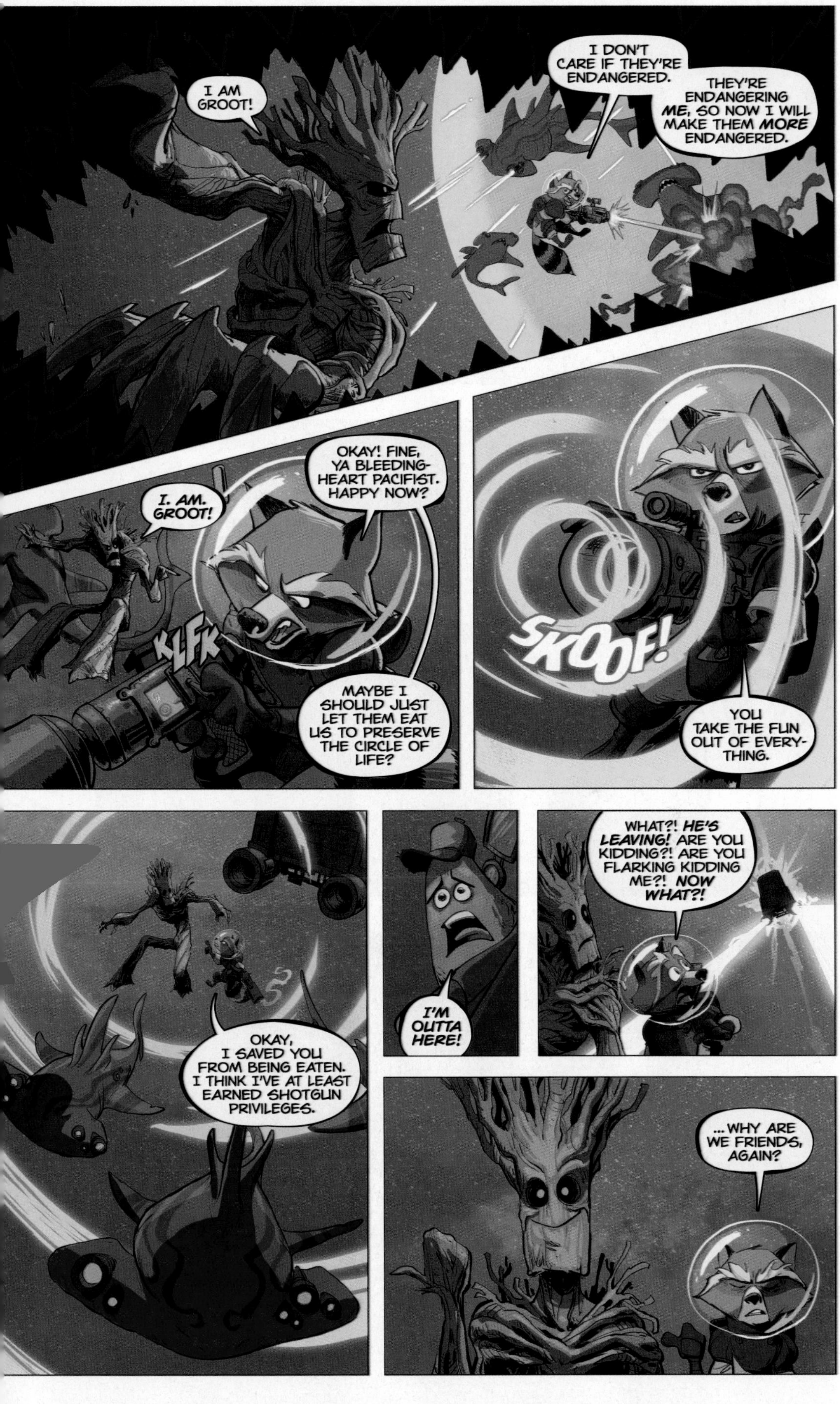
I AM GROOT!
I DON'T CARE IF THEY'RE ENDANGERED.
THEY'RE ENDANGERING *ME*, SO NOW I WILL MAKE THEM *MORE* ENDANGERED.
I. AM. GROOT!
OKAY! FINE, YA BLEEDING-HEART PACIFIST. HAPPY NOW?
KLFK
MAYBE I SHOULD JUST LET THEM EAT US TO PRESERVE THE CIRCLE OF LIFE?
SKOOF!
YOU TAKE THE FUN OUT OF EVERY-THING.
OKAY, I SAVED YOU FROM BEING EATEN. I THINK I'VE AT LEAST EARNED SHOTGUN PRIVILEGES.
I'M OUTTA HERE!
WHAT?! *HE'S LEAVING!* ARE YOU KIDDING?! ARE YOU FLARKING KIDDING ME?! *NOW WHAT?!*
...WHY ARE WE FRIENDS, AGAIN?

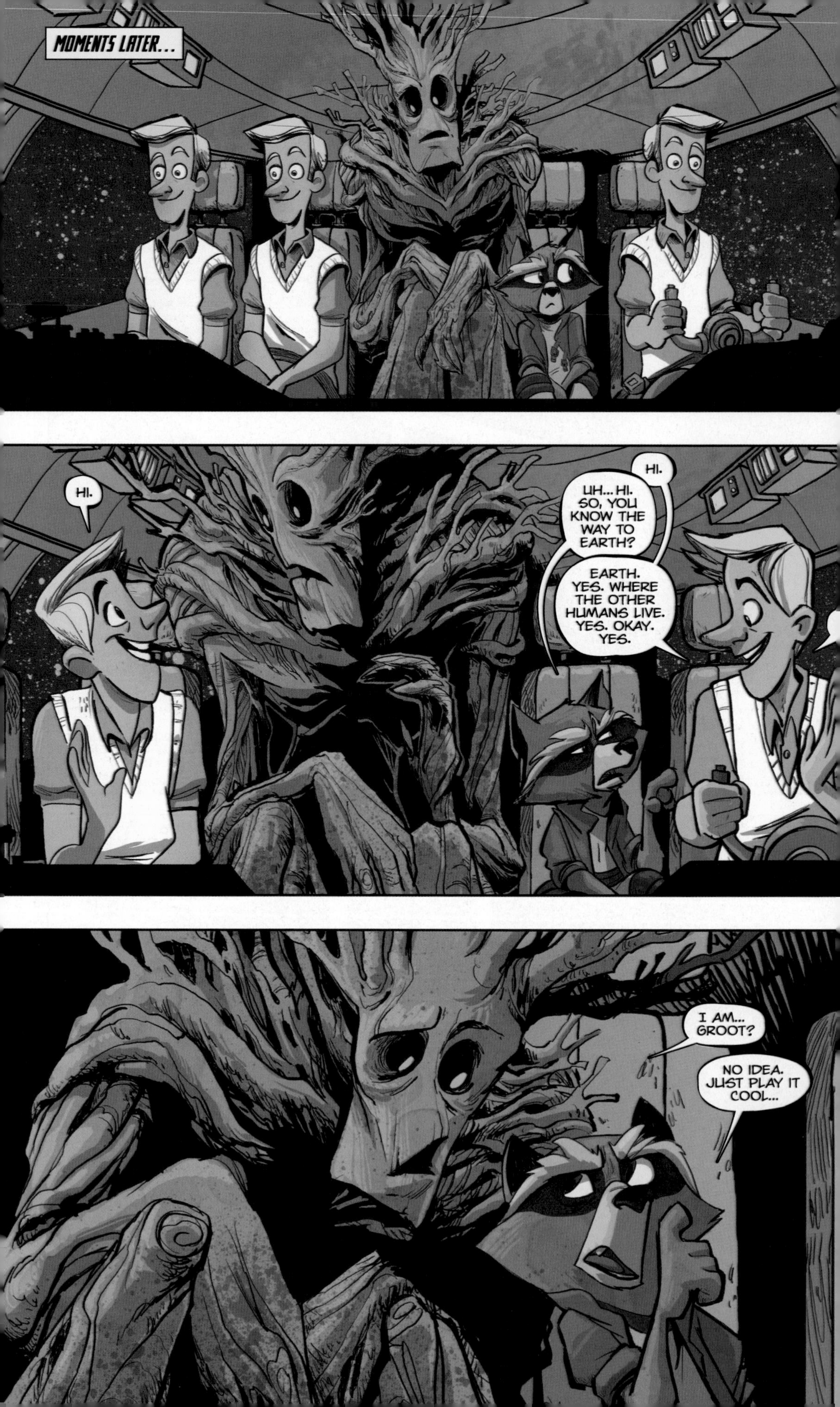
MOMENTS LATER...
HI.
HI.
UH... HI. SO, YOU KNOW THE WAY TO EARTH?
EARTH. YES. WHERE THE OTHER HUMANS LIVE. YES. OKAY. YES.
I AM... GROOT?
NO IDEA. JUST PLAY IT COOL...

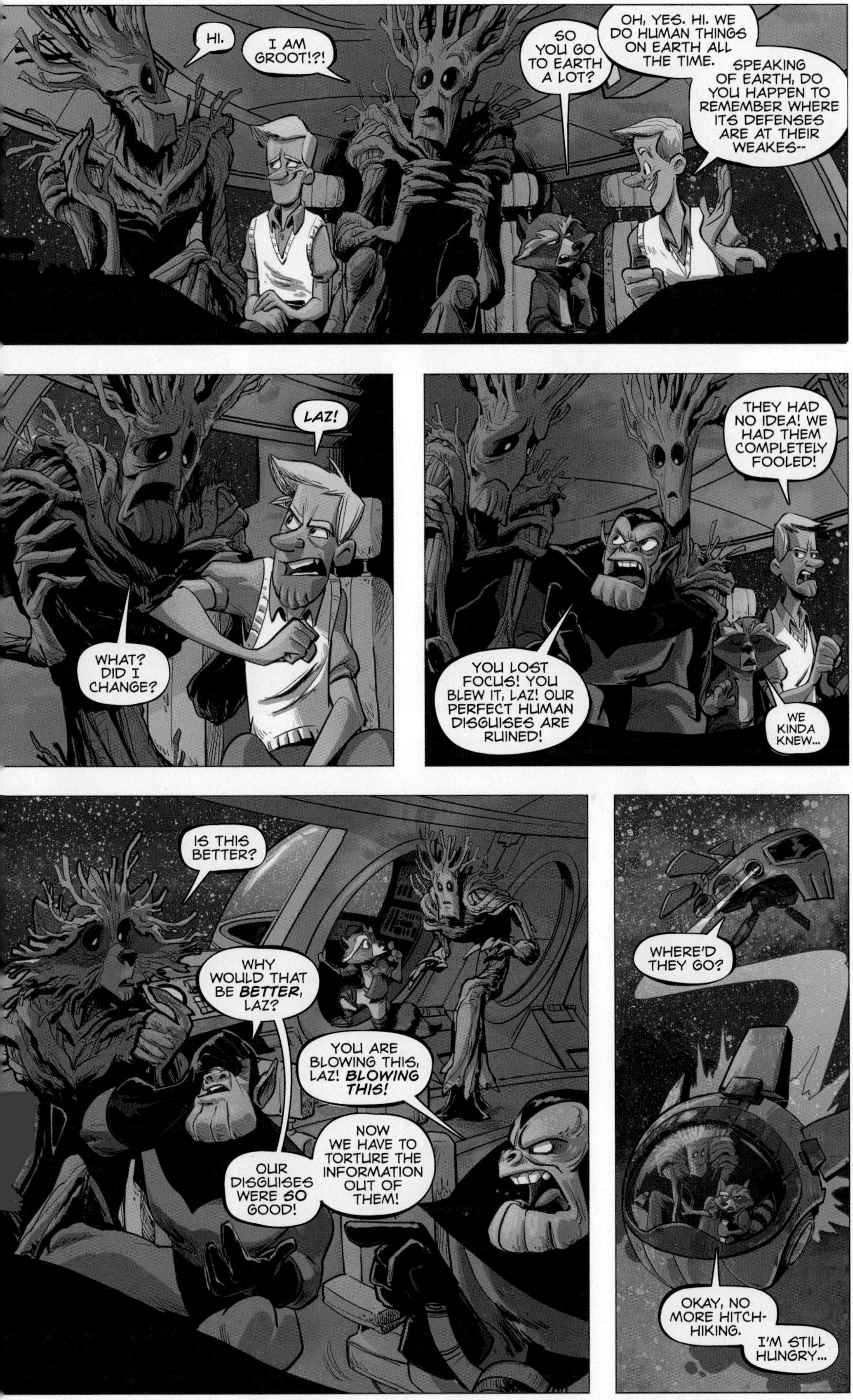
HI.
I AM GROOT!?!
SO YOU GO TO EARTH A LOT?
OH, YES. HI. WE DO HUMAN THINGS ON EARTH ALL THE TIME.
SPEAKING OF EARTH, DO YOU HAPPEN TO REMEMBER WHERE ITS DEFENSES ARE AT THEIR WEAKES--
LAZ!
WHAT? DID I CHANGE?
THEY HAD NO IDEA! WE HAD THEM COMPLETELY FOOLED!
YOU LOST FOCUS! YOU BLEW IT, LAZ! OUR PERFECT HUMAN DISGUISES ARE RUINED!
WE KINDA KNEW...
IS THIS BETTER?
WHY WOULD THAT BE BETTER, LAZ?
YOU ARE BLOWING THIS, LAZ! BLOWING THIS!
OUR DISGUISES WERE SO GOOD!
NOW WE HAVE TO TORTURE THE INFORMATION OUT OF THEM!
WHERE'D THEY GO?
OKAY, NO MORE HITCH-HIKING.
I'M STILL HUNGRY...

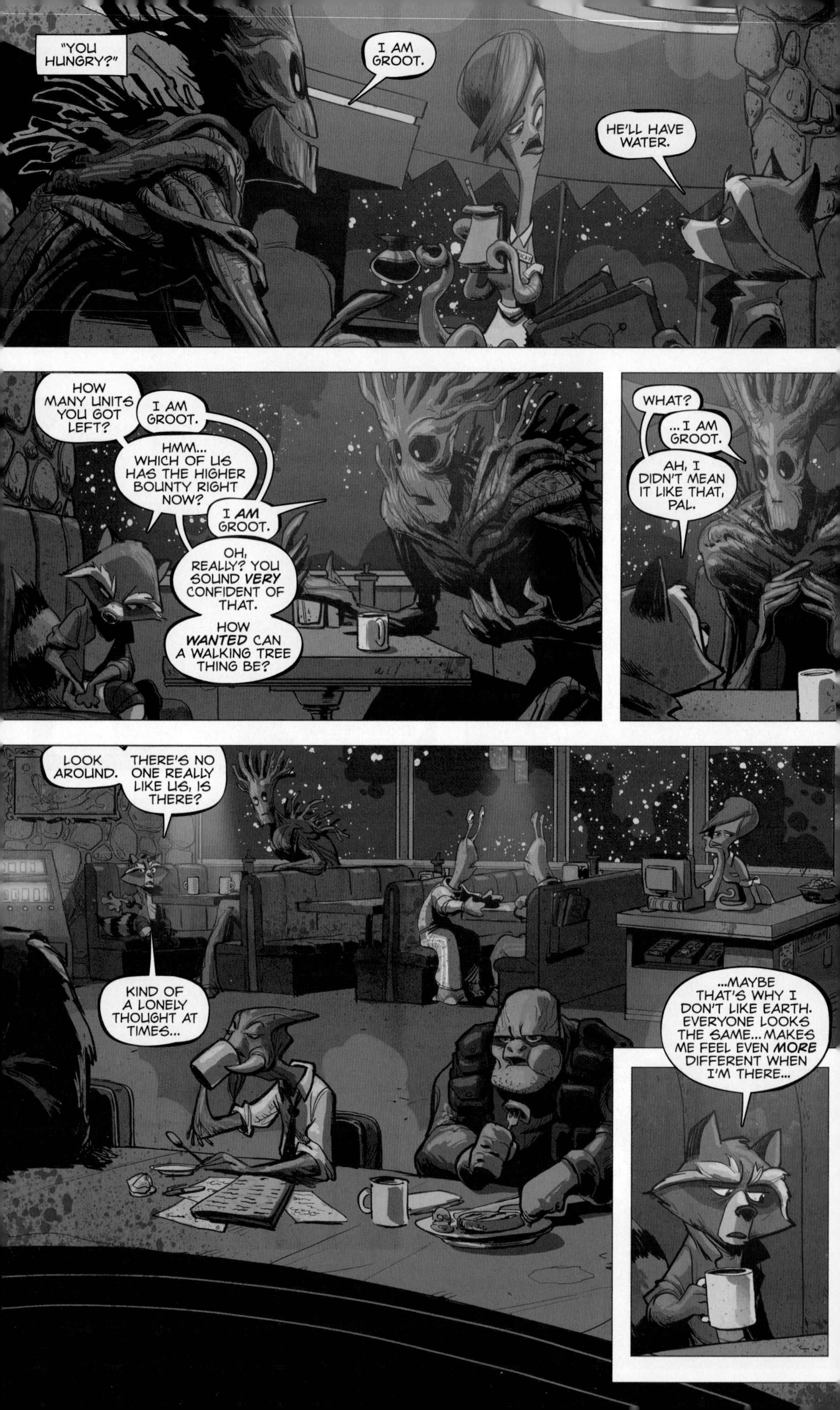
"YOU HUNGRY?"
I AM GROOT.
HE'LL HAVE WATER.
HOW MANY UNITS YOU GOT LEFT?
I AM GROOT.
HMM... WHICH OF US HAS THE HIGHER BOUNTY RIGHT NOW?
I *AM* GROOT.
OH, REALLY? YOU SOUND *VERY* CONFIDENT OF THAT.
HOW *WANTED* CAN A WALKING TREE THING BE?
WHAT?
...I AM GROOT.
AH, I DIDN'T MEAN IT LIKE THAT, PAL.
LOOK AROUND.
THERE'S NO ONE REALLY LIKE US, IS THERE?
KIND OF A LONELY THOUGHT AT TIMES...
...MAYBE THAT'S WHY I DON'T LIKE EARTH. EVERYONE LOOKS THE SAME... MAKES ME FEEL EVEN *MORE* DIFFERENT WHEN I'M THERE...

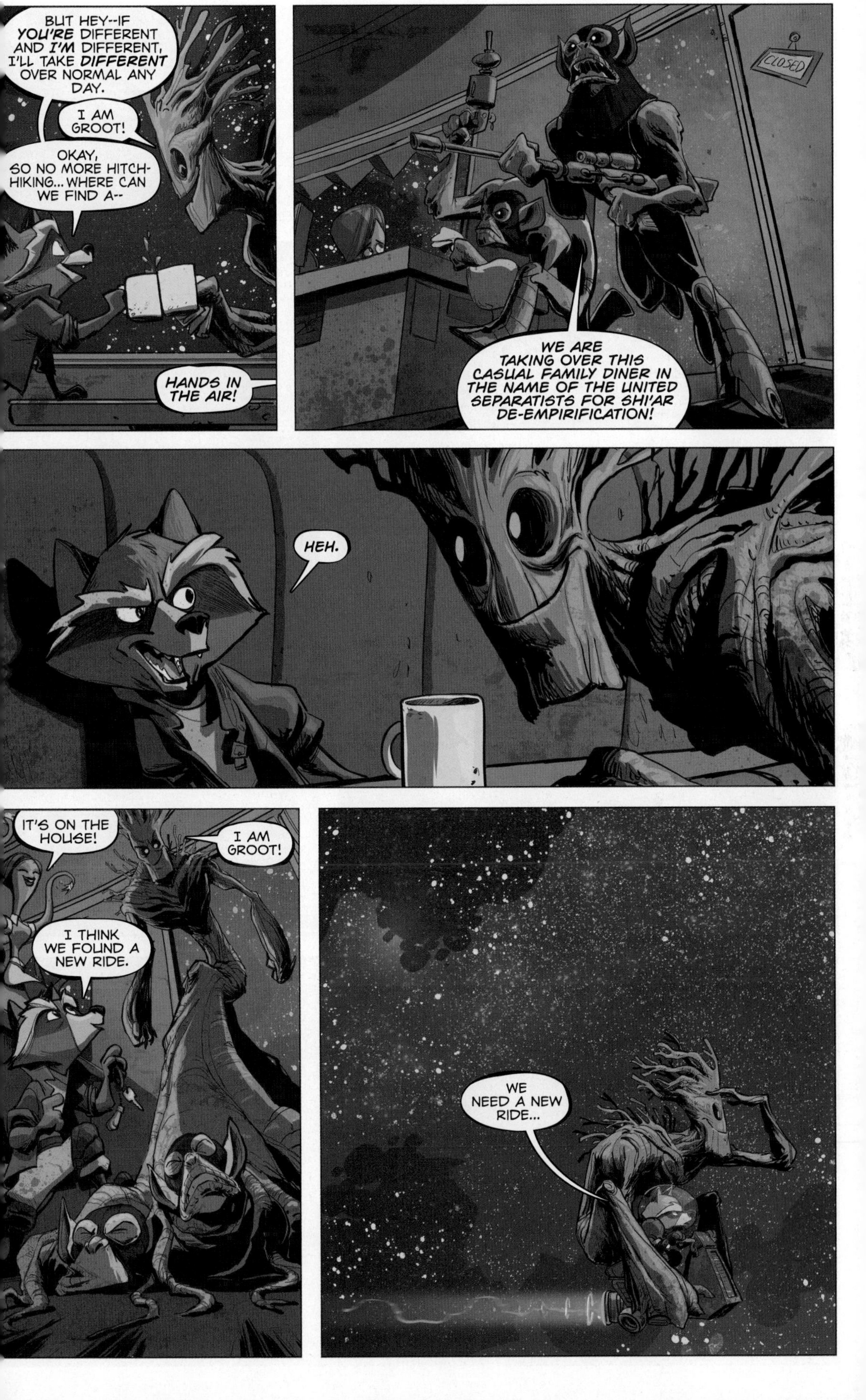

BUT HEY--IF YOU'RE DIFFERENT AND I'M DIFFERENT, I'LL TAKE DIFFERENT OVER NORMAL ANY DAY.
I AM GROOT!
OKAY, SO NO MORE HITCH-HIKING... WHERE CAN WE FIND A--
HANDS IN THE AIR!
CLOSED
WE ARE TAKING OVER THIS CASUAL FAMILY DINER IN THE NAME OF THE UNITED SEPARATISTS FOR SHI'AR DE-EMPIRIFICATION!
HEH.
IT'S ON THE HOUSE!
I AM GROOT!
I THINK WE FOUND A NEW RIDE.
WE NEED A NEW RIDE...

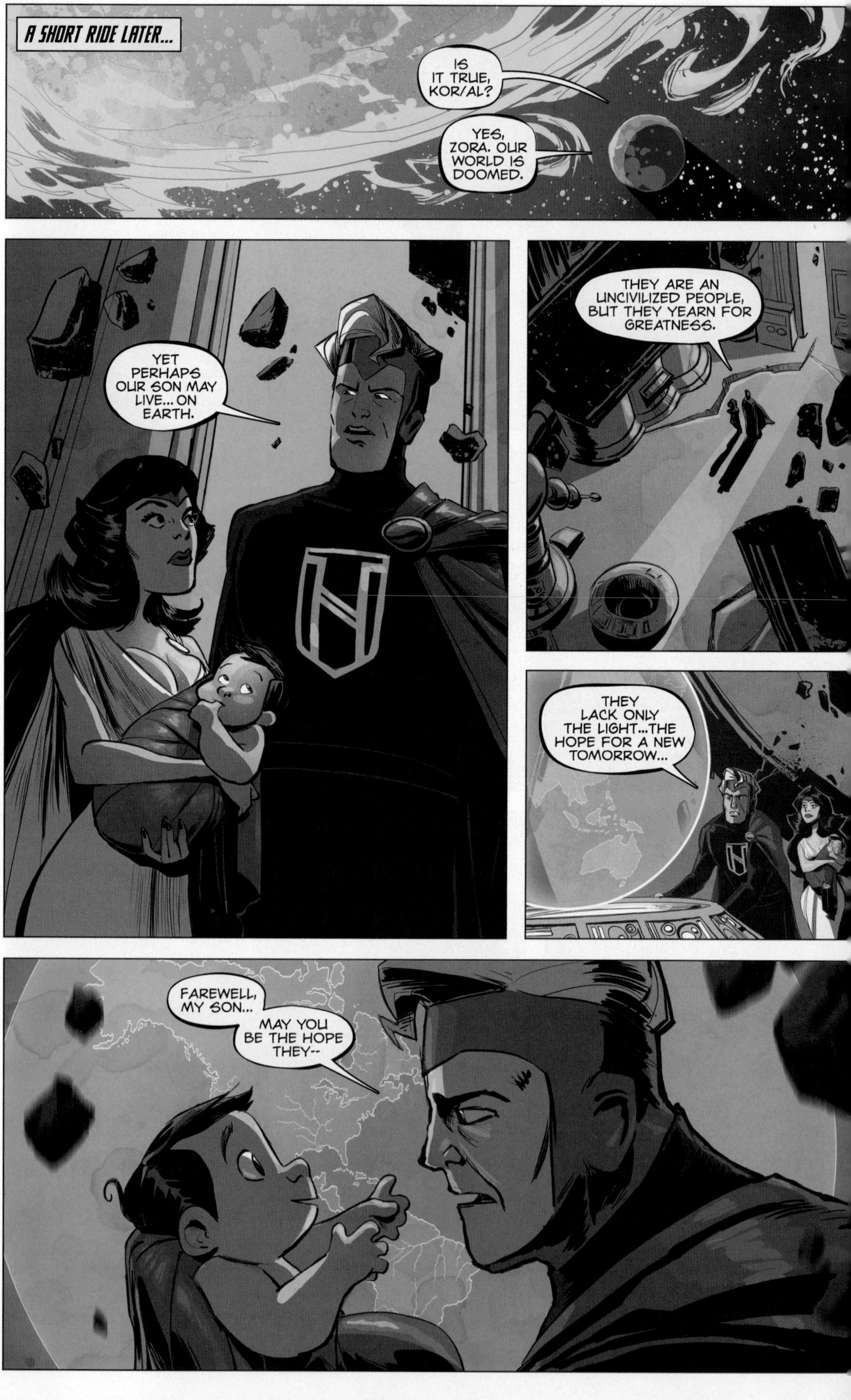
A SHORT RIDE LATER...
IS IT TRUE, KOR/AL?
YES, ZORA. OUR WORLD IS DOOMED.
YET PERHAPS OUR SON MAY LIVE... ON EARTH.
THEY ARE AN UNCIVILIZED PEOPLE, BUT THEY YEARN FOR GREATNESS.
THEY LACK ONLY THE LIGHT...THE HOPE FOR A NEW TOMORROW...
FAREWELL, MY SON...
MAY YOU BE THE HOPE THEY--

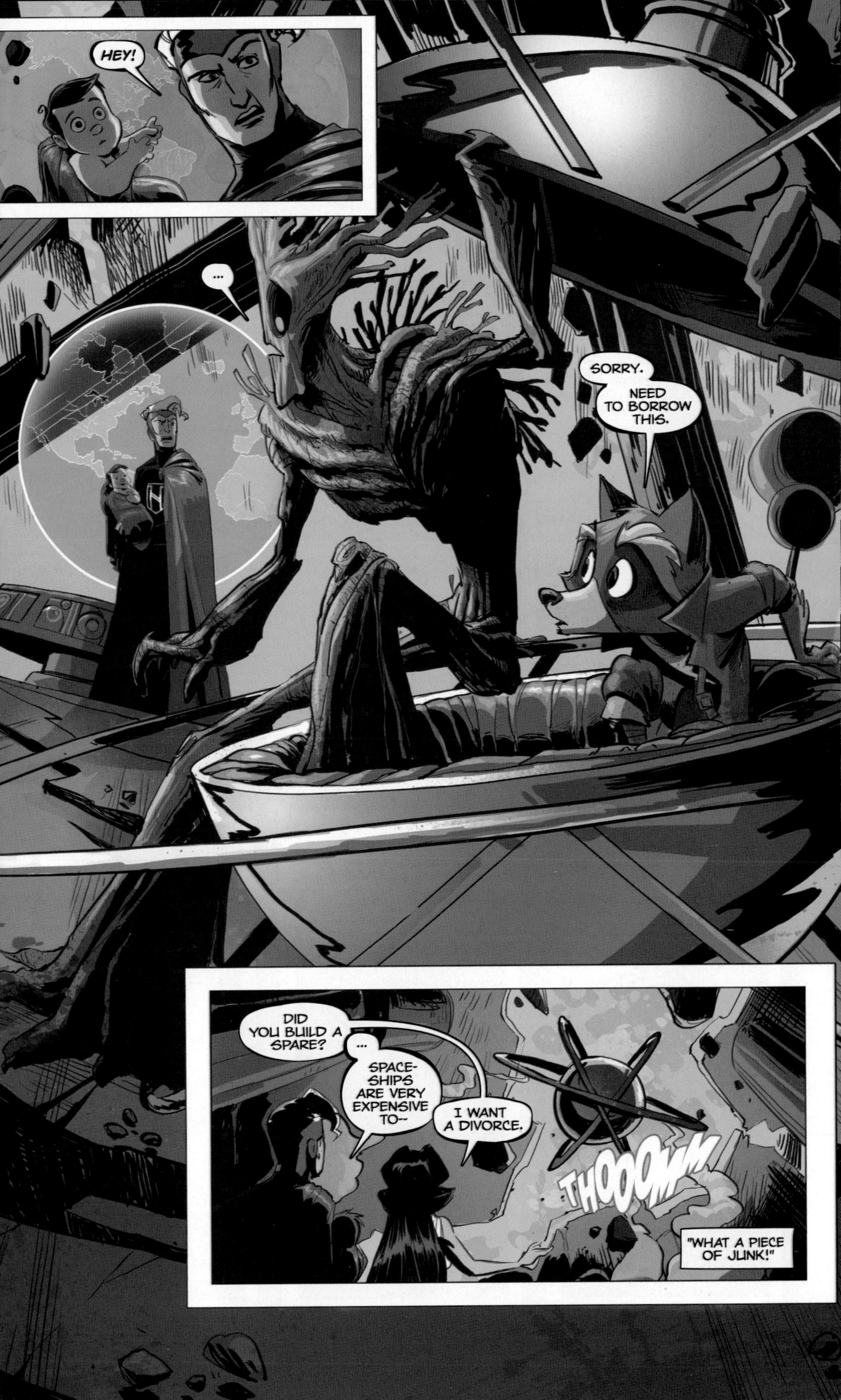
HEY!
...
SORRY.
NEED TO BORROW THIS.
DID YOU BUILD A SPARE?
...
SPACE-SHIPS ARE VERY EXPENSIVE TO--
I WANT A DIVORCE.
THOOOMM
"WHAT A PIECE OF JUNK!"

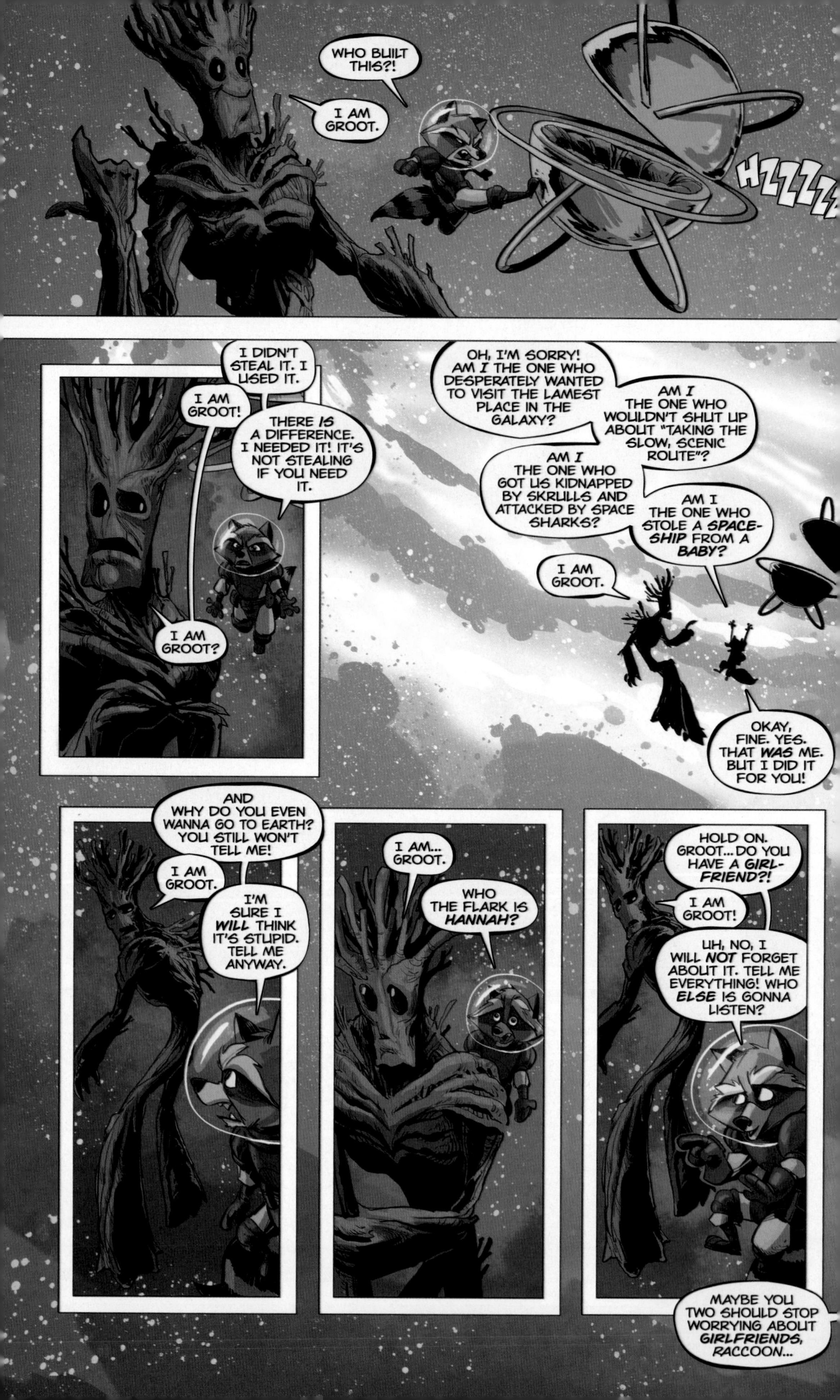
WHO BUILT THIS?!
I AM GROOT.
HZZZZZ
I DIDN'T STEAL IT. I USED IT.
I AM GROOT!
THERE IS A DIFFERENCE. I NEEDED IT! IT'S NOT STEALING IF YOU NEED IT.
I AM GROOT?
OH, I'M SORRY! AM I THE ONE WHO DESPERATELY WANTED TO VISIT THE LAMEST PLACE IN THE GALAXY?
AM I THE ONE WHO WOULDN'T SHUT UP ABOUT "TAKING THE SLOW, SCENIC ROUTE"?
AM I THE ONE WHO GOT US KIDNAPPED BY SKRULLS AND ATTACKED BY SPACE SHARKS?
AM I THE ONE WHO STOLE A SPACE-SHIP FROM A BABY?
I AM GROOT.
OKAY, FINE. YES. THAT WAS ME. BUT I DID IT FOR YOU!
AND WHY DO YOU EVEN WANNA GO TO EARTH? YOU STILL WON'T TELL ME!
I AM GROOT.
I'M SURE I WILL THINK IT'S STUPID. TELL ME ANYWAY.
I AM... GROOT.
WHO THE FLARK IS HANNAH?
HOLD ON. GROOT... DO YOU HAVE A GIRL-FRIEND?!
I AM GROOT!
UH, NO, I WILL NOT FORGET ABOUT IT. TELL ME EVERYTHING! WHO ELSE IS GONNA LISTEN?
MAYBE YOU TWO SHOULD STOP WORRYING ABOUT GIRLFRIENDS, RACCOON...

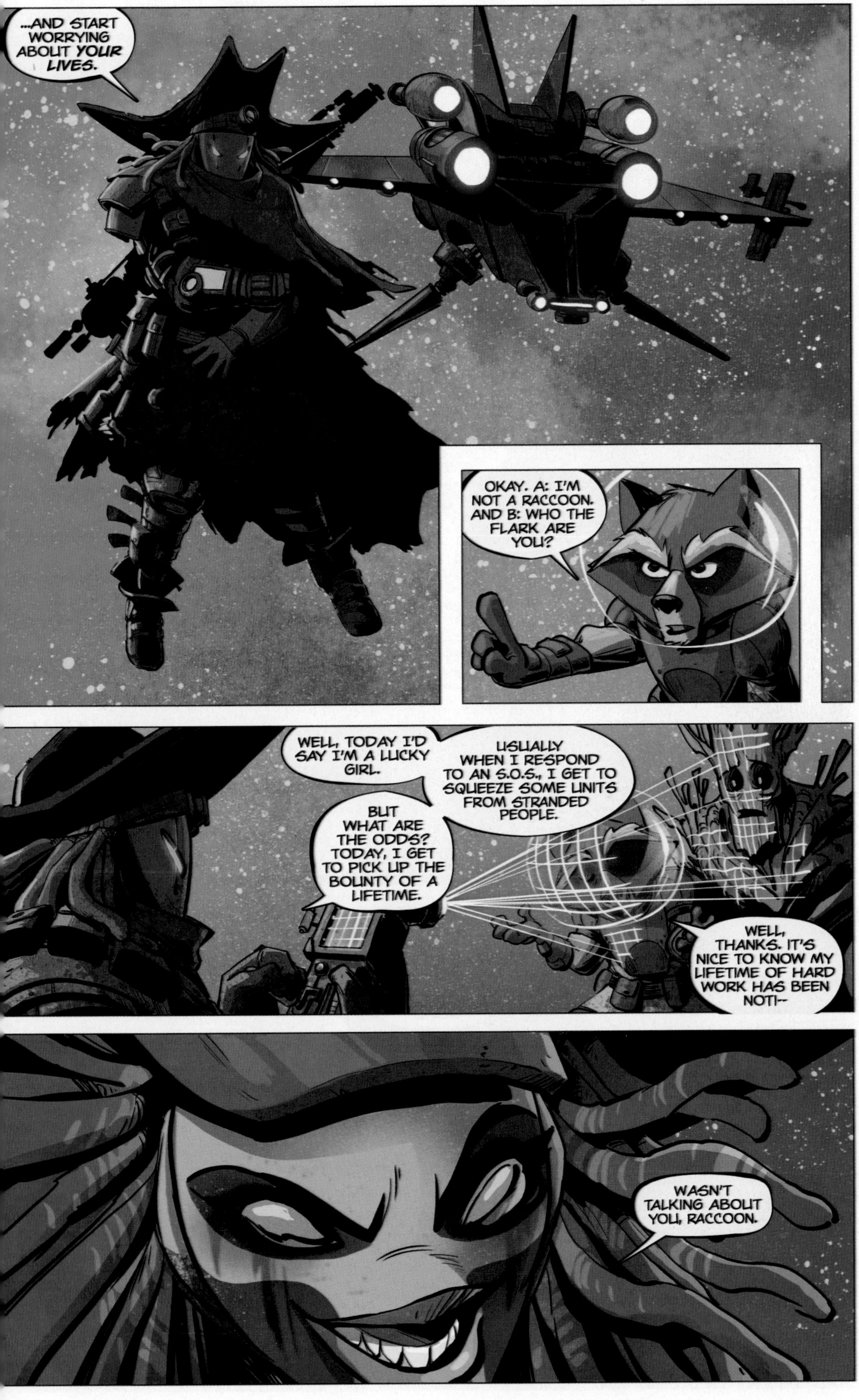
...AND START WORRYING ABOUT YOUR LIVES.
OKAY. A: I'M NOT A RACCOON. AND B: WHO THE FLARK ARE YOU?
WELL, TODAY I'D SAY I'M A LUCKY GIRL.
USUALLY WHEN I RESPOND TO AN S.O.S., I GET TO SQUEEZE SOME UNITS FROM STRANDED PEOPLE.
BUT WHAT ARE THE ODDS? TODAY, I GET TO PICK UP THE BOUNTY OF A LIFETIME.
WELL, THANKS. IT'S NICE TO KNOW MY LIFETIME OF HARD WORK HAS BEEN NOTI--
WASN'T TALKING ABOUT YOU, RACCOON.

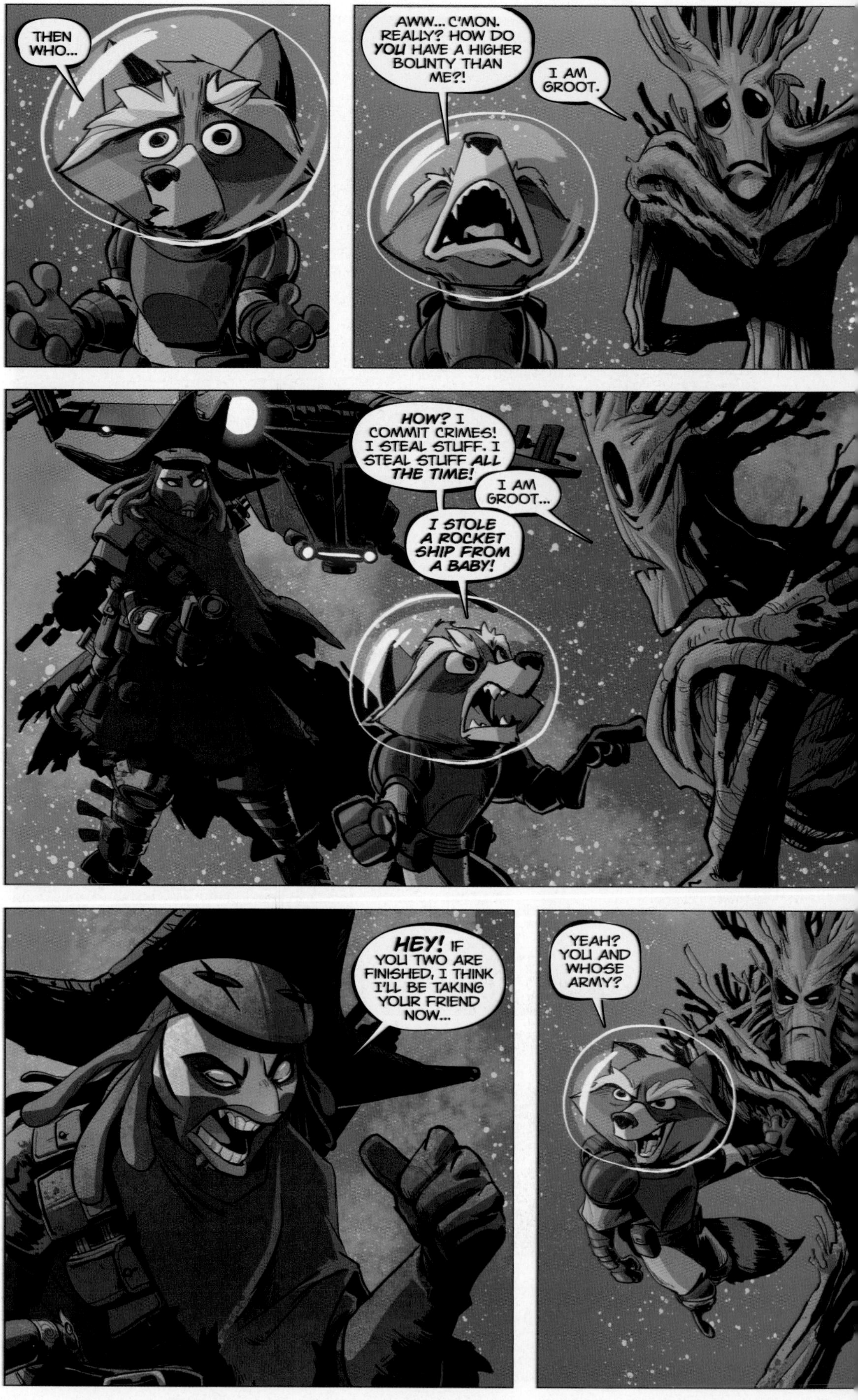
THEN WHO...
AWW... C'MON. REALLY? HOW DO YOU HAVE A HIGHER BOUNTY THAN ME?!
I AM GROOT.
HOW? I COMMIT CRIMES! I STEAL STUFF. I STEAL STUFF ALL THE TIME!
I AM GROOT...
I STOLE A ROCKET SHIP FROM A BABY!
HEY! IF YOU TWO ARE FINISHED, I THINK I'LL BE TAKING YOUR FRIEND NOW...
YEAH? YOU AND WHOSE ARMY?

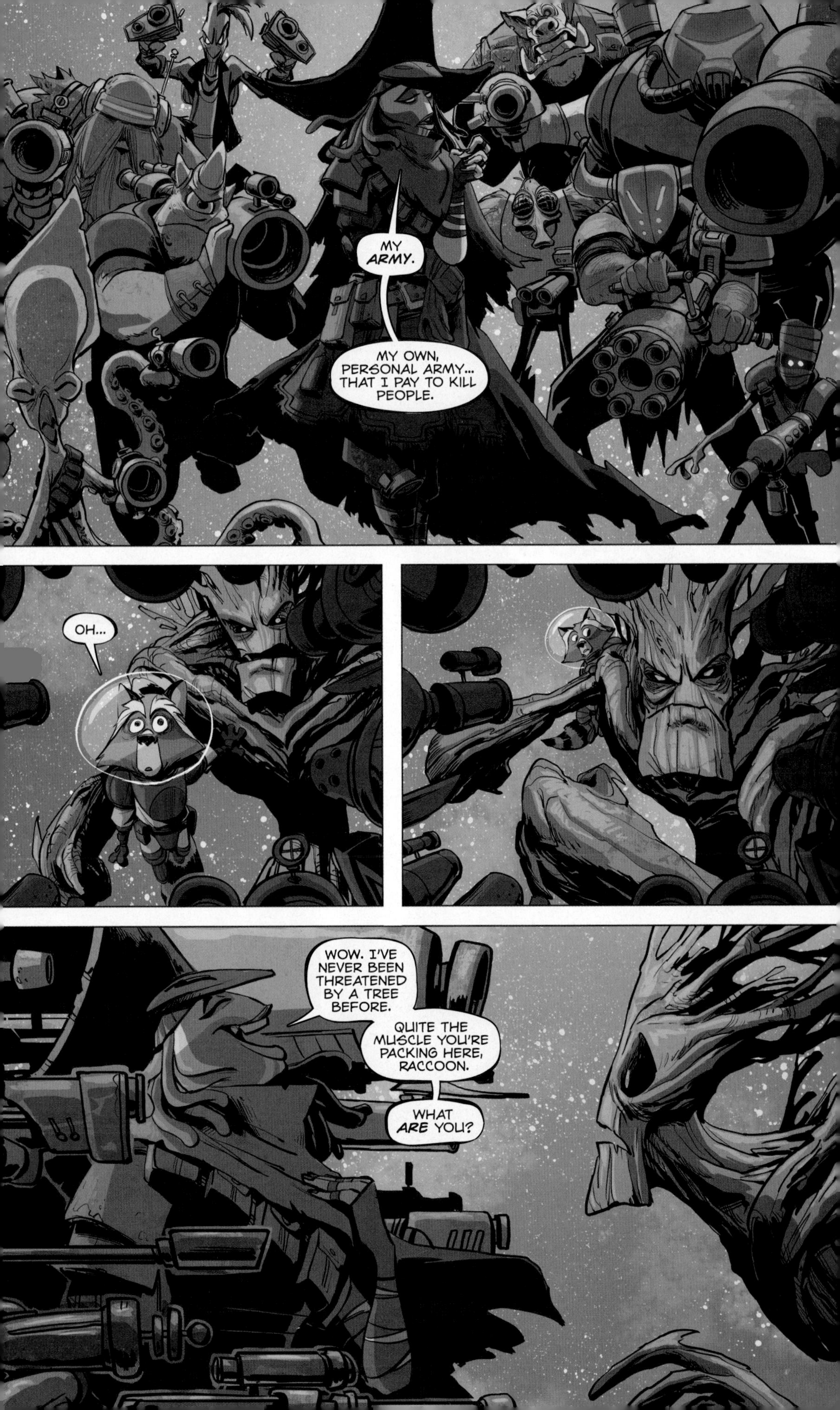
MY ARMY.
MY OWN, PERSONAL ARMY... THAT I PAY TO KILL PEOPLE.
OH...
WOW. I'VE NEVER BEEN THREATENED BY A TREE BEFORE.
QUITE THE MUSCLE YOU'RE PACKING HERE, RACCOON.
WHAT ARE YOU?

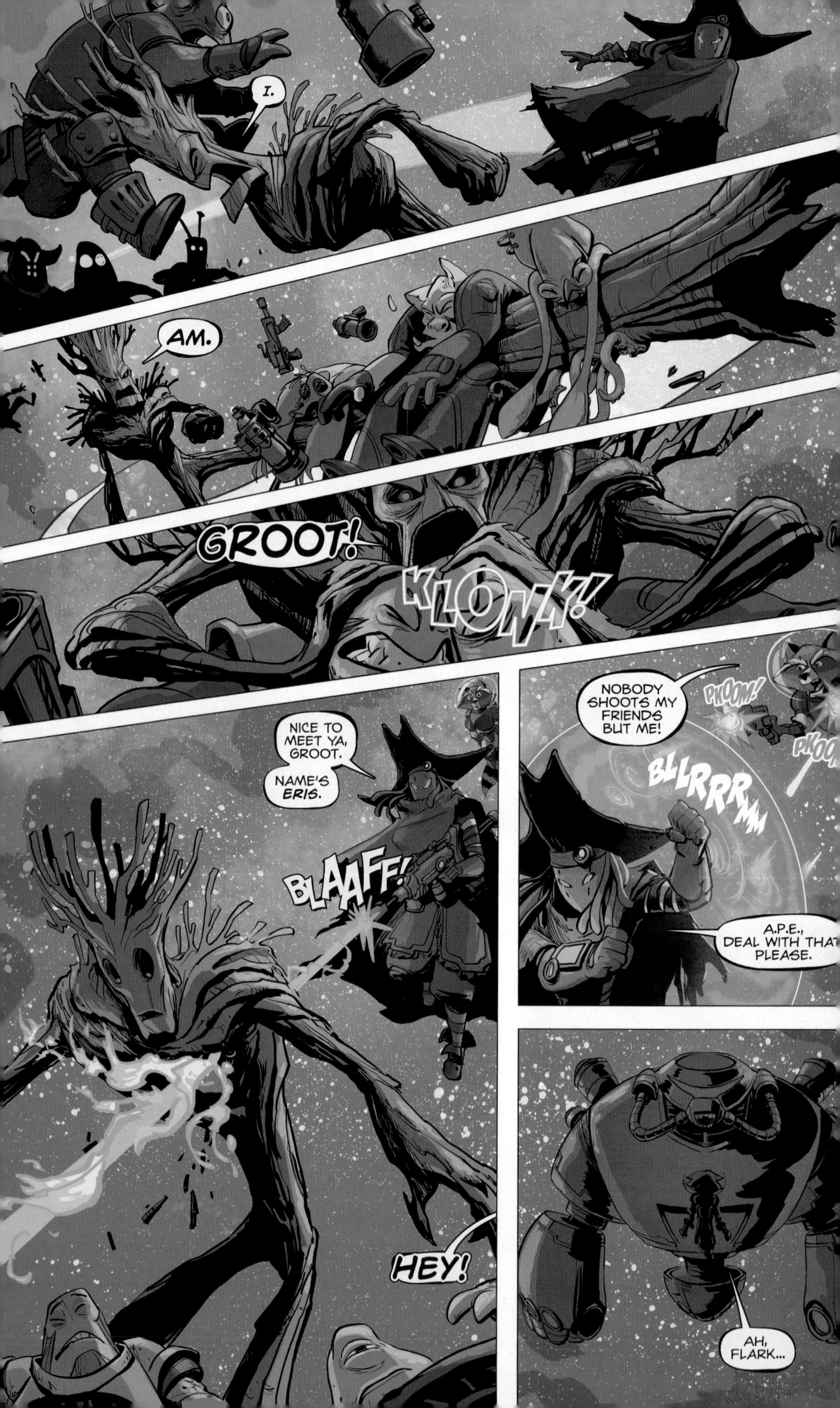
I.
AM.
GROOT!
KLONK!
NOBODY SHOOTS MY FRIENDS BUT ME!
PKOOM!
PKOOM
BLLRRRRMM
A.P.E., DEAL WITH THAT PLEASE.
NICE TO MEET YA, GROOT.
NAME'S ERIS.
BLAAFF!
HEY!
AH, FLARK...

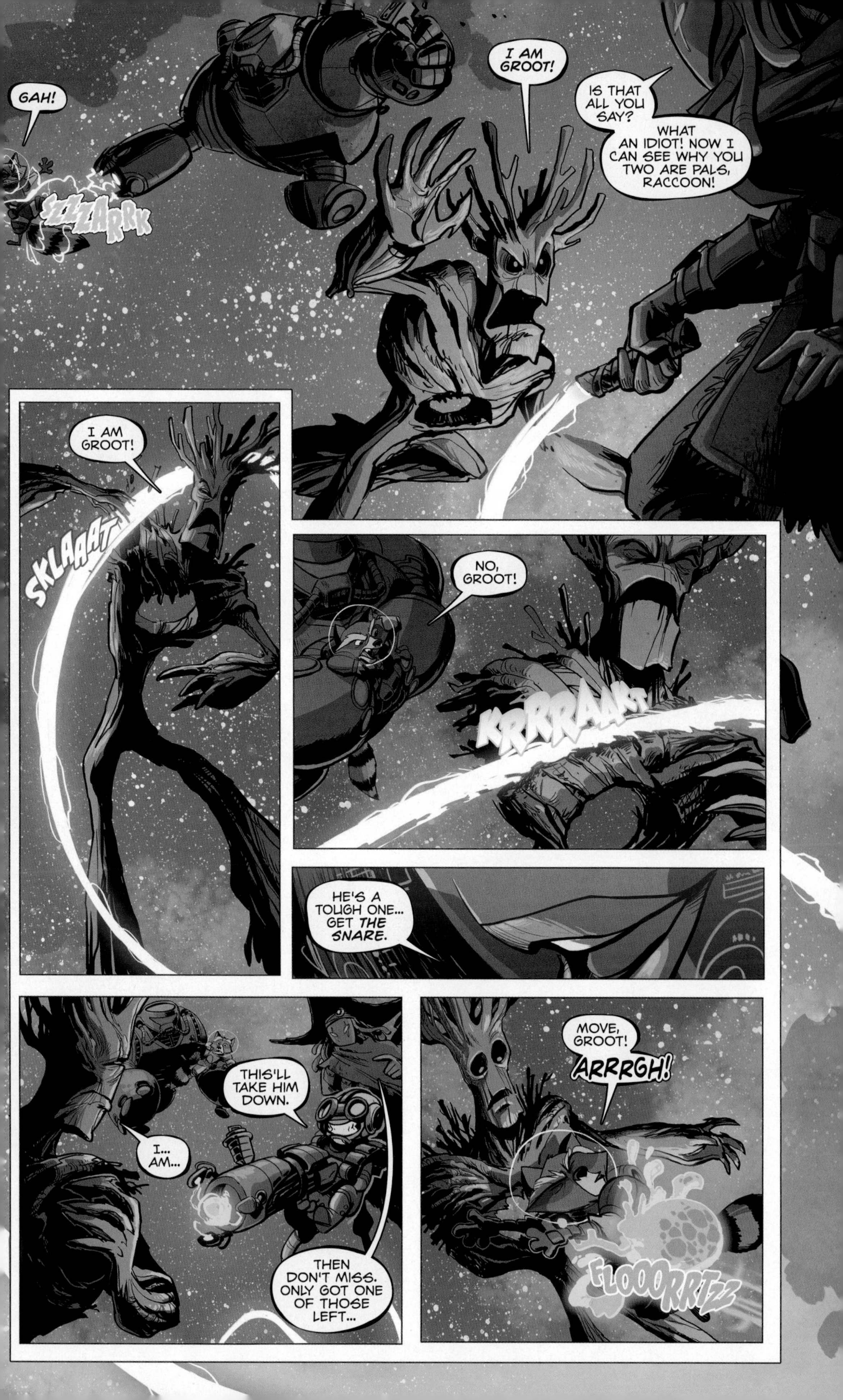
GAH!
SZZZZARRK
I AM GROOT!
IS THAT ALL YOU SAY?
WHAT AN IDIOT! NOW I CAN SEE WHY YOU TWO ARE PALS, RACCOON!
I AM GROOT!
SKLAAAT
NO, GROOT!
KRRRAAKT
HE'S A TOUGH ONE... GET THE SNARE.
THIS'LL TAKE HIM DOWN.
I... AM...
THEN DON'T MISS. ONLY GOT ONE OF THOSE LEFT...
MOVE, GROOT!
ARRRGH!
FLOOORRTZZ

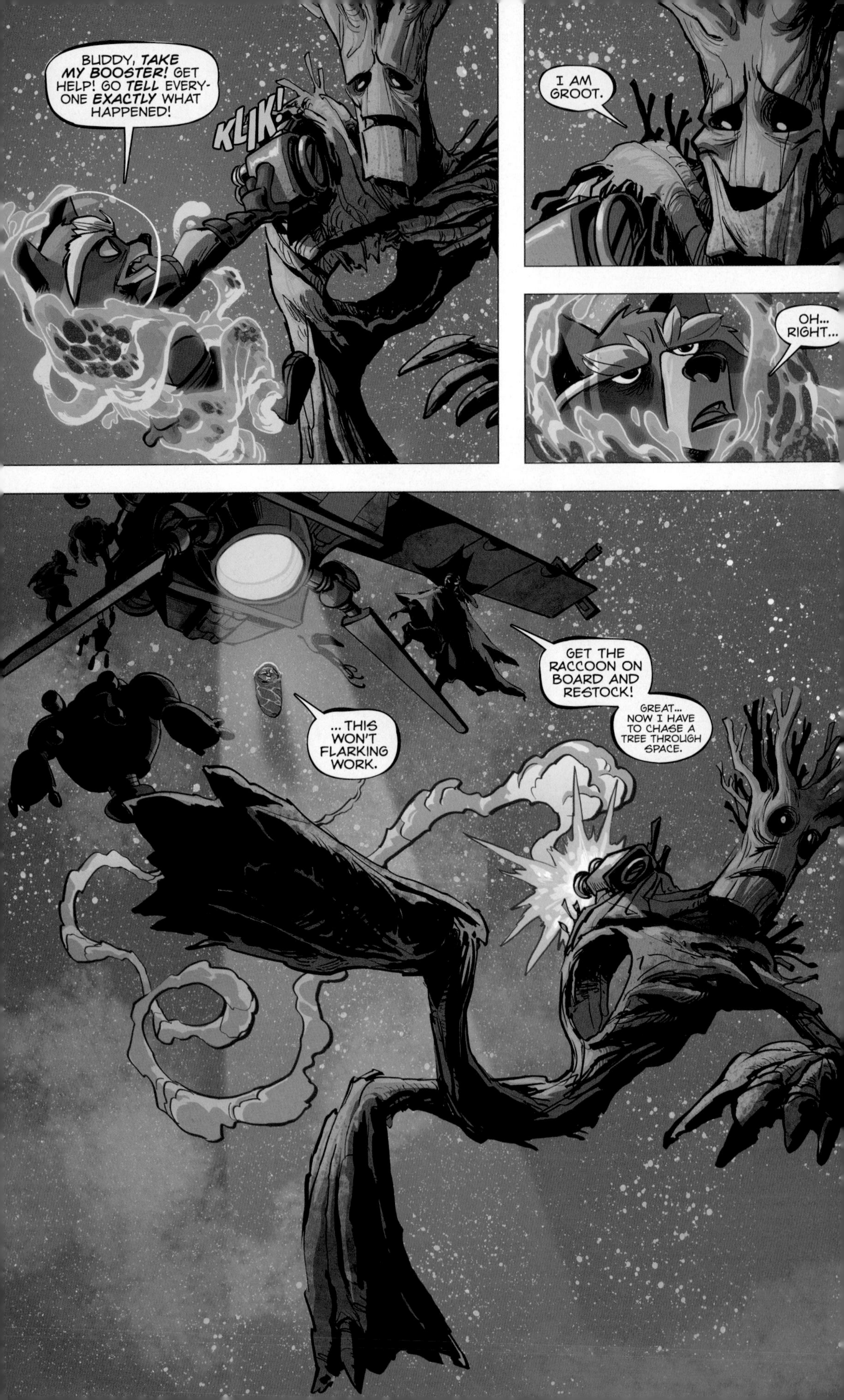
BUDDY, TAKE MY BOOSTER! GET HELP! GO TELL EVERY-ONE EXACTLY WHAT HAPPENED!
KLIK!
I AM GROOT.
OH... RIGHT...
GET THE RACCOON ON BOARD AND RESTOCK!
GREAT... NOW I HAVE TO CHASE A TREE THROUGH SPACE.
... THIS WON'T FLARKING WORK.

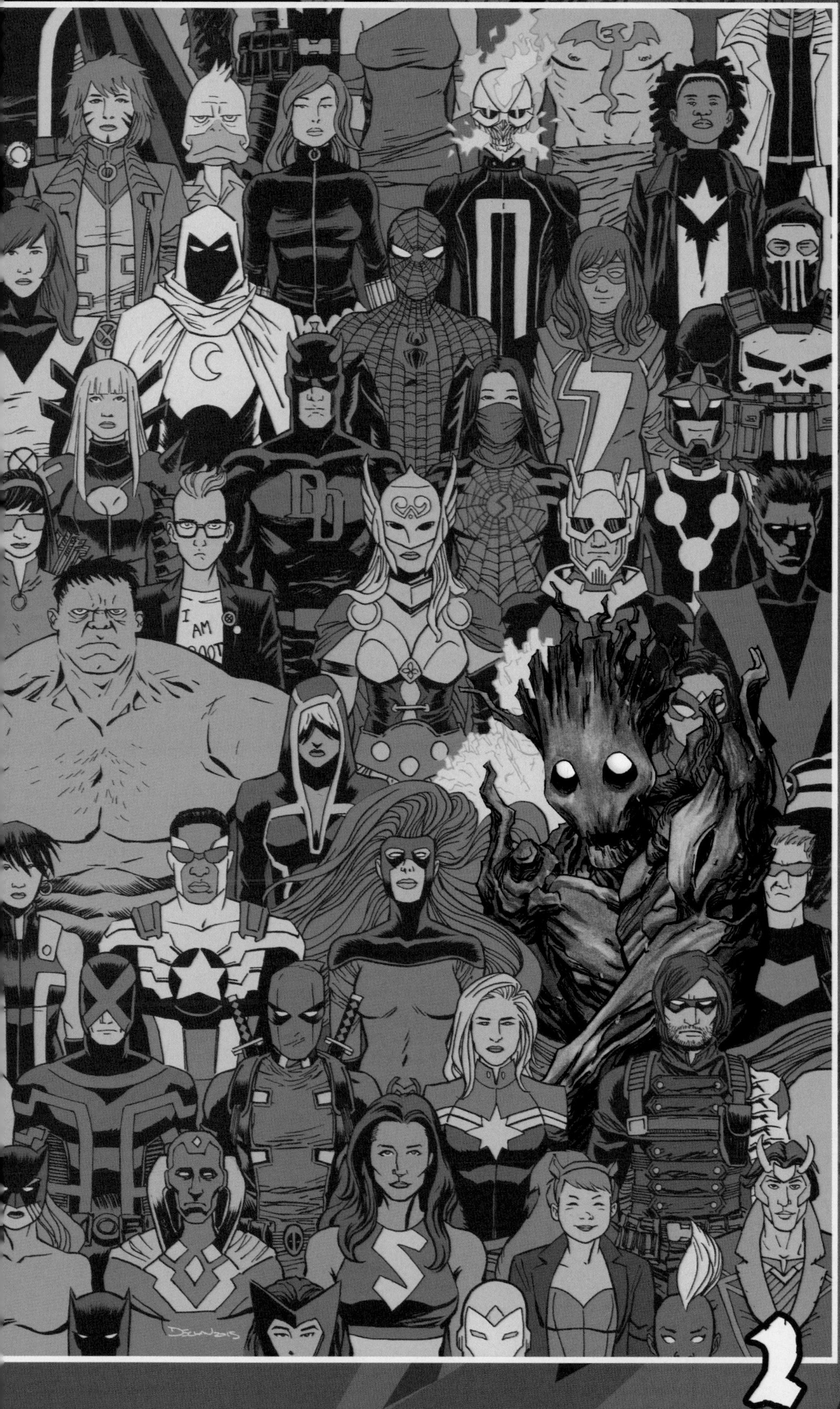
I
AM

2

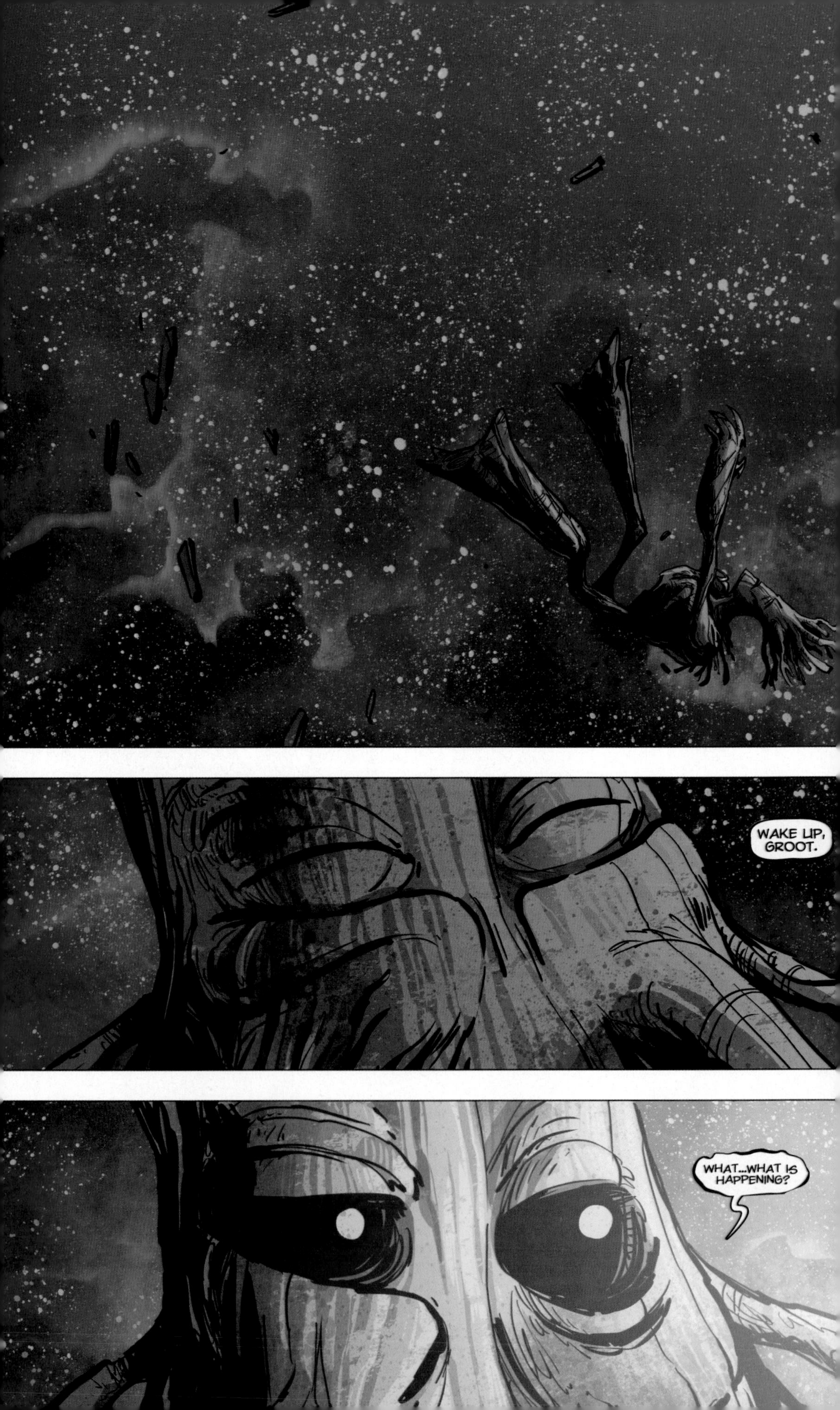
WAKE UP, GROOT.
WHAT...WHAT IS HAPPENING?

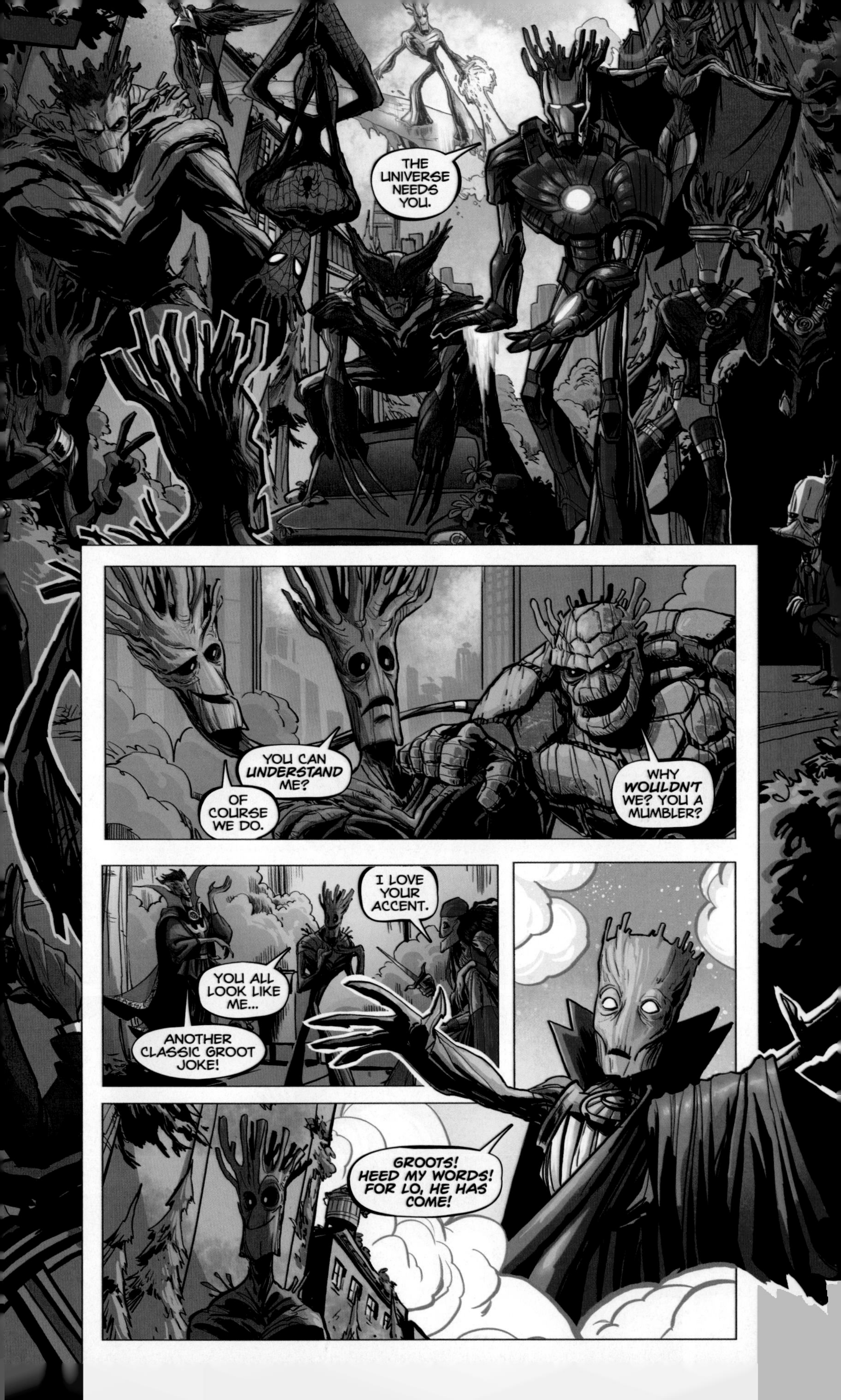

THE UNIVERSE NEEDS YOU.
YOU CAN *UNDERSTAND* ME?
OF COURSE WE DO.
WHY *WOULDN'T* WE? YOU A MUMBLER?
I LOVE YOUR ACCENT.
YOU ALL LOOK LIKE ME...
ANOTHER CLASSIC GROOT JOKE!
GROOTS! HEED MY WORDS! FOR LO, HE HAS COME!

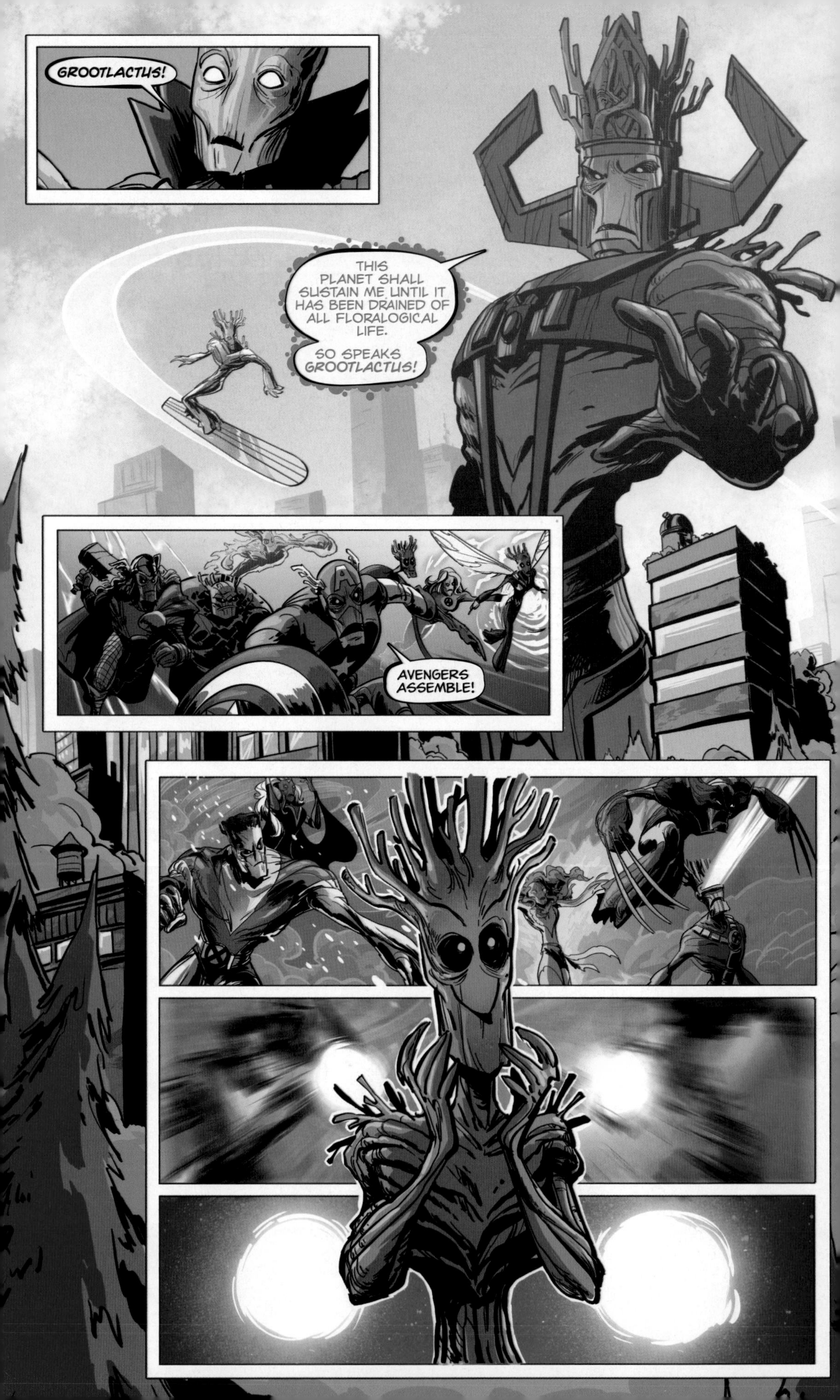
GROOTLACTUS!
THIS PLANET SHALL SUSTAIN ME UNTIL IT HAS BEEN DRAINED OF ALL FLORALOGICAL LIFE.
SO SPEAKS GROOTLACTUS!
AVENGERS ASSEMBLE!

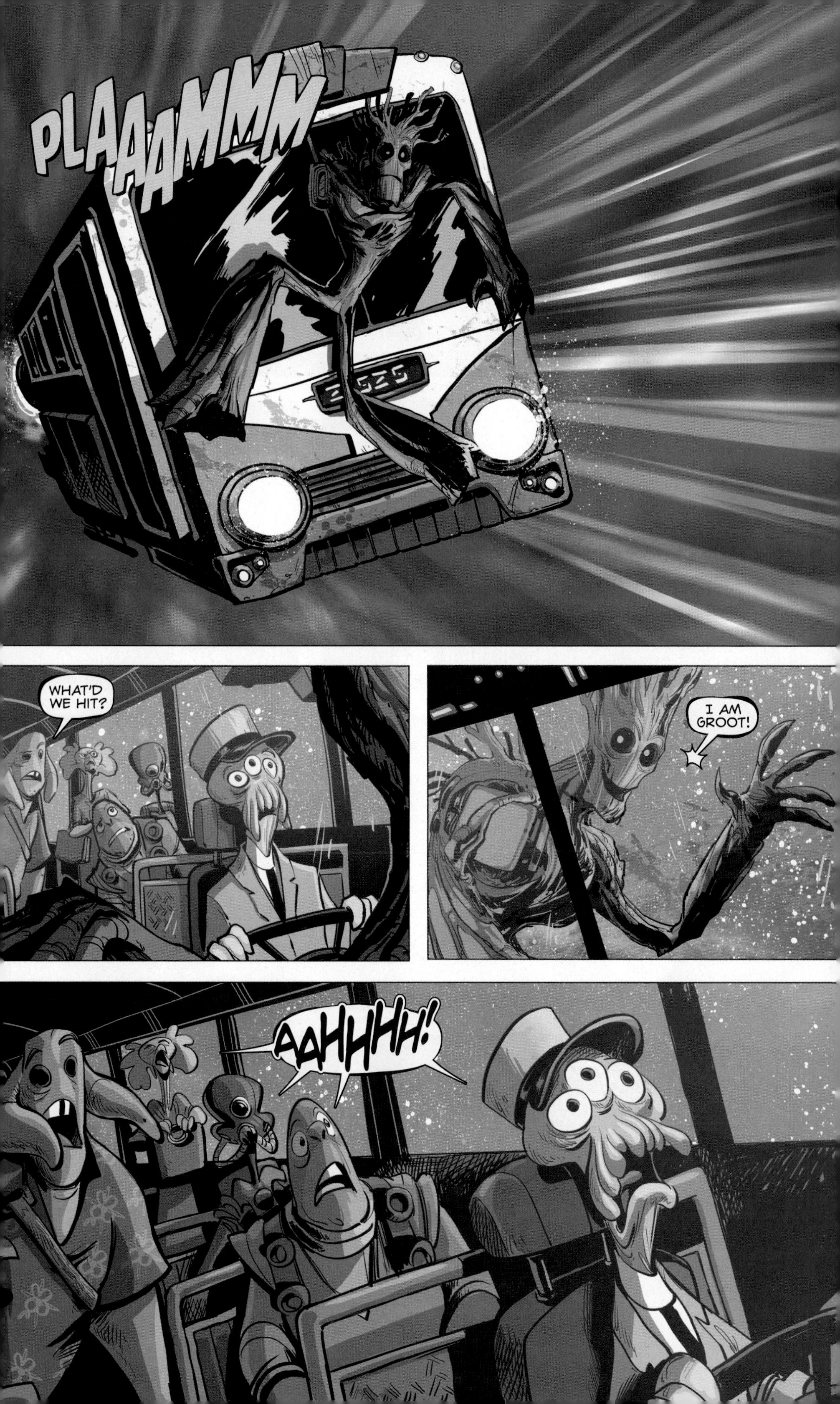
PLAAAMMM
WHAT'D WE HIT?
I AM GROOT!
AAHHHH!

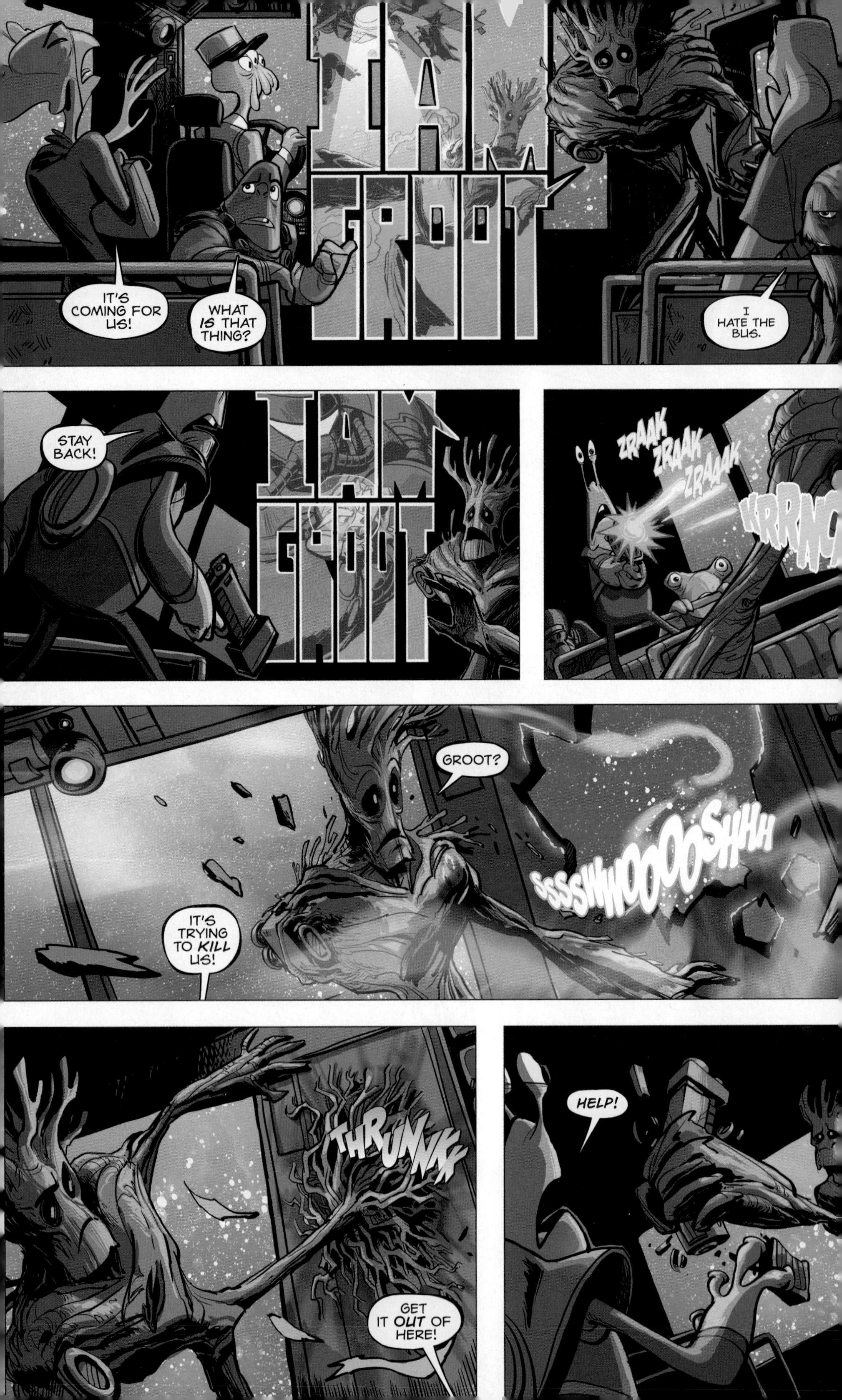
I AM GROOT
IT'S COMING FOR US!
WHAT IS THAT THING?
I HATE THE BUS.
STAY BACK!
I AM GROOT
ZRAAK ZRAAK ZRAAAK
KRRNCH
GROOT?
SSSSWHOOOOSHHH
IT'S TRYING TO KILL US!
THRUNKK
GET IT OUT OF HERE!
HELP!

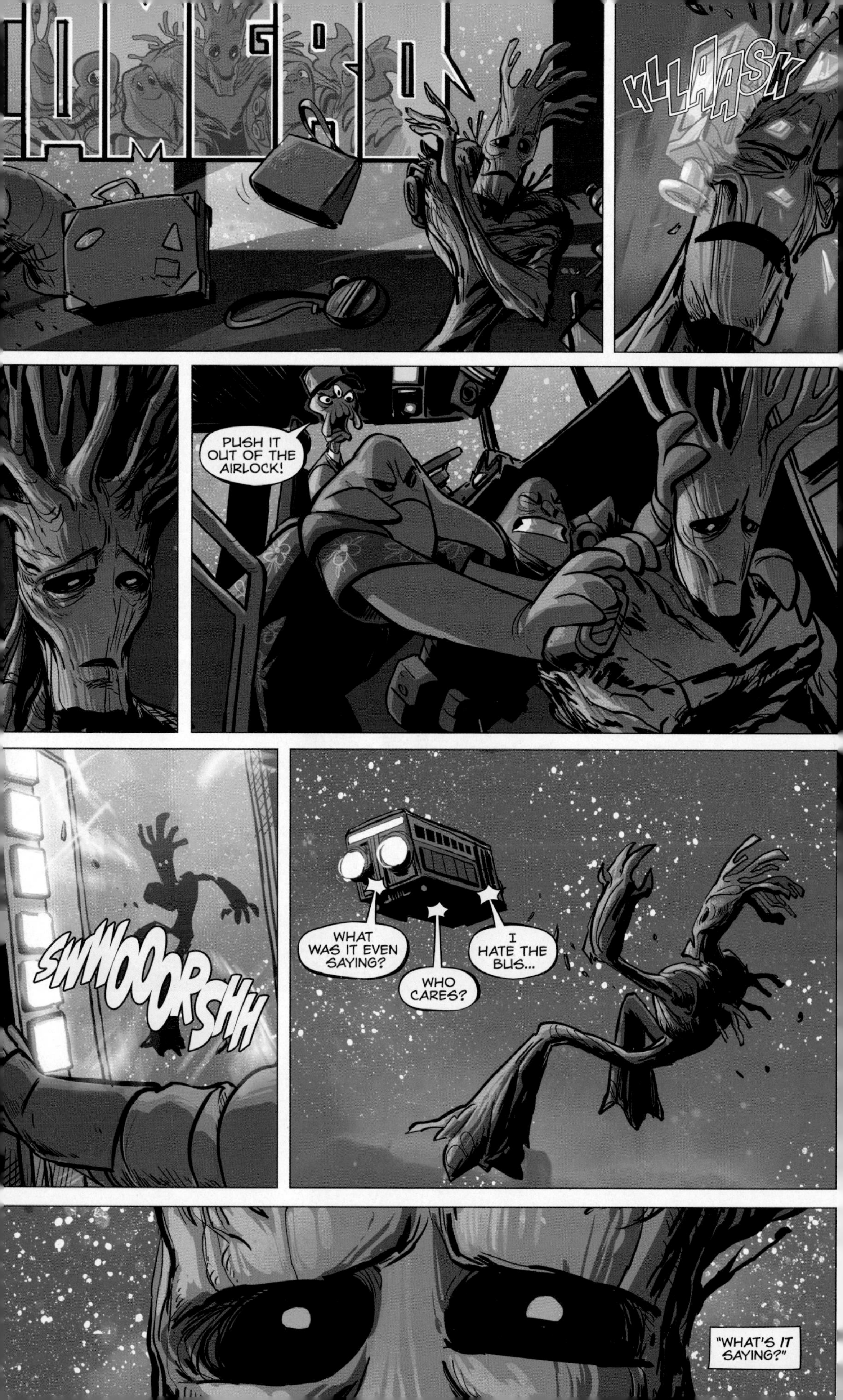
KLLAASK
PUSH IT OUT OF THE AIRLOCK!
SWWOOORSHH
WHAT WAS IT EVEN SAYING?
WHO CARES?
I HATE THE BUS...
"WHAT'S *IT* SAYING?"

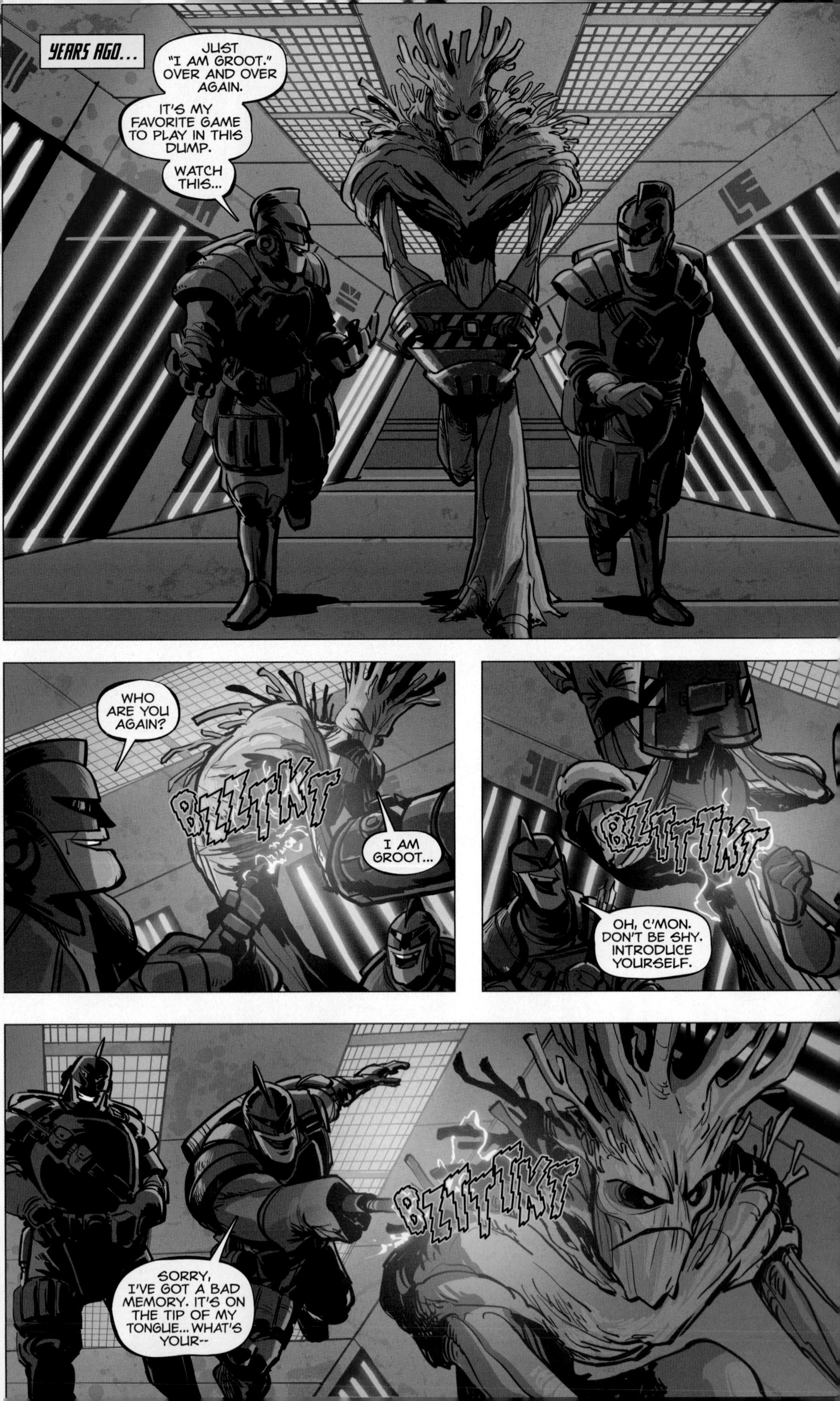
YEARS AGO...
JUST "I AM GROOT." OVER AND OVER AGAIN.
IT'S MY FAVORITE GAME TO PLAY IN THIS DUMP.
WATCH THIS...
WHO ARE YOU AGAIN?
BZZTTKT
I AM GROOT...
BZZTTKT
OH, C'MON. DON'T BE SHY. INTRODUCE YOURSELF.
BZZTTKT
SORRY, I'VE GOT A BAD MEMORY. IT'S ON THE TIP OF MY TONGUE... WHAT'S YOUR--

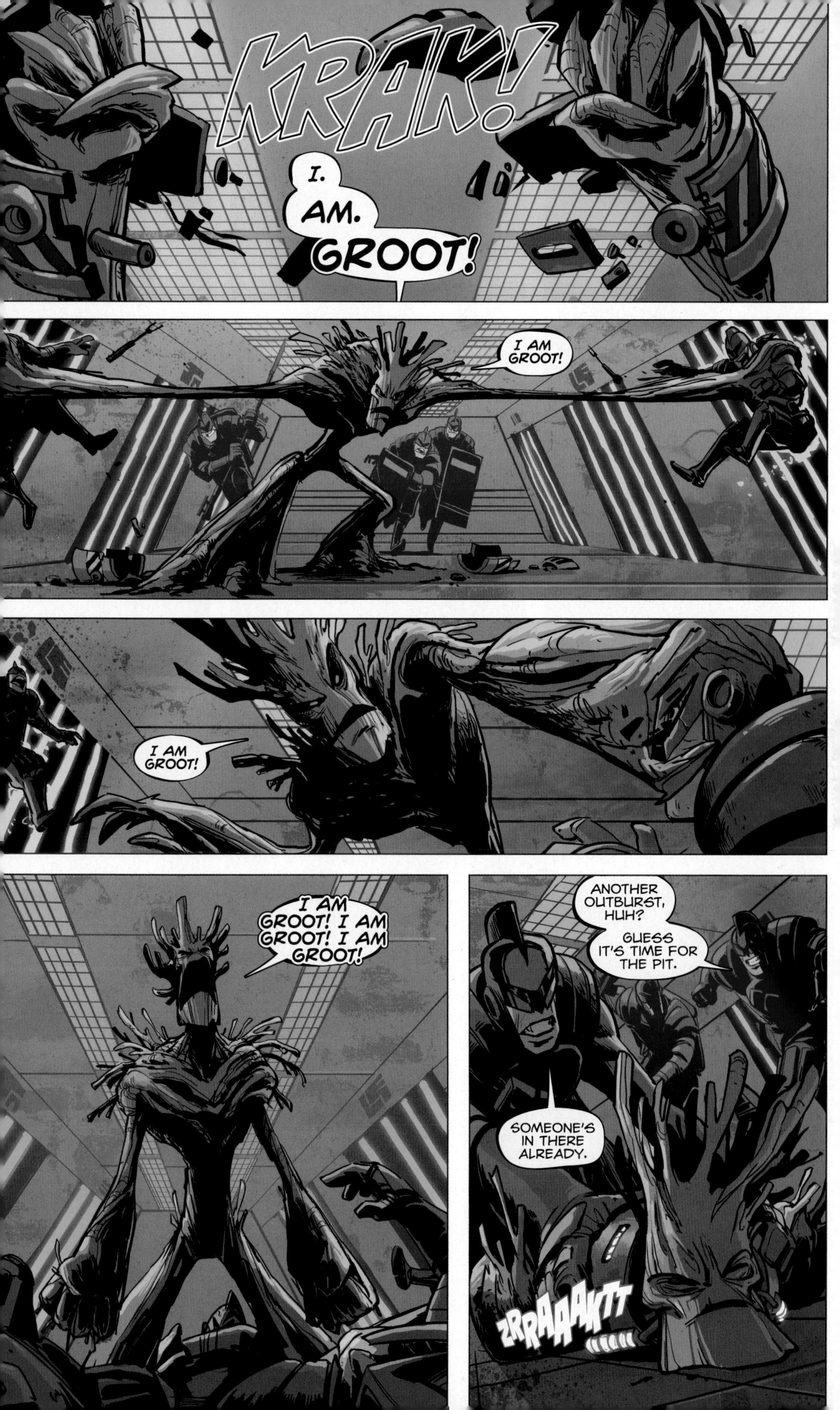
KRAK!
I. AM. GROOT!
I AM GROOT!
I AM GROOT!
I AM GROOT! I AM GROOT! I AM GROOT!
ANOTHER OUTBURST, HUH?
GUESS IT'S TIME FOR THE PIT.
SOMEONE'S IN THERE ALREADY.
ZRRAAAKTT

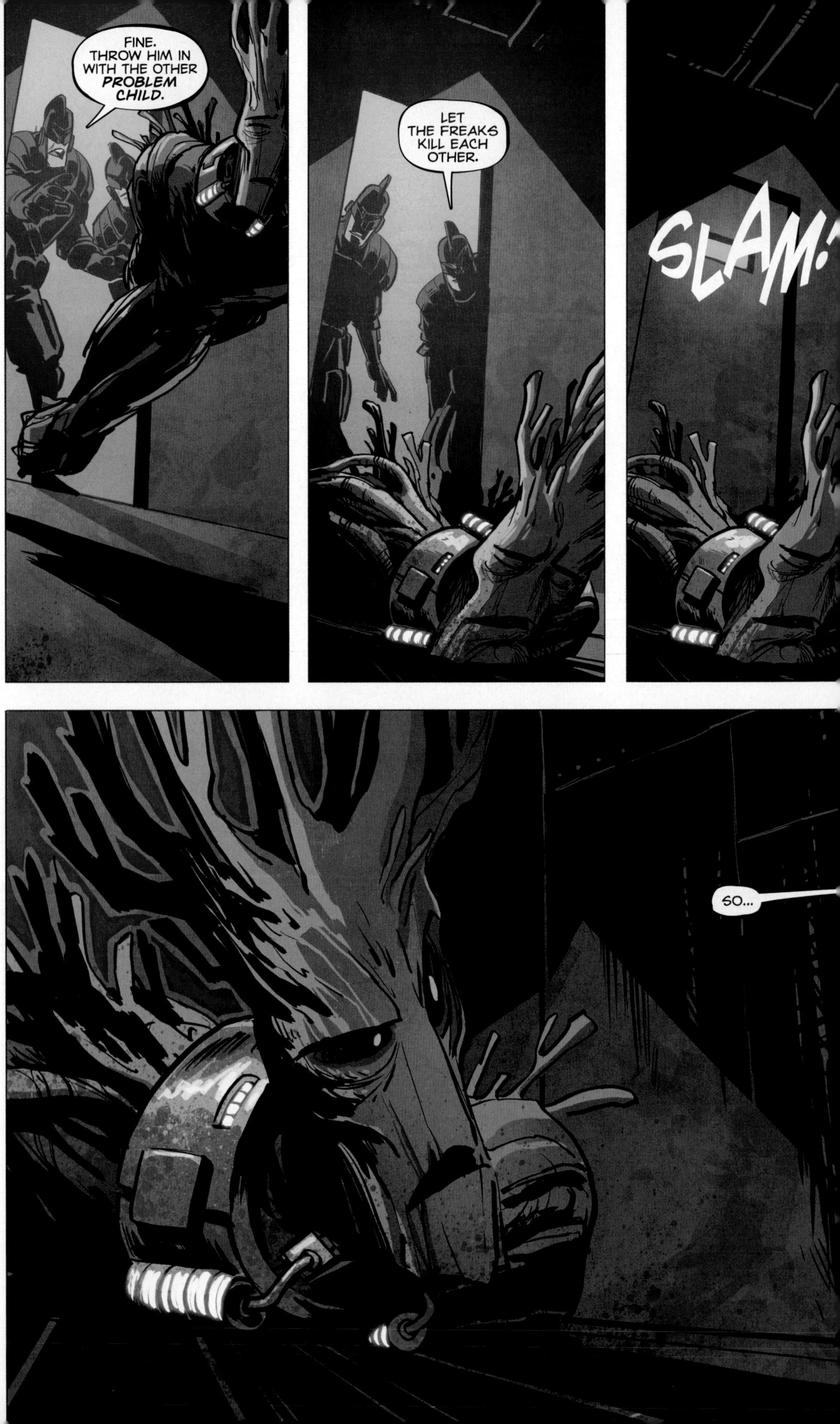
FINE. THROW HIM IN WITH THE OTHER *PROBLEM CHILD.*
LET THE FREAKS KILL EACH OTHER.
SLAM!
SO...

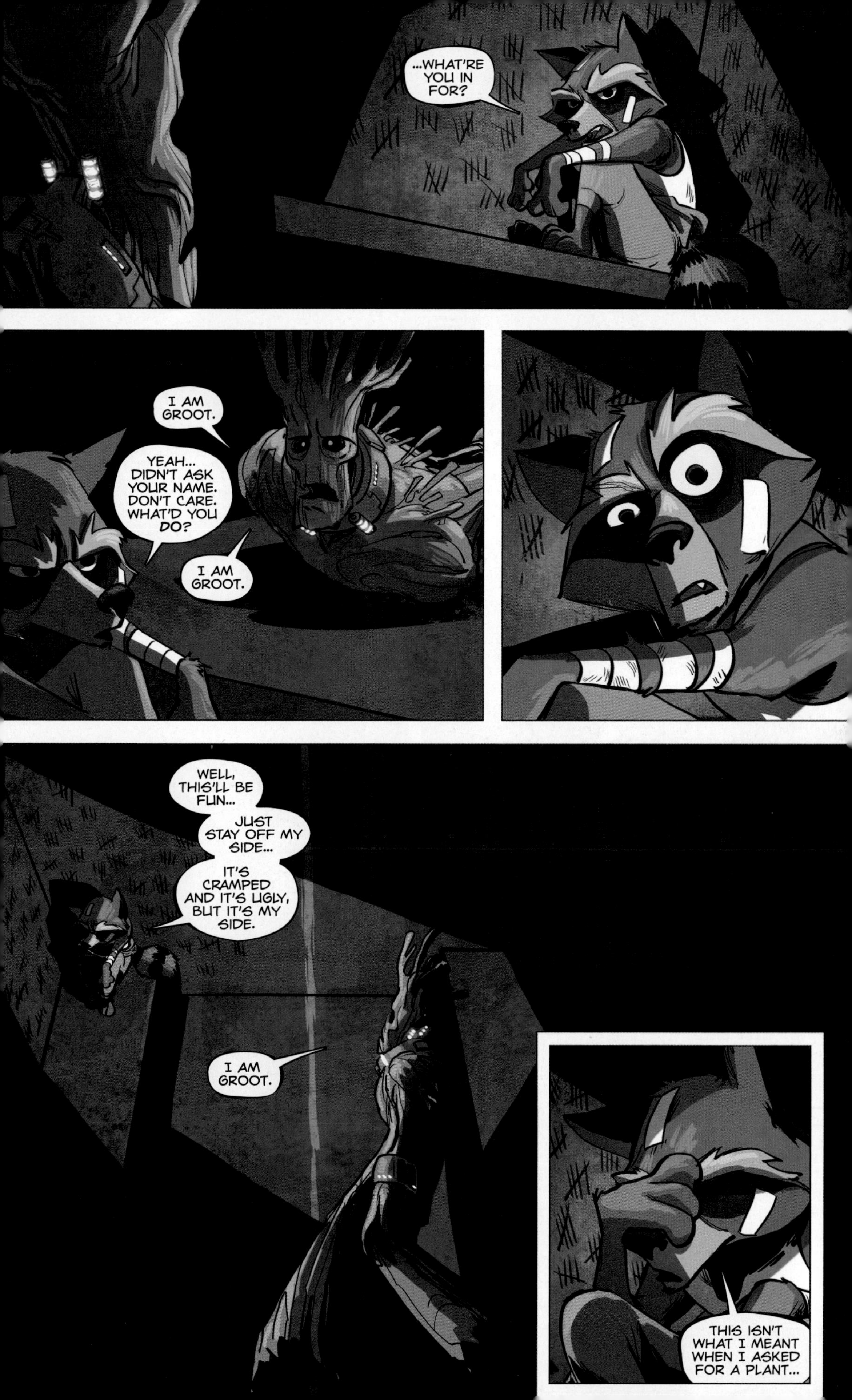
...WHAT'RE YOU IN FOR?
I AM GROOT.
YEAH... DIDN'T ASK YOUR NAME. DON'T CARE. WHAT'D YOU DO?
I AM GROOT.
WELL, THIS'LL BE FUN...
JUST STAY OFF MY SIDE...
IT'S CRAMPED AND IT'S UGLY, BUT IT'S MY SIDE.
I AM GROOT.
THIS ISN'T WHAT I MEANT WHEN I ASKED FOR A PLANT...

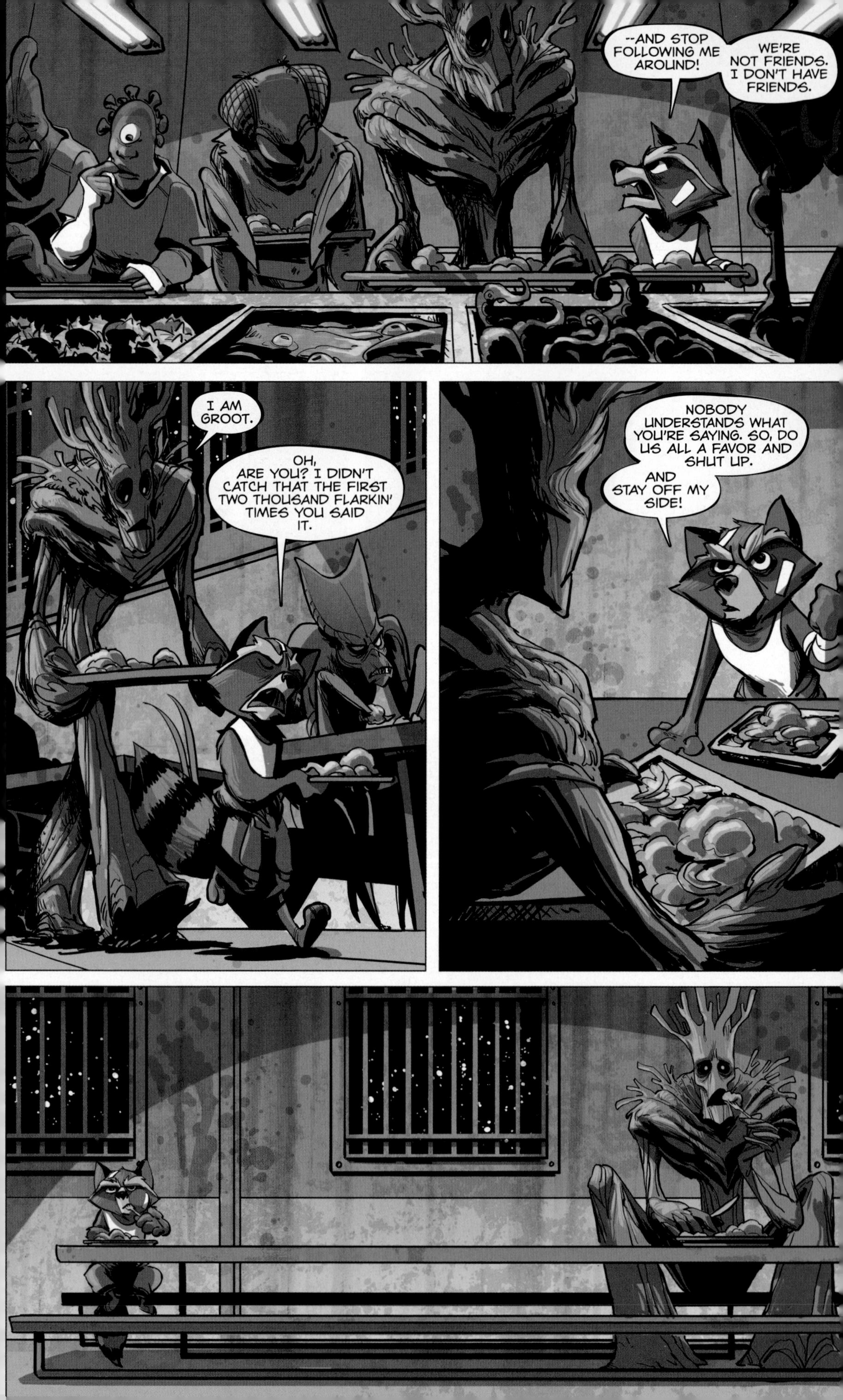
--AND STOP FOLLOWING ME AROUND!
WE'RE NOT FRIENDS. I DON'T HAVE FRIENDS.
I AM GROOT.
OH, ARE YOU? I DIDN'T CATCH THAT THE FIRST TWO THOUSAND FLARKIN' TIMES YOU SAID IT.
NOBODY UNDERSTANDS WHAT YOU'RE SAYING. SO, DO US ALL A FAVOR AND SHUT UP.
AND STAY OFF MY SIDE!

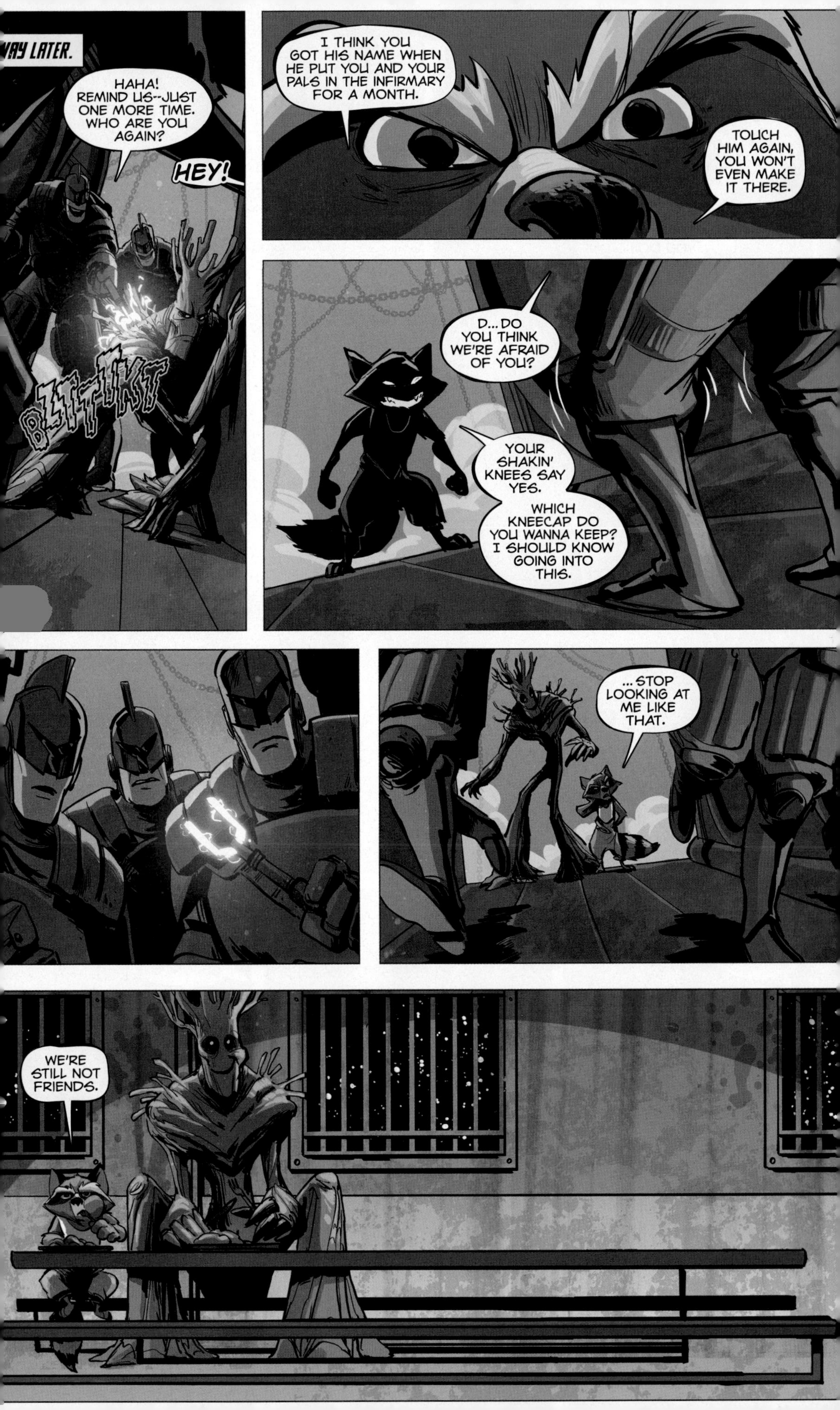

...WAY LATER.
HAHA! REMIND US--JUST ONE MORE TIME. WHO ARE YOU AGAIN?
HEY!
BZZTTZKT
I THINK YOU GOT HIS NAME WHEN HE PUT YOU AND YOUR PALS IN THE INFIRMARY FOR A MONTH.
TOUCH HIM AGAIN, YOU WON'T EVEN MAKE IT THERE.
D...DO YOU THINK WE'RE AFRAID OF YOU?
YOUR SHAKIN' KNEES SAY YES.
WHICH KNEECAP DO YOU WANNA KEEP? I SHOULD KNOW GOING INTO THIS.
...STOP LOOKING AT ME LIKE THAT.
WE'RE STILL NOT FRIENDS.

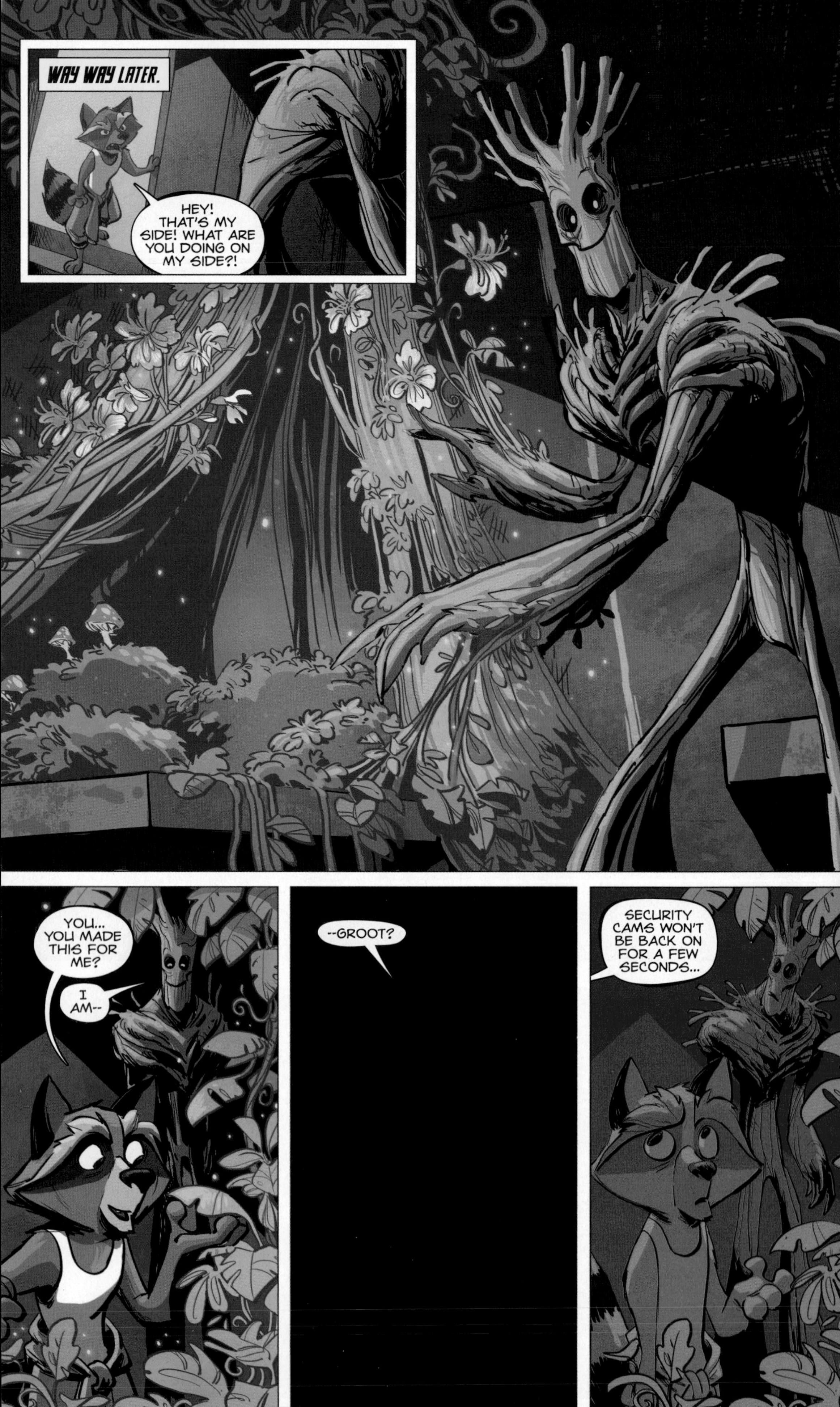
WAY WAY LATER.
HEY! THAT'S MY SIDE! WHAT ARE YOU DOING ON MY SIDE?!
YOU... YOU MADE THIS FOR ME?
I AM--
--GROOT?
SECURITY CAMS WON'T BE BACK ON FOR A FEW SECONDS...

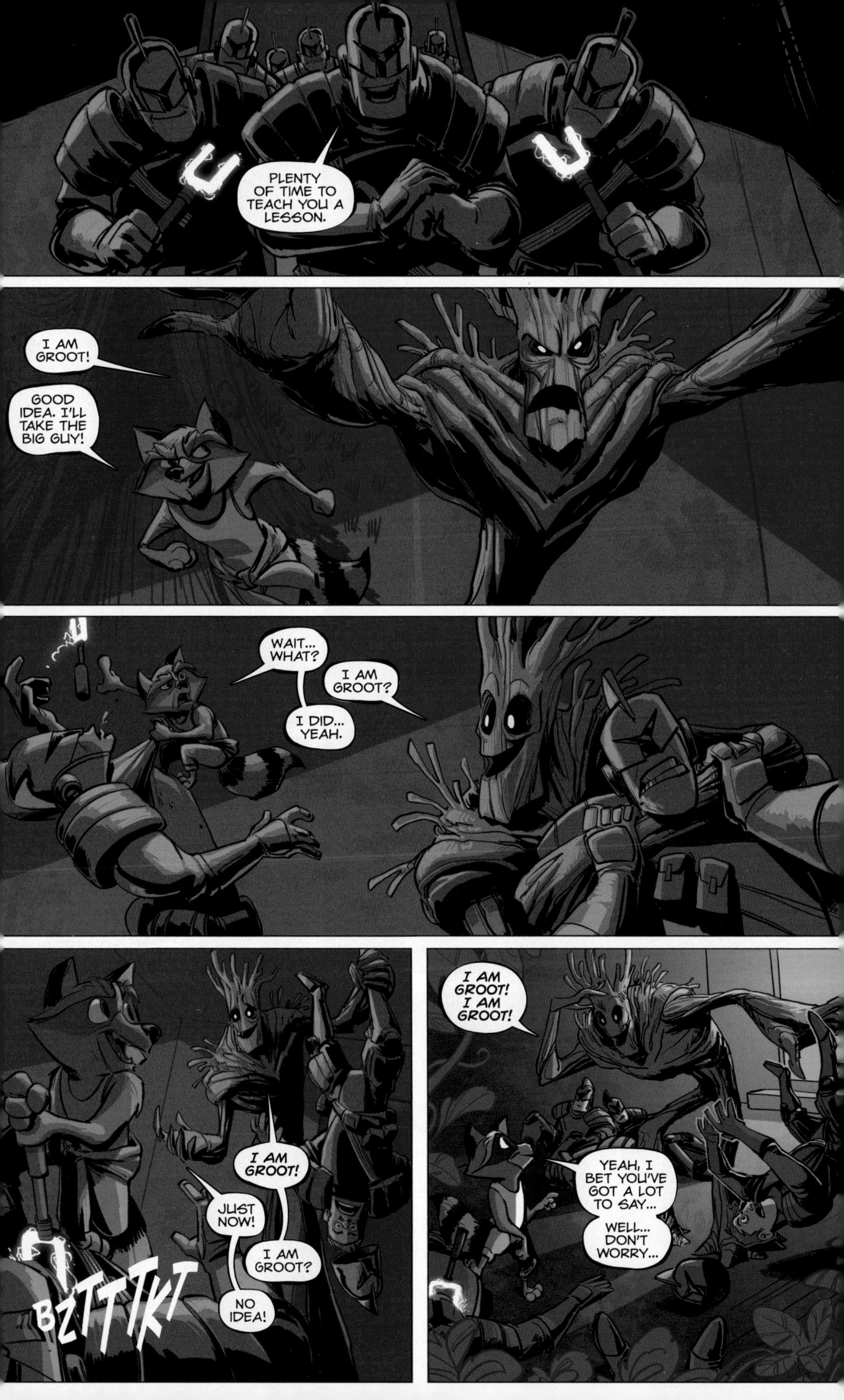
PLENTY OF TIME TO TEACH YOU A LESSON.
I AM GROOT!
GOOD IDEA. I'LL TAKE THE BIG GUY!
WAIT... WHAT?
I AM GROOT?
I DID... YEAH.
I AM GROOT!
JUST NOW!
I AM GROOT?
NO IDEA!
BZTTTKT
I AM GROOT! I AM GROOT!
YEAH, I BET YOU'VE GOT A LOT TO SAY...
WELL... DON'T WORRY...

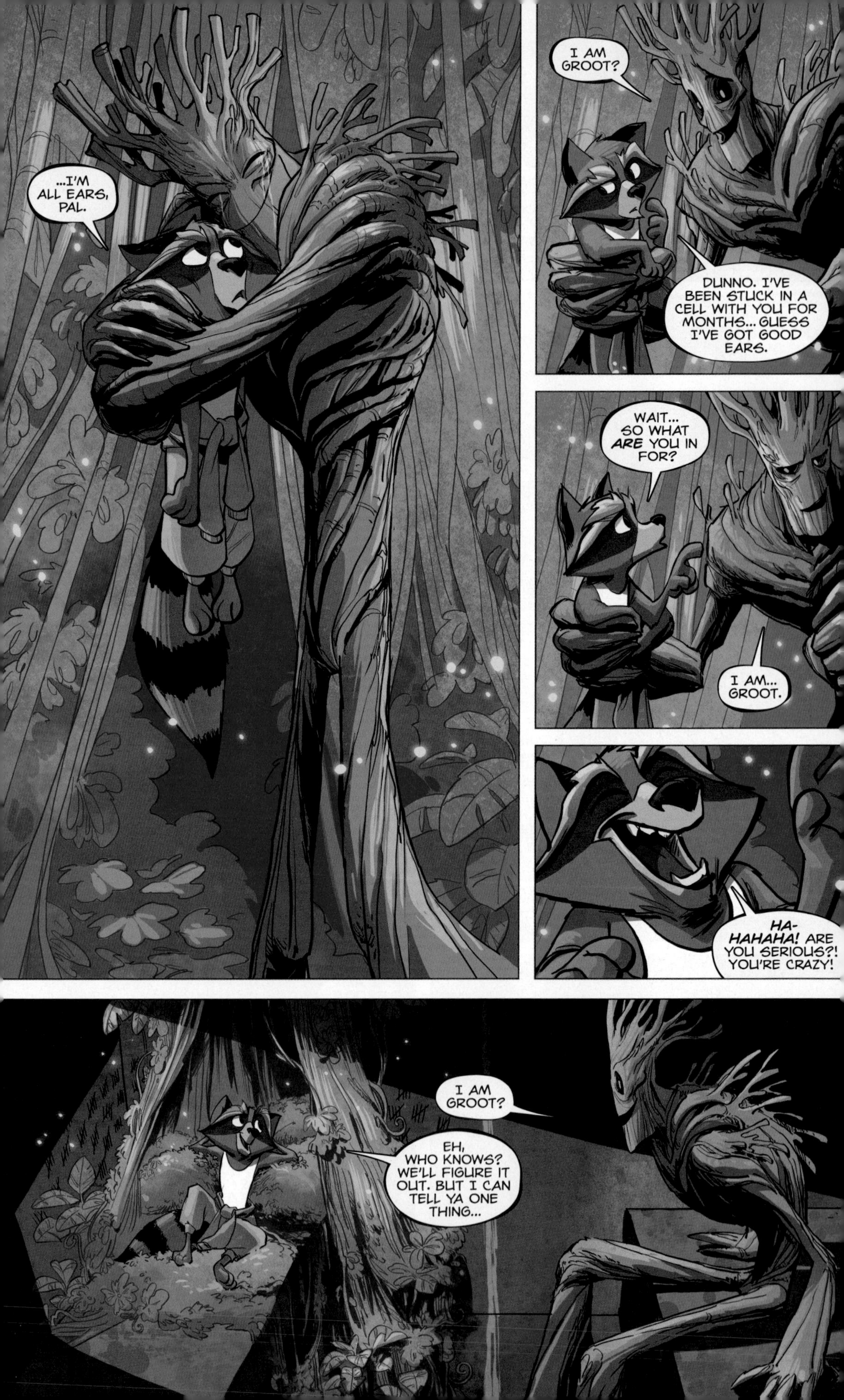
...I'M ALL EARS, PAL.
I AM GROOT?
DUNNO. I'VE BEEN STUCK IN A CELL WITH YOU FOR MONTHS... GUESS I'VE GOT GOOD EARS.
WAIT... SO WHAT *ARE* YOU IN FOR?
I AM... GROOT.
HA-HAHAHA! ARE YOU SERIOUS?! YOU'RE CRAZY!
I AM GROOT?
EH, WHO KNOWS? WE'LL FIGURE IT OUT. BUT I CAN TELL YA ONE THING...

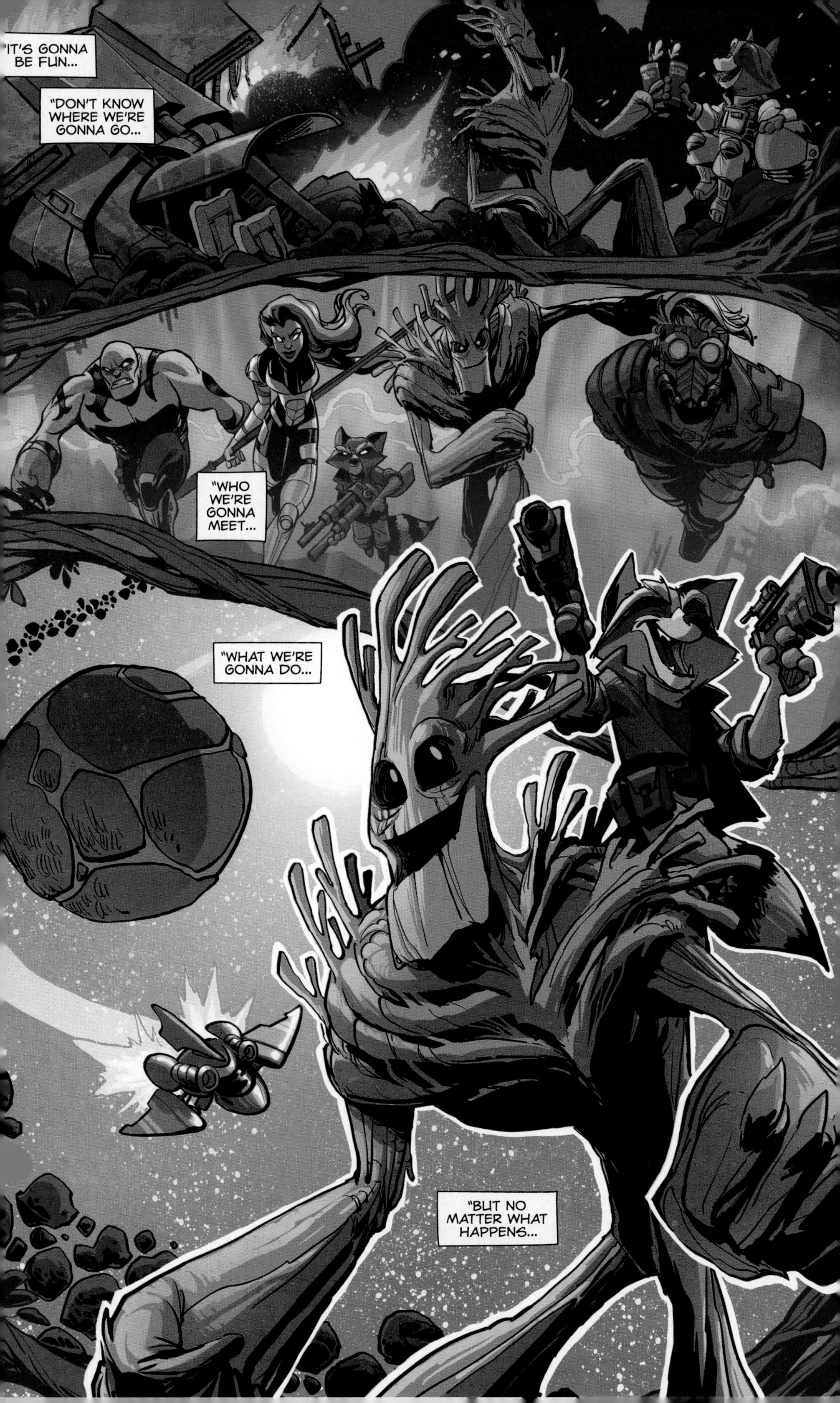
"IT'S GONNA BE FUN...
"DON'T KNOW WHERE WE'RE GONNA GO...
"WHO WE'RE GONNA MEET...
"WHAT WE'RE GONNA DO...
"BUT NO MATTER WHAT HAPPENS...

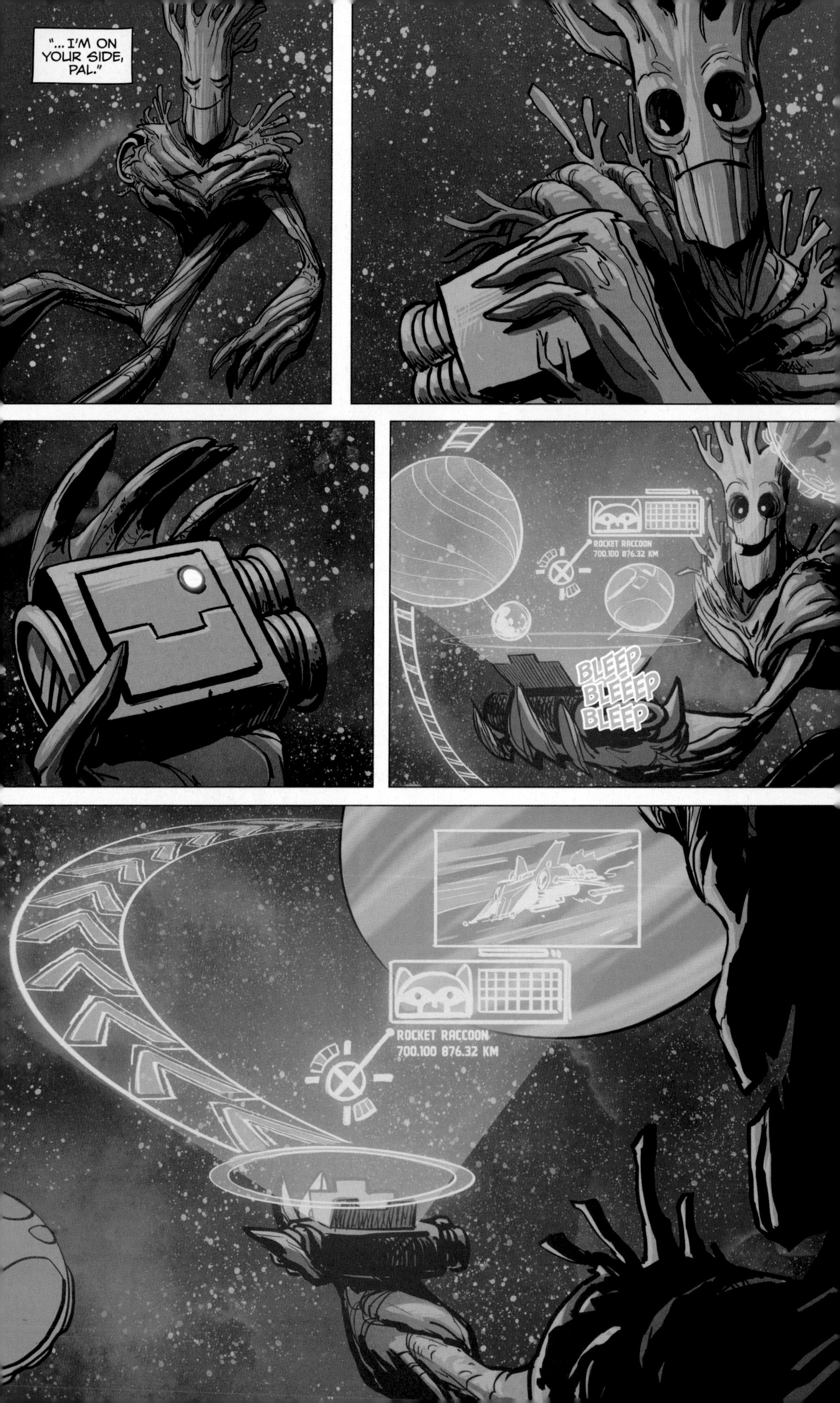
"...I'M ON YOUR SIDE, PAL."
ROCKET RACCOON
700.100 876.32 KM
BLEEP
BLEEEP
BLEEP
ROCKET RACCOON
700.100 876.32 KM

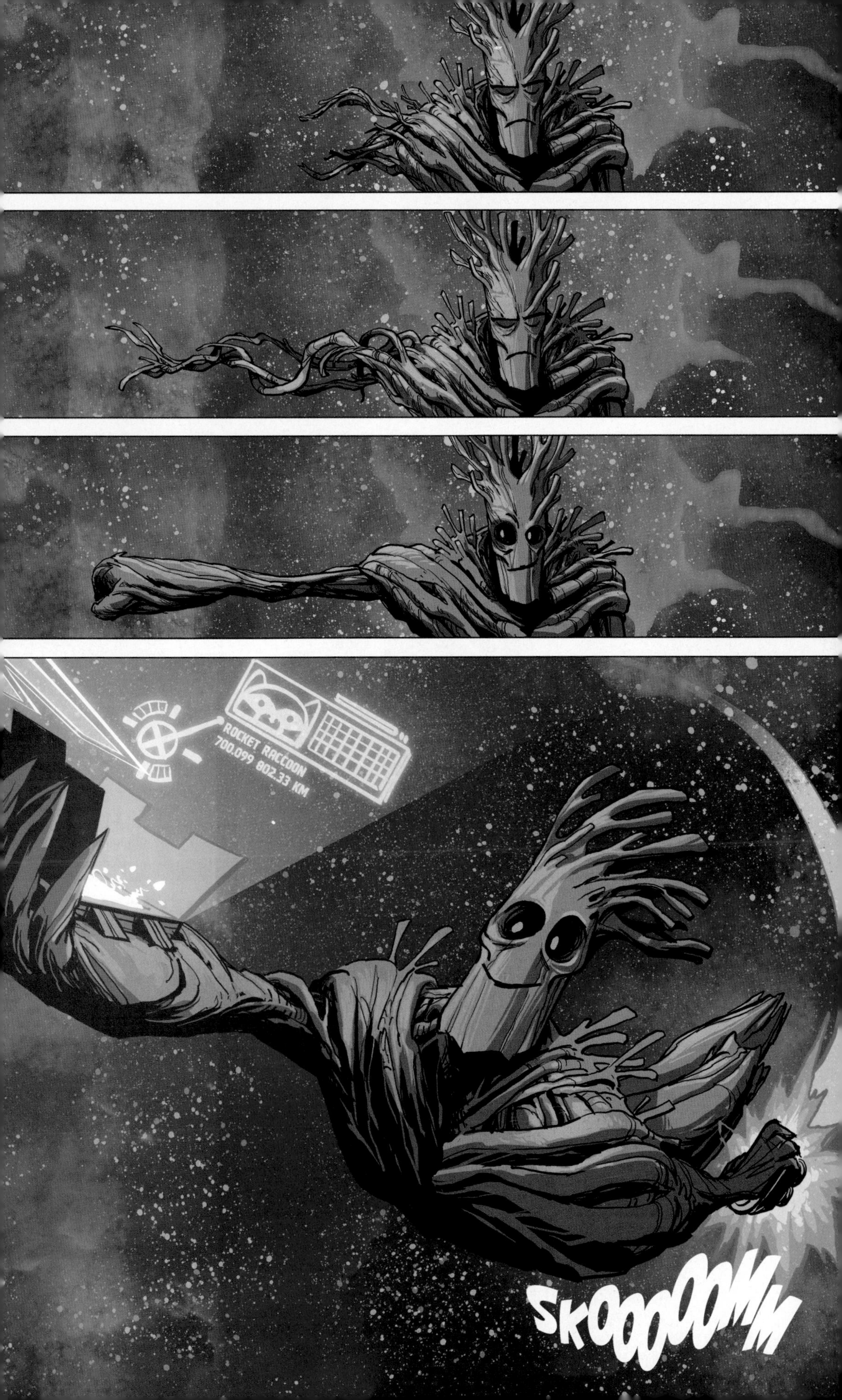

ROCKET RACCOON
700.099 802.33 KM
SKOOOOOMM

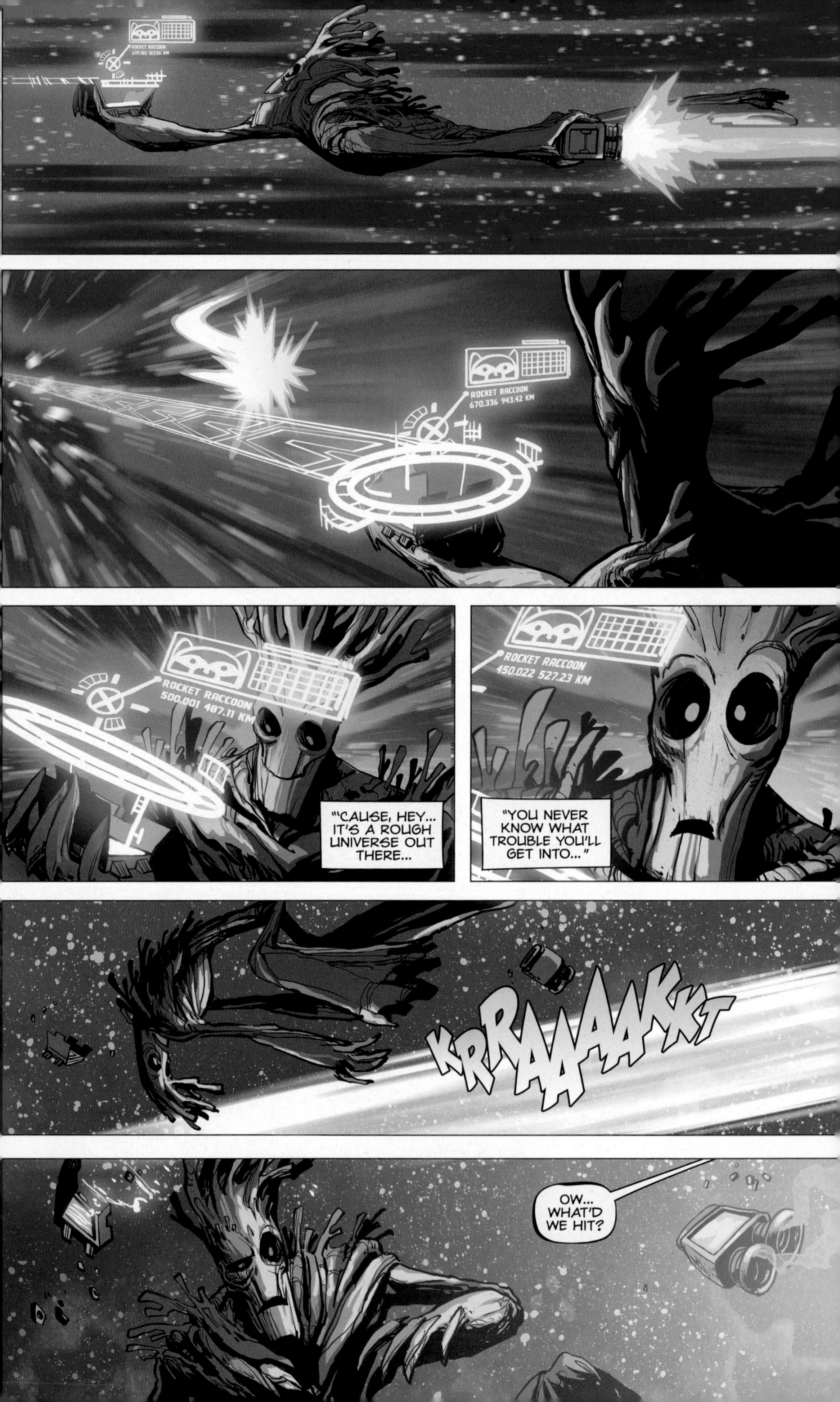
ROCKET RACCOON
699.150 103.56 KM
ROCKET RACCOON
670.336 943.42 KM
ROCKET RACCOON
500.001 487.11 KM
"'CAUSE, HEY... IT'S A ROUGH UNIVERSE OUT THERE...
ROCKET RACCOON
450.022 527.23 KM
"YOU NEVER KNOW WHAT TROUBLE YOU'LL GET INTO..."
KRRAAAAKKT
OW... WHAT'D WE HIT?

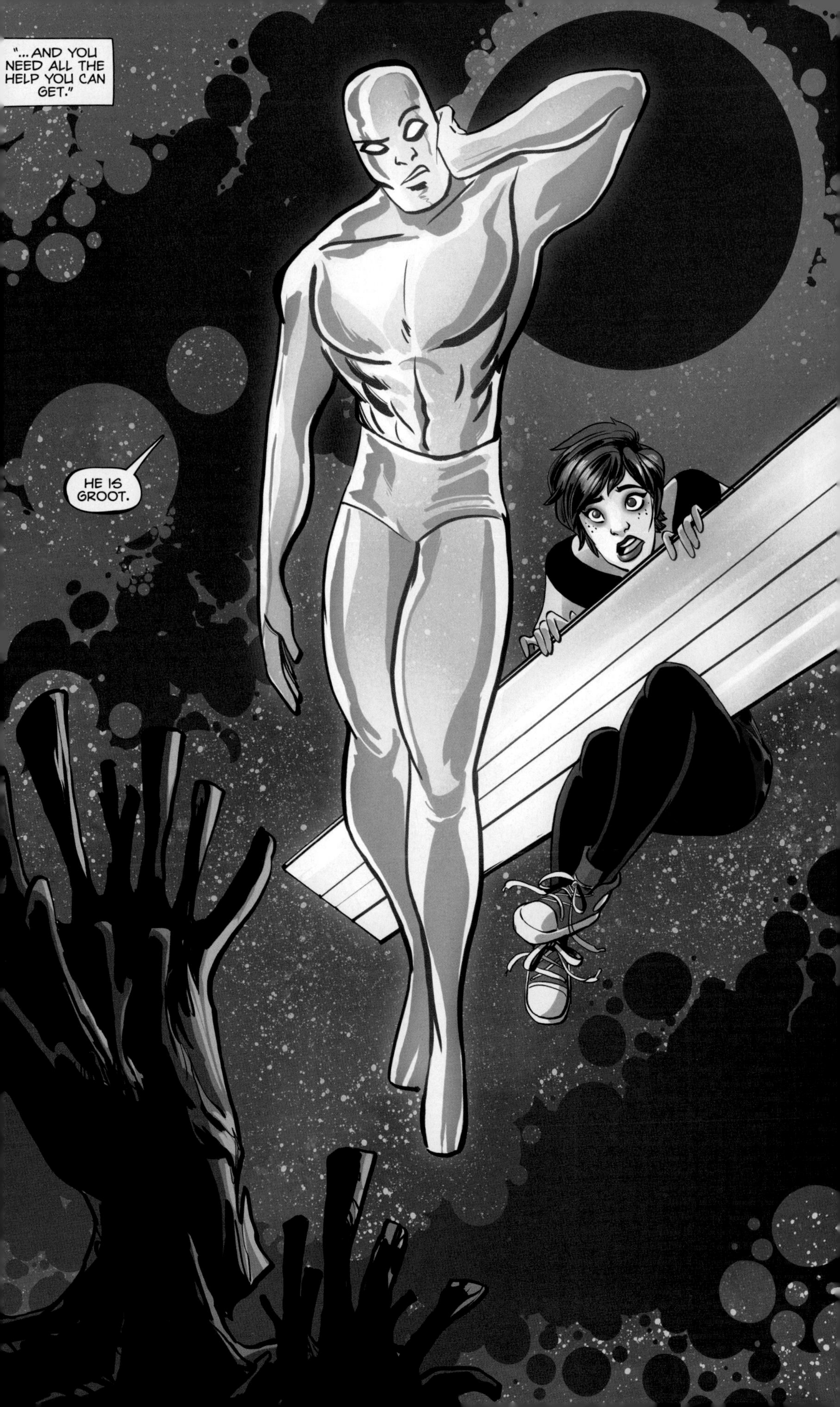
"...AND YOU NEED ALL THE HELP YOU CAN GET."
HE IS GROOT.

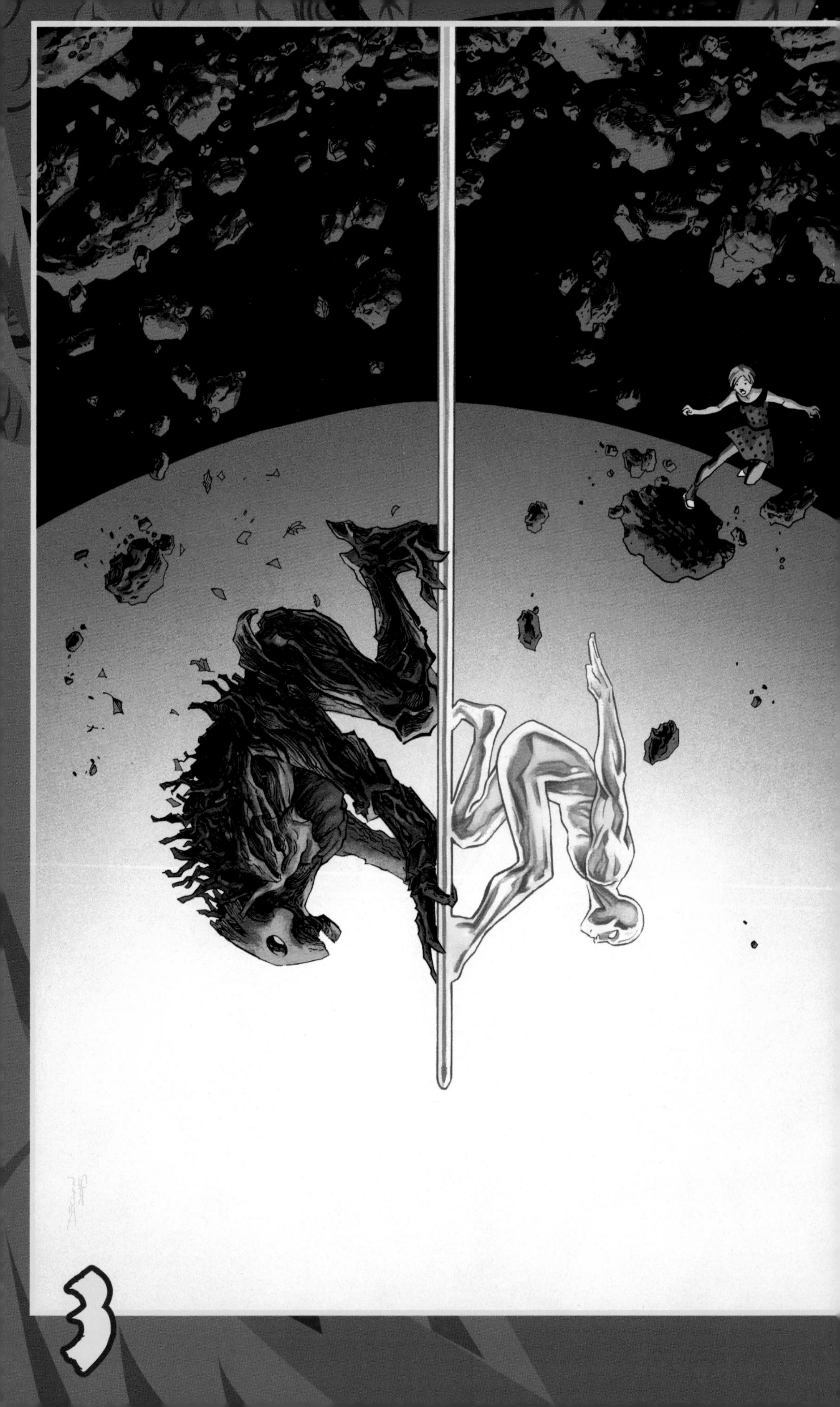
3

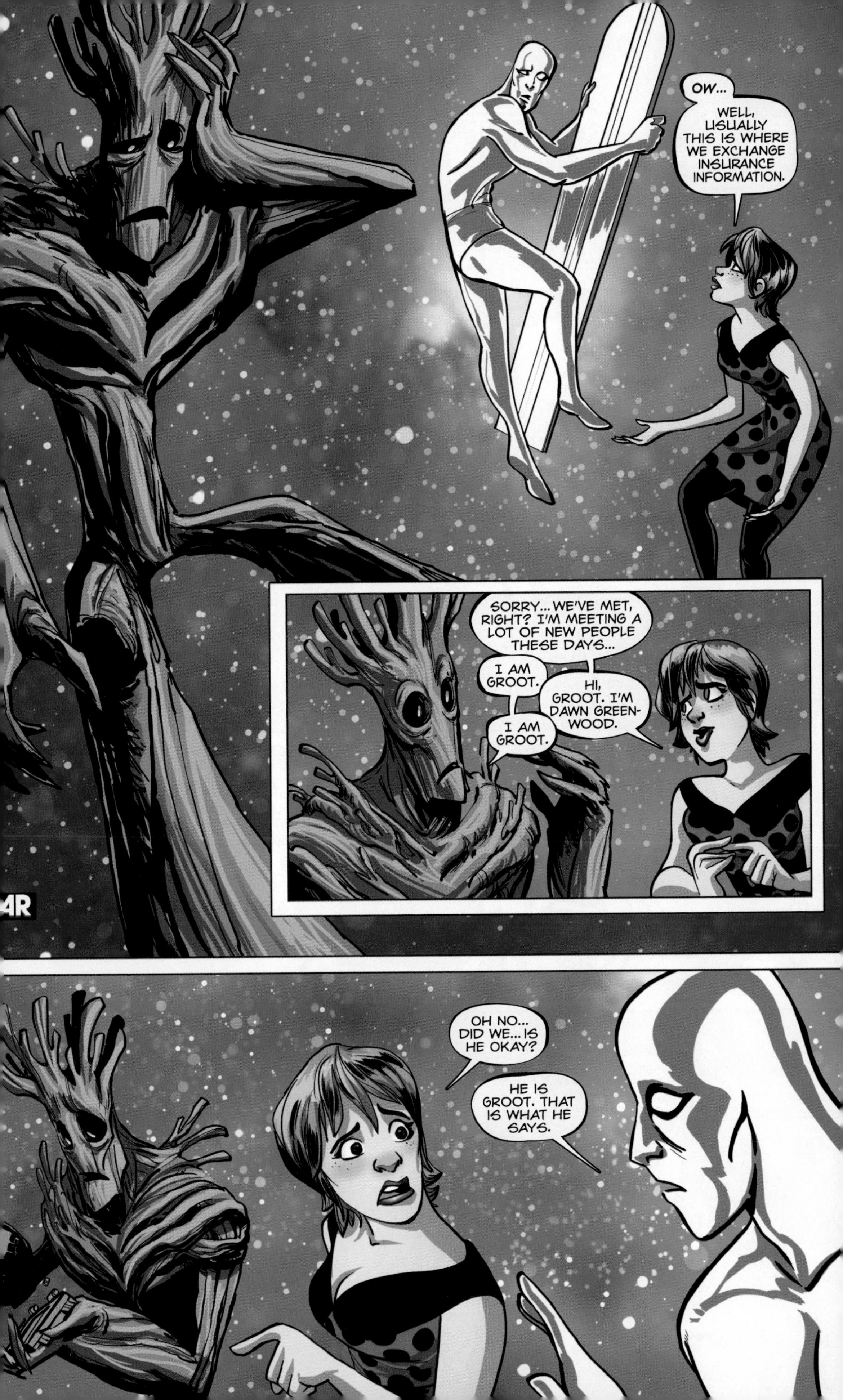
OW...
WELL, USUALLY THIS IS WHERE WE EXCHANGE INSURANCE INFORMATION.
SORRY... WE'VE MET, RIGHT? I'M MEETING A LOT OF NEW PEOPLE THESE DAYS...
I AM GROOT.
HI, GROOT. I'M DAWN GREEN-WOOD.
I AM GROOT.
OH NO... DID WE... IS HE OKAY?
HE IS GROOT. THAT IS WHAT HE SAYS.

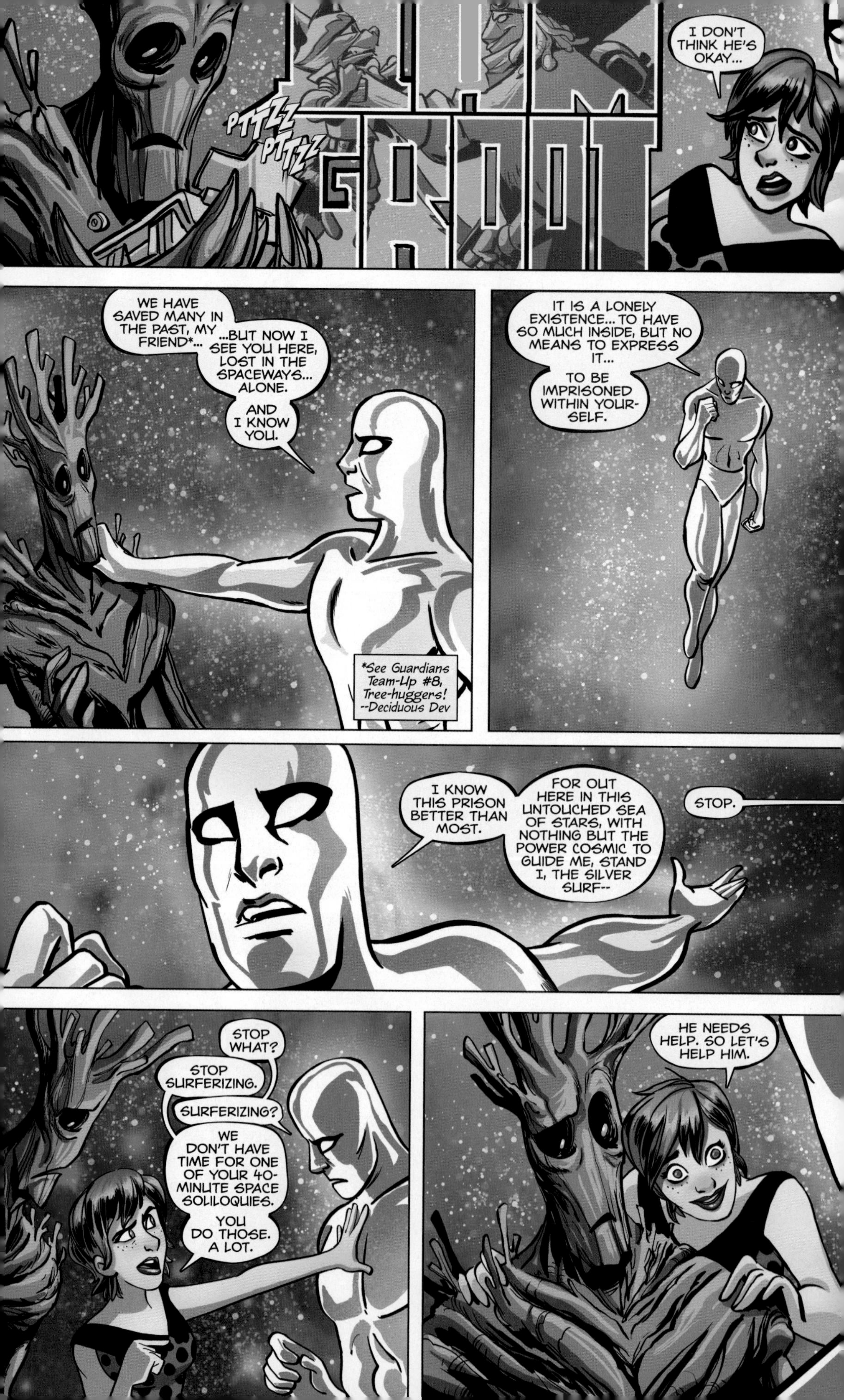
PTTZZ
PTTZZ
I DON'T THINK HE'S OKAY...
WE HAVE SAVED MANY IN THE PAST, MY FRIEND*...
...BUT NOW I SEE YOU HERE, LOST IN THE SPACEWAYS... ALONE.
AND I KNOW YOU.
*See Guardians Team-Up #8, Tree-huggers! --Deciduous Dev
IT IS A LONELY EXISTENCE... TO HAVE SO MUCH INSIDE, BUT NO MEANS TO EXPRESS IT...
TO BE IMPRISONED WITHIN YOURSELF.
I KNOW THIS PRISON BETTER THAN MOST.
FOR OUT HERE IN THIS UNTOUCHED SEA OF STARS, WITH NOTHING BUT THE POWER COSMIC TO GUIDE ME, STAND I, THE SILVER SURF--
STOP.
STOP WHAT?
STOP SURFERIZING.
SURFERIZING?
WE DON'T HAVE TIME FOR ONE OF YOUR 40-MINUTE SPACE SOLILOQUIES.
YOU DO THOSE. A LOT.
HE NEEDS HELP. SO LET'S HELP HIM.

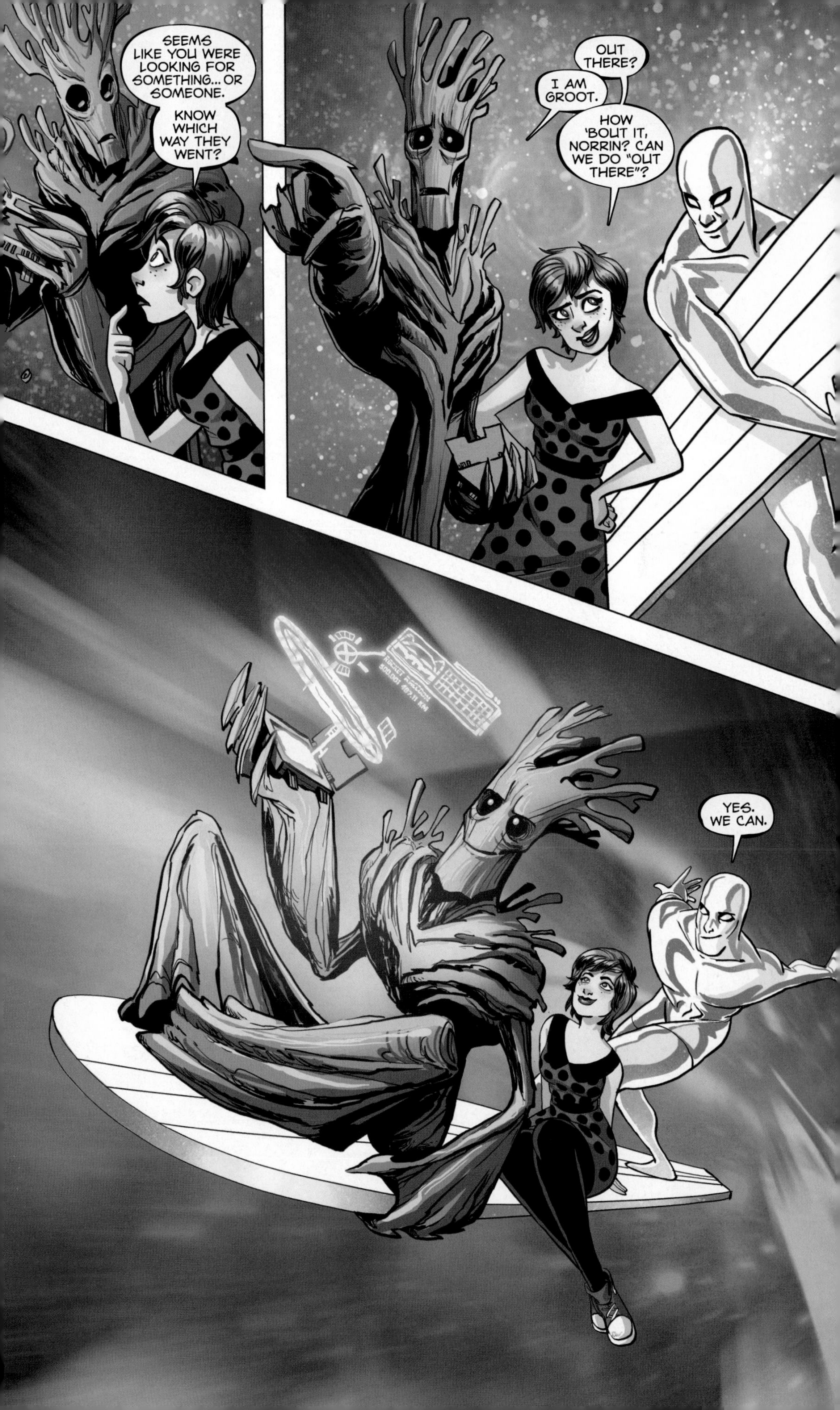
SEEMS LIKE YOU WERE LOOKING FOR SOMETHING...OR SOMEONE.
KNOW WHICH WAY THEY WENT?
I AM GROOT.
OUT THERE?
HOW 'BOUT IT, NORRIN? CAN WE DO "OUT THERE"?
YES. WE CAN.

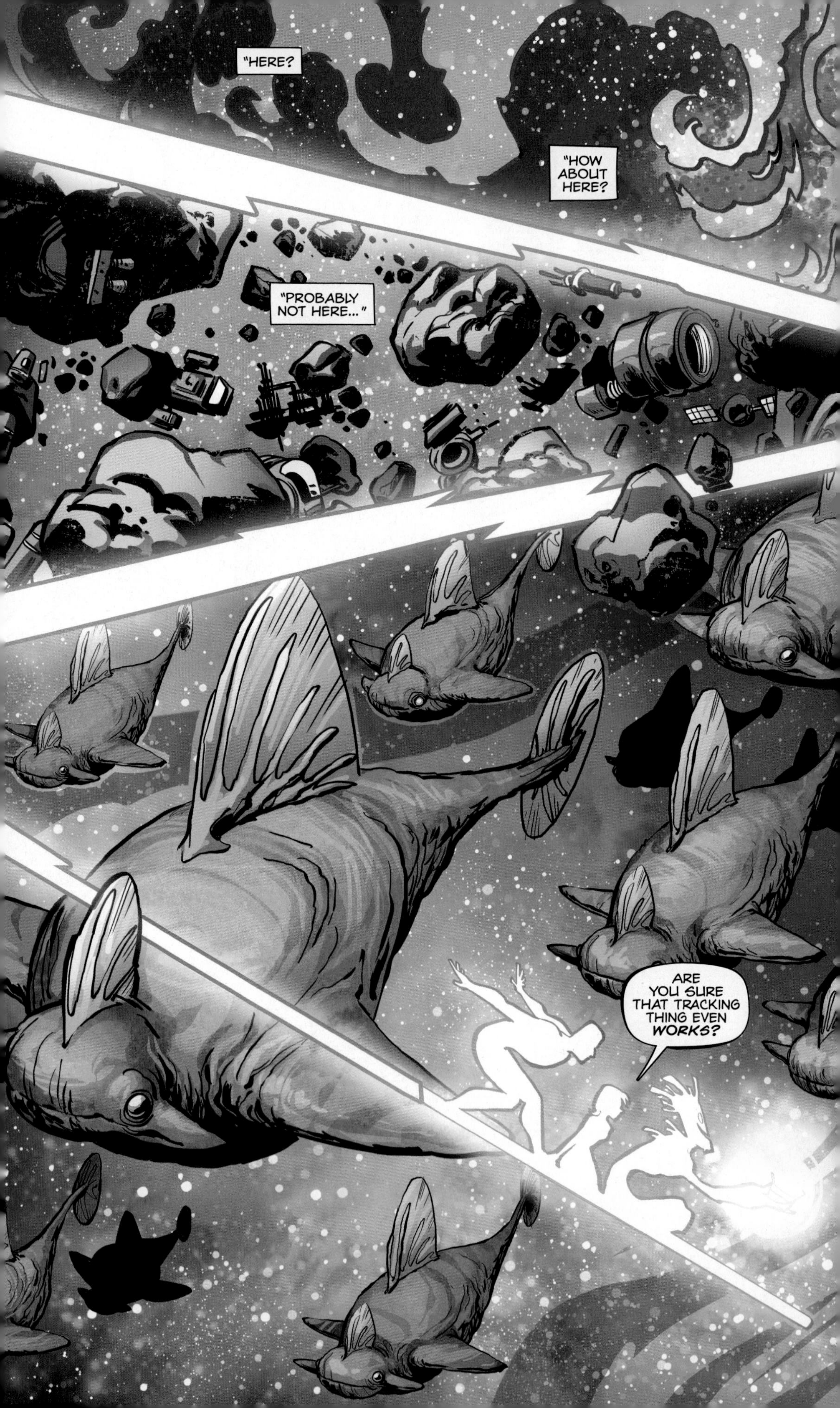
"HERE?
"HOW ABOUT HERE?
"PROBABLY NOT HERE..."
ARE YOU SURE THAT TRACKING THING EVEN WORKS?

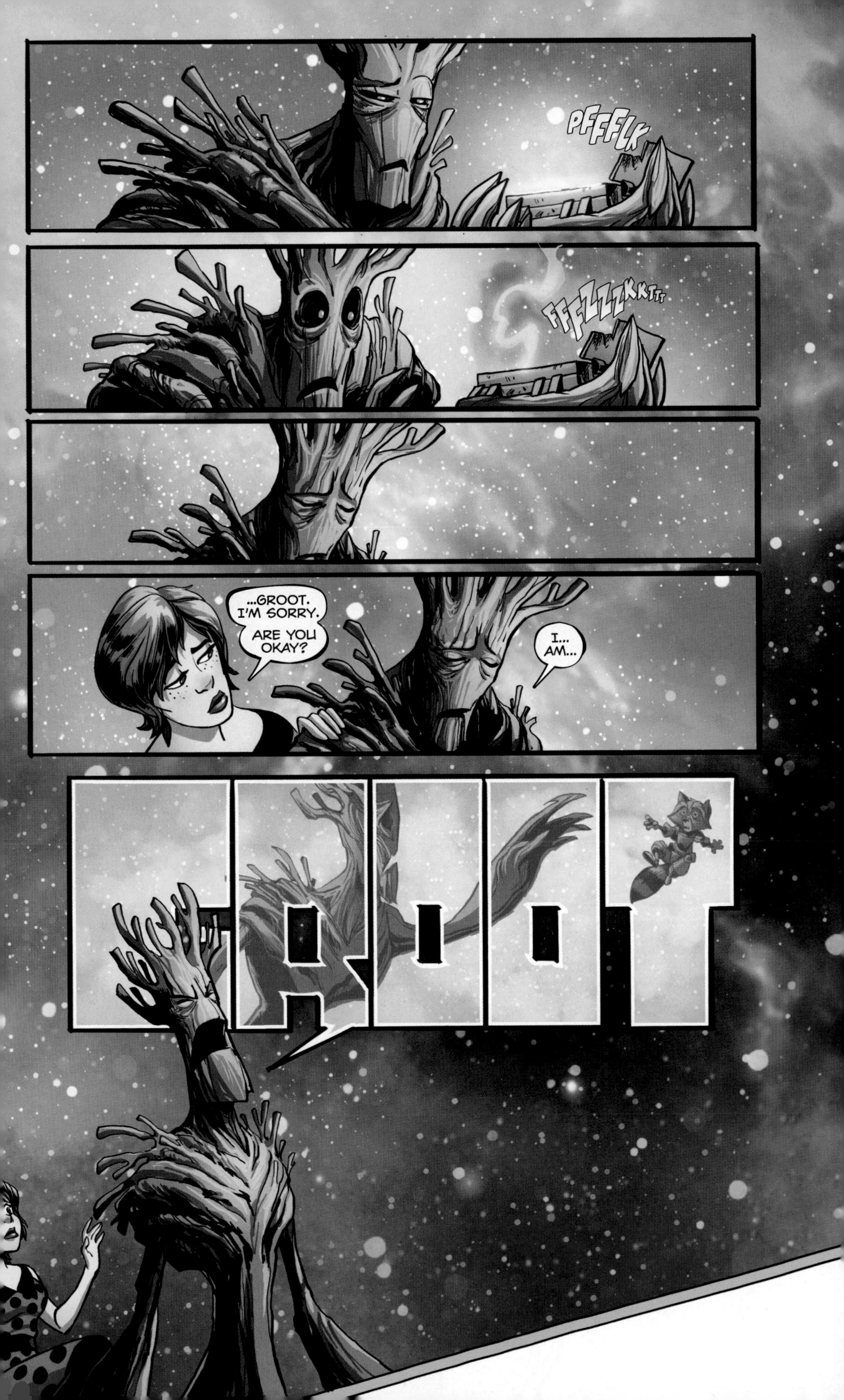
PFFFLK
FFFZZZKKTTT
...GROOT. I'M SORRY. ARE YOU OKAY?
I... AM...
GROOT

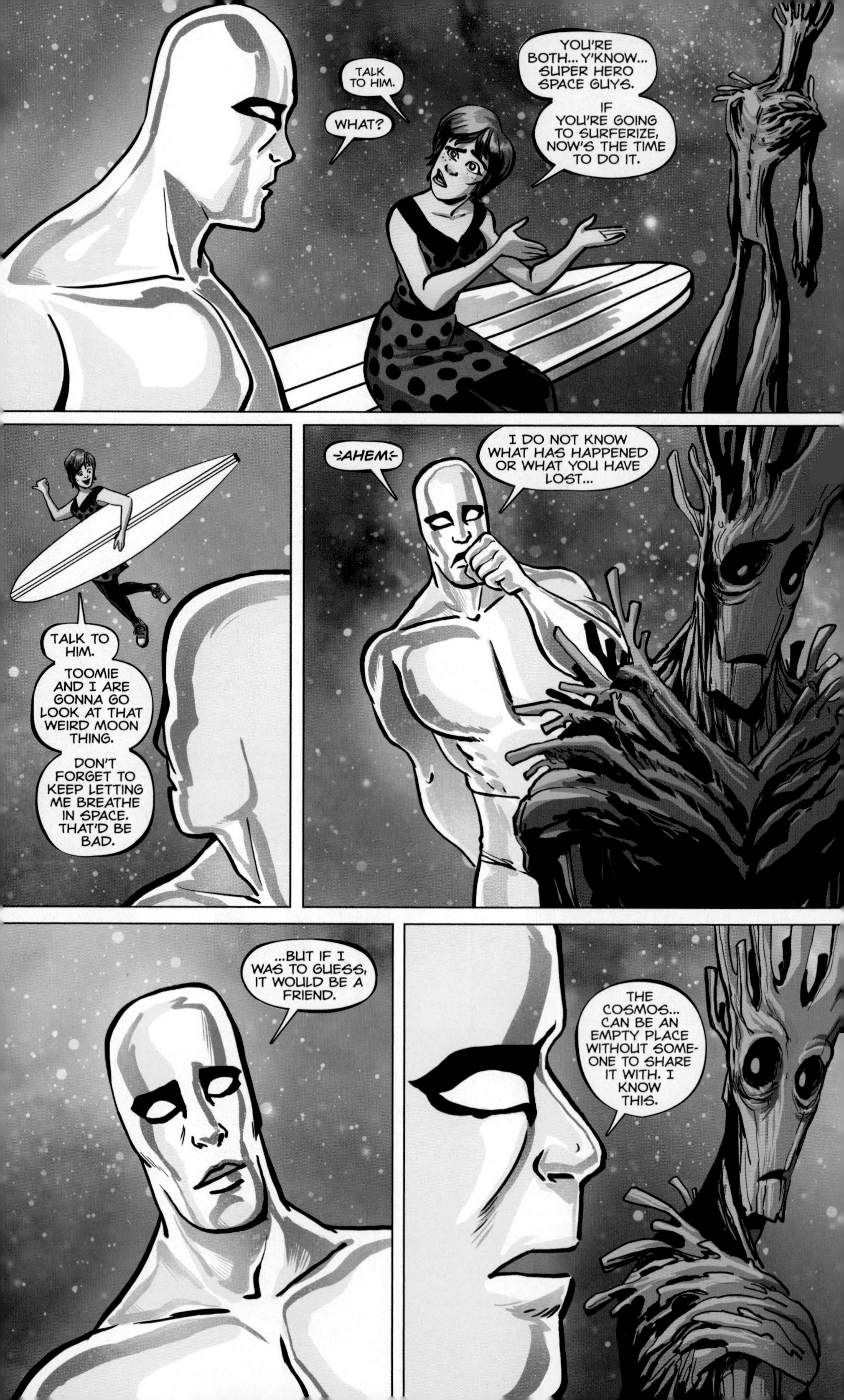
TALK TO HIM.
WHAT?
YOU'RE BOTH... Y'KNOW... SUPER HERO SPACE GUYS.
IF YOU'RE GOING TO SURFERIZE, NOW'S THE TIME TO DO IT.
TALK TO HIM.
TOOMIE AND I ARE GONNA GO LOOK AT THAT WEIRD MOON THING.
DON'T FORGET TO KEEP LETTING ME BREATHE IN SPACE. THAT'D BE BAD.
AHEM
I DO NOT KNOW WHAT HAS HAPPENED OR WHAT YOU HAVE LOST...
...BUT IF I WAS TO GUESS, IT WOULD BE A FRIEND.
THE COSMOS... CAN BE AN EMPTY PLACE WITHOUT SOME-ONE TO SHARE IT WITH. I KNOW THIS.

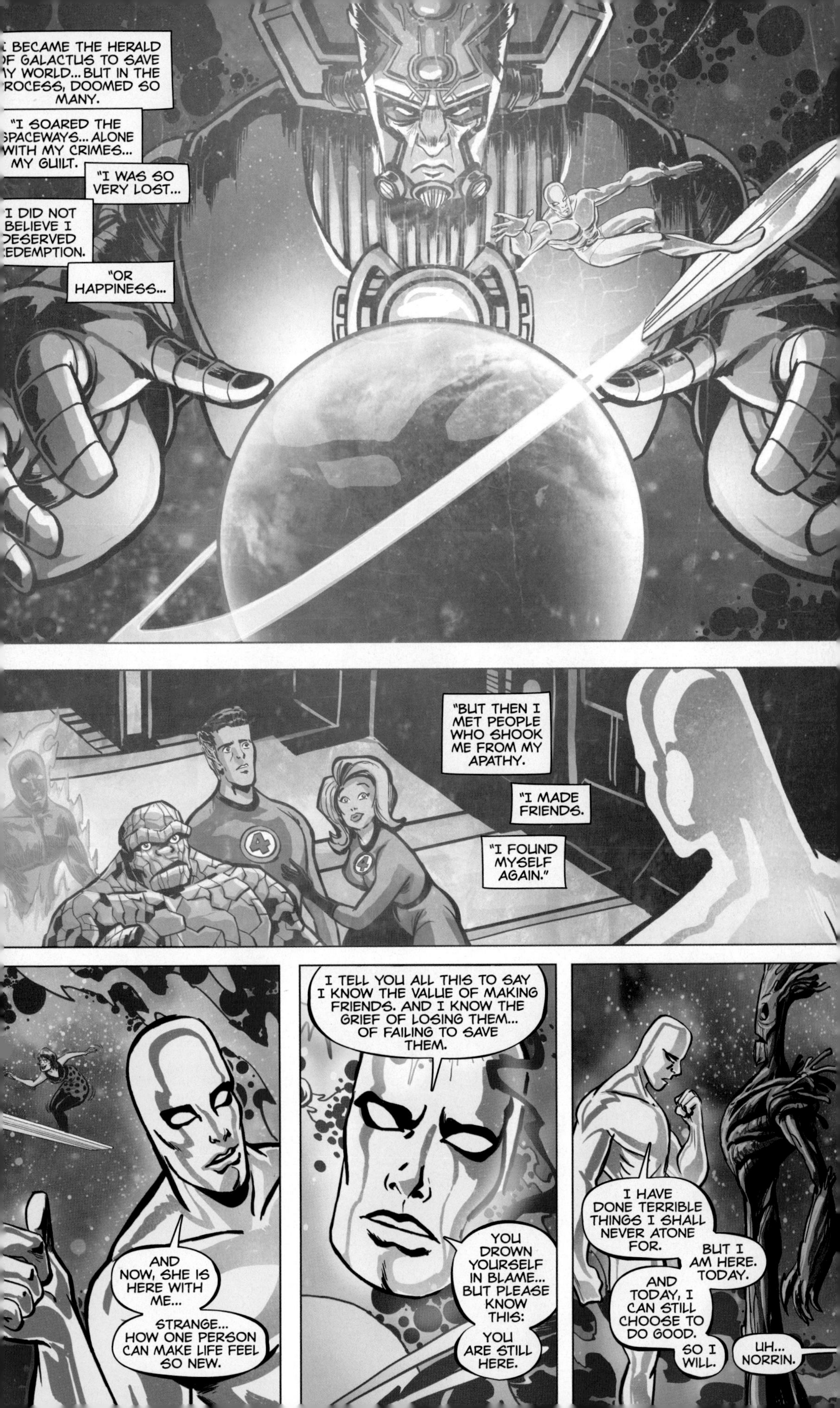

I BECAME THE HERALD OF GALACTUS TO SAVE MY WORLD... BUT IN THE PROCESS, DOOMED SO MANY.
"I SOARED THE SPACEWAYS... ALONE WITH MY CRIMES... MY GUILT.
"I WAS SO VERY LOST...
"I DID NOT BELIEVE I DESERVED REDEMPTION.
"OR HAPPINESS...
"BUT THEN I MET PEOPLE WHO SHOOK ME FROM MY APATHY.
"I MADE FRIENDS.
"I FOUND MYSELF AGAIN."
AND NOW, SHE IS HERE WITH ME...
STRANGE... HOW ONE PERSON CAN MAKE LIFE FEEL SO NEW.
I TELL YOU ALL THIS TO SAY I KNOW THE VALUE OF MAKING FRIENDS. AND I KNOW THE GRIEF OF LOSING THEM... OF FAILING TO SAVE THEM.
YOU DROWN YOURSELF IN BLAME... BUT PLEASE KNOW THIS:
YOU ARE STILL HERE.
I HAVE DONE TERRIBLE THINGS I SHALL NEVER ATONE FOR.
BUT I AM HERE. TODAY.
AND TODAY, I CAN STILL CHOOSE TO DO GOOD.
SO I WILL.
UH... NORRIN.

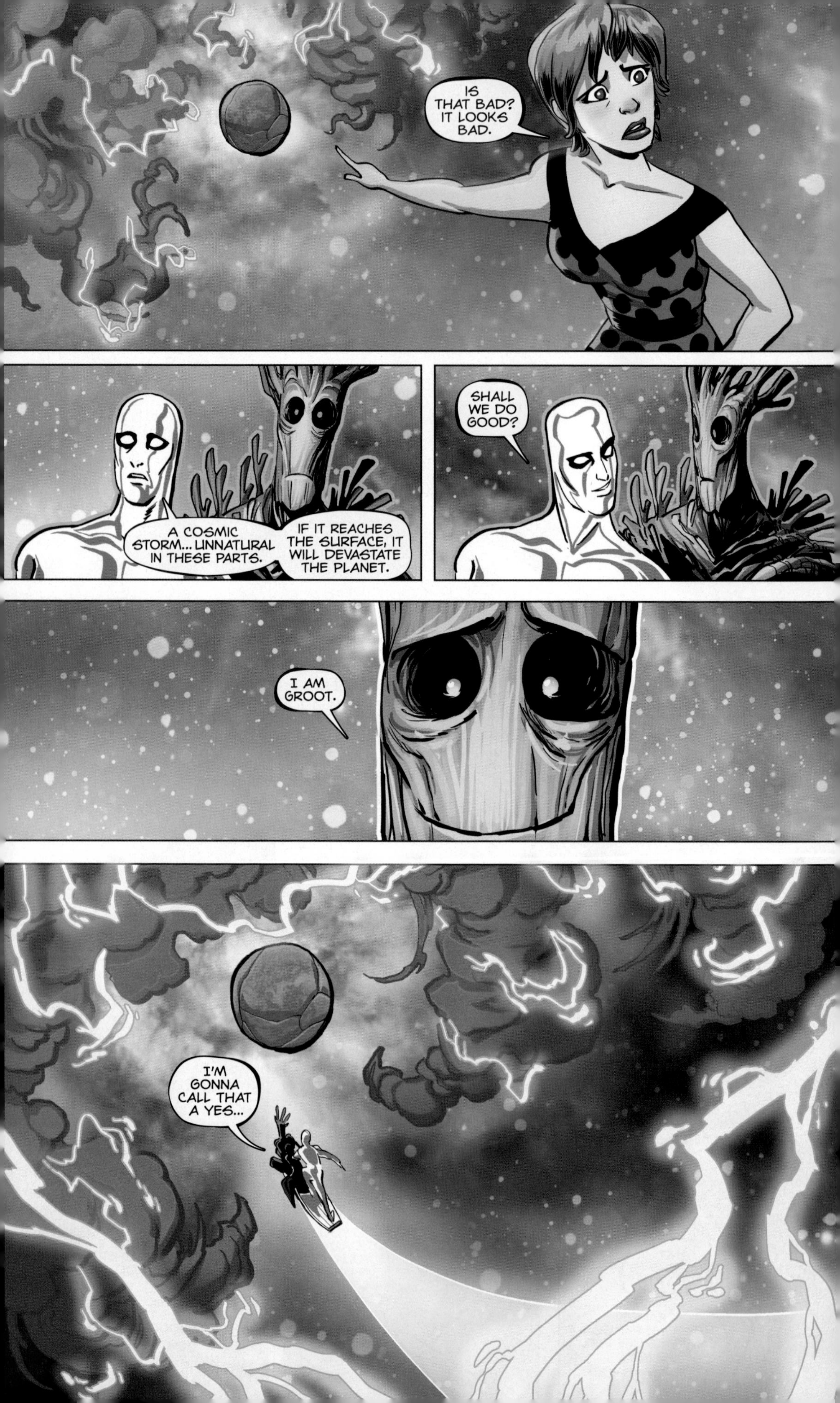
IS THAT BAD? IT LOOKS BAD.
A COSMIC STORM... UNNATURAL IN THESE PARTS.
IF IT REACHES THE SURFACE, IT WILL DEVASTATE THE PLANET.
SHALL WE DO GOOD?
I AM GROOT.
I'M GONNA CALL THAT A YES...

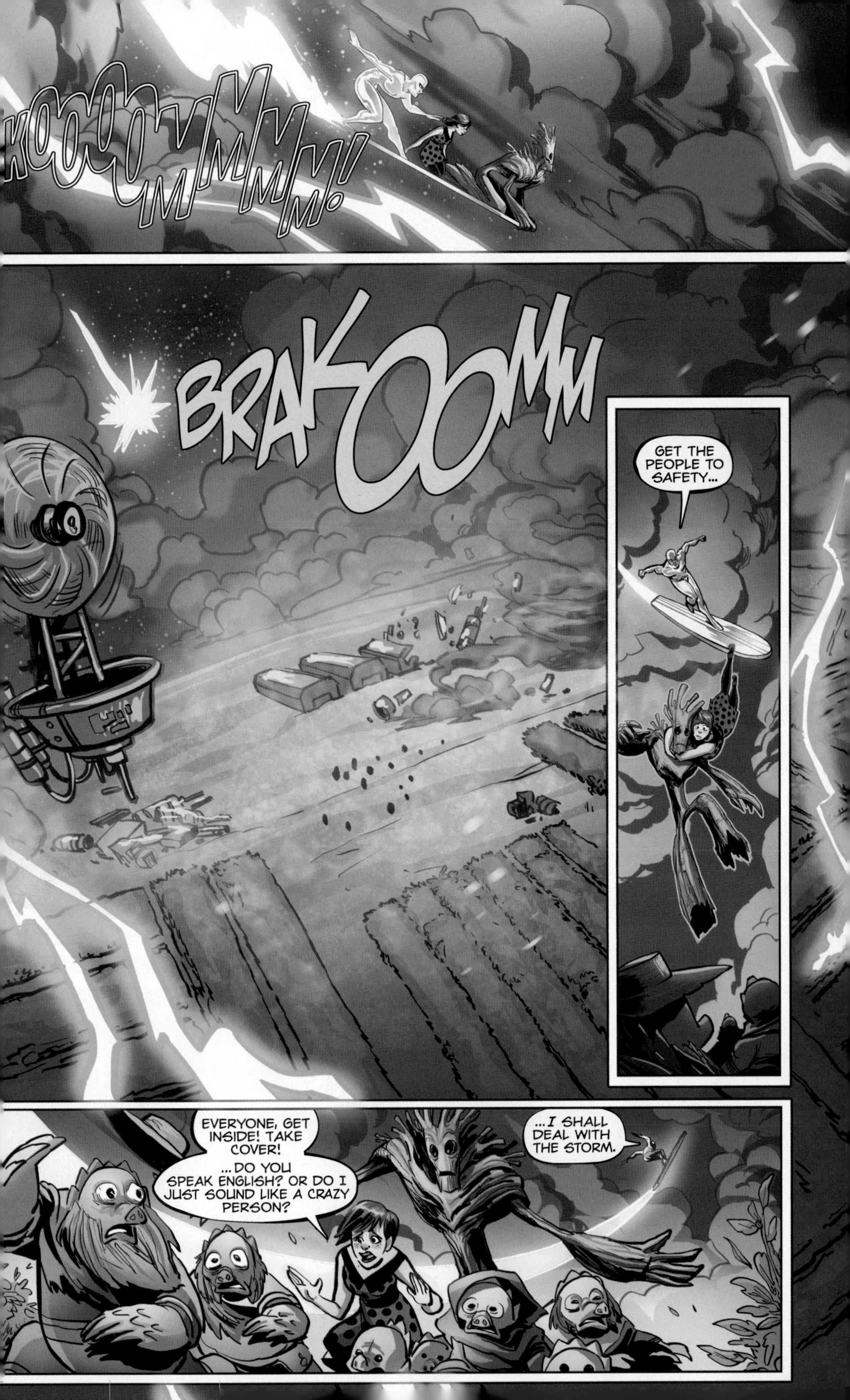
KOOOOMMMMMM!
BRAKOOMMM
GET THE PEOPLE TO SAFETY...
EVERYONE, GET INSIDE! TAKE COVER!
...DO YOU SPEAK ENGLISH? OR DO I JUST SOUND LIKE A CRAZY PERSON?
...I SHALL DEAL WITH THE STORM.

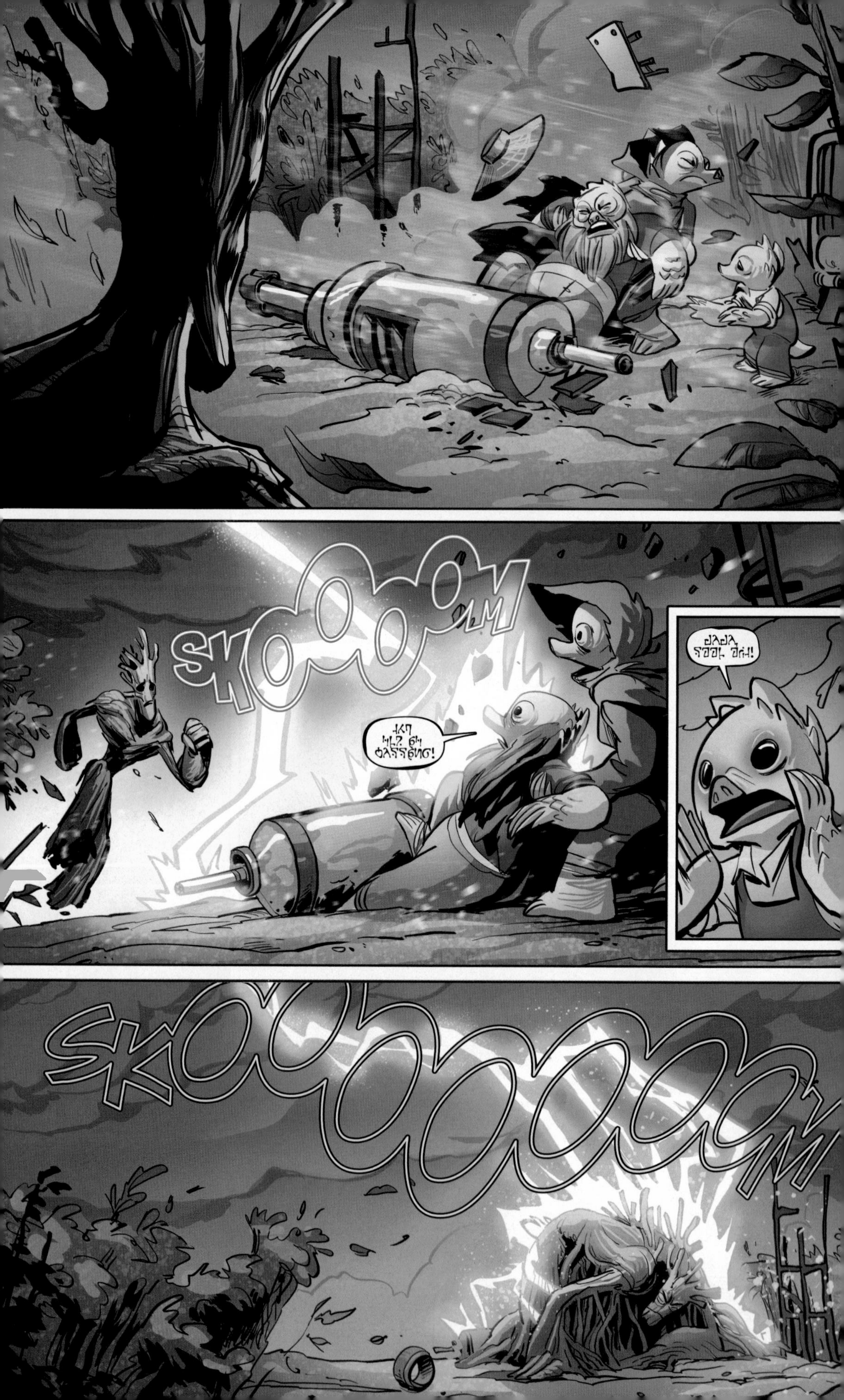
SKOOOOM
SKOOOOOOOM

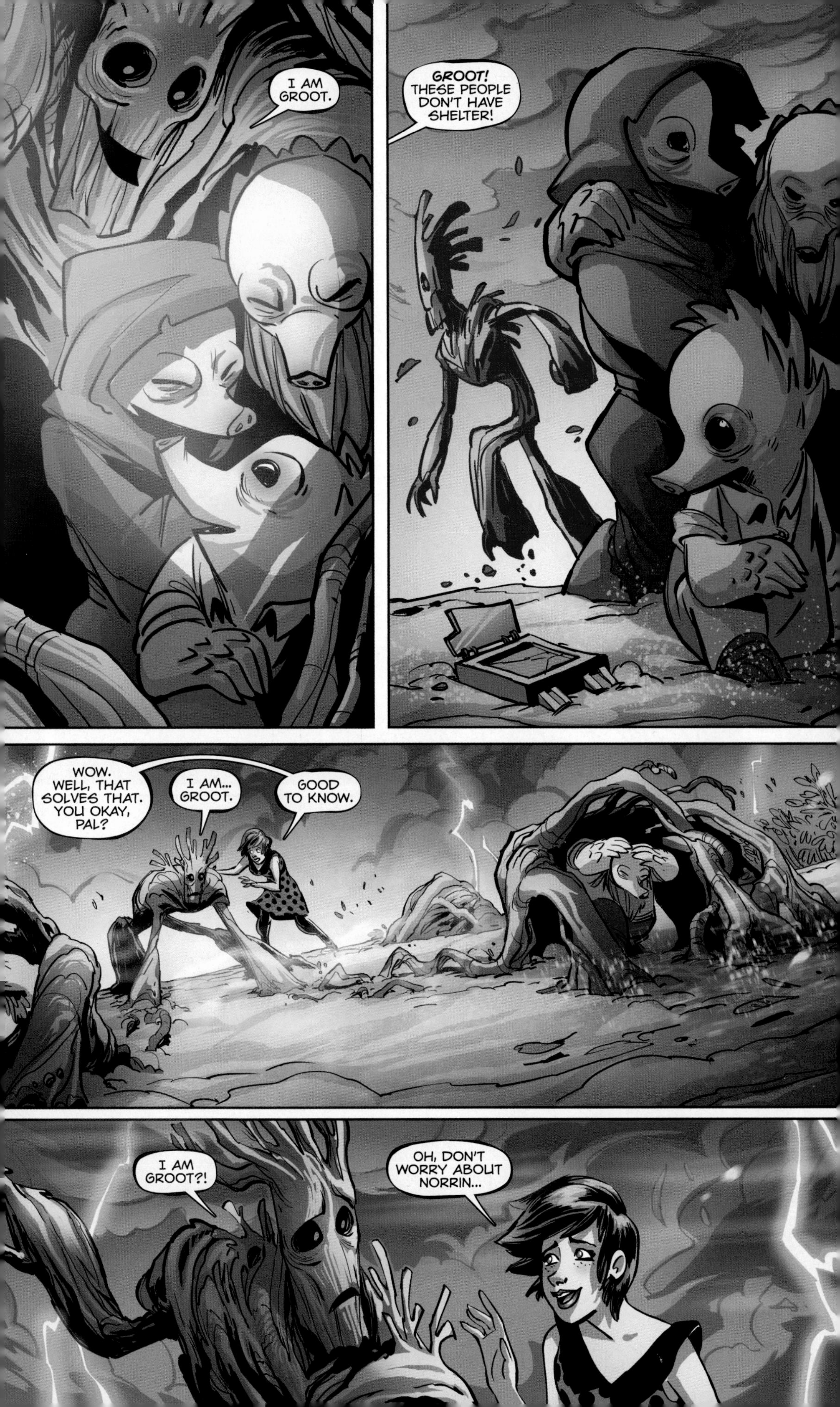
I AM GROOT.
GROOT! THESE PEOPLE DON'T HAVE SHELTER!
WOW. WELL, THAT SOLVES THAT. YOU OKAY, PAL?
I AM... GROOT.
GOOD TO KNOW.
I AM GROOT?!
OH, DON'T WORRY ABOUT NORRIN...

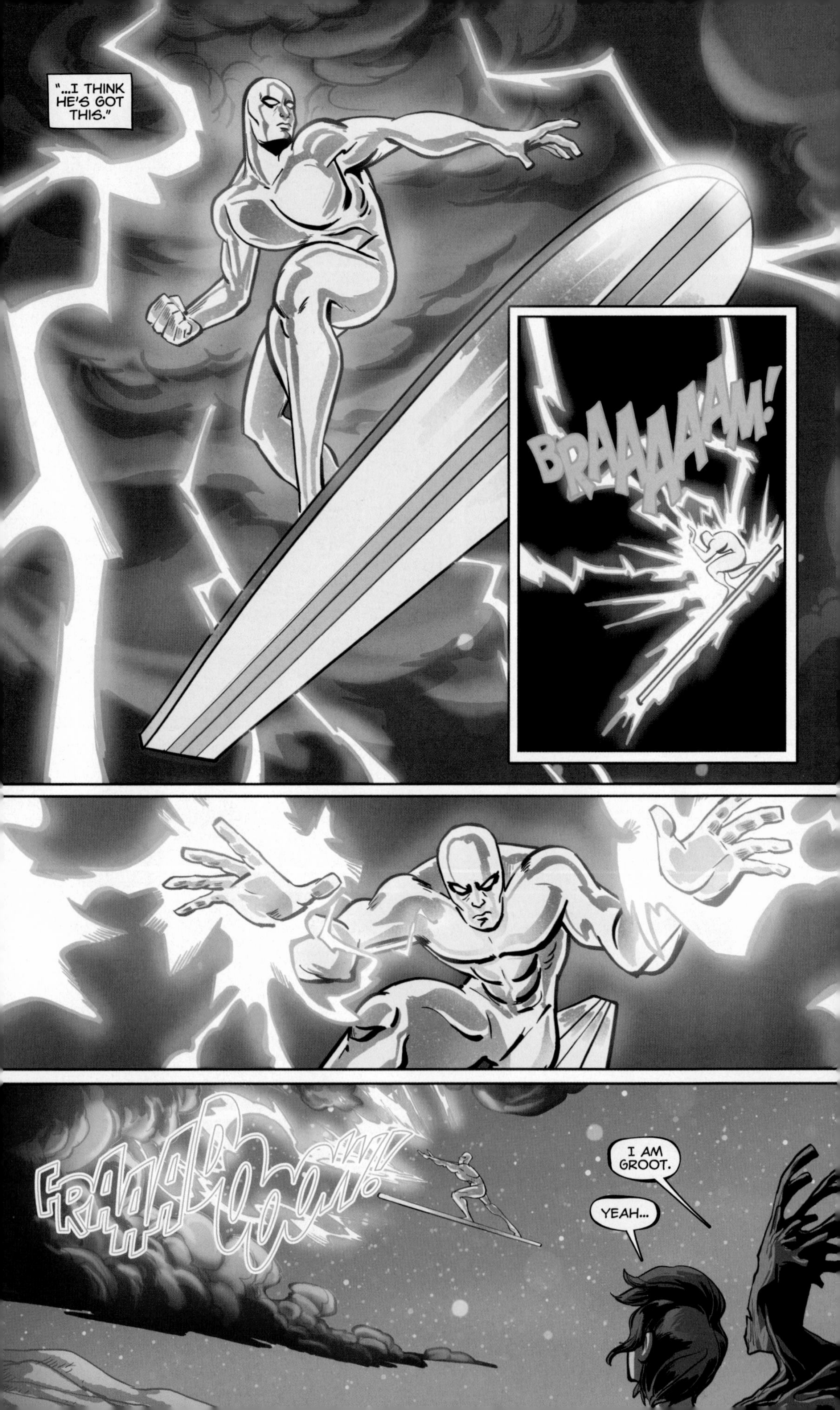
"...I THINK HE'S GOT THIS."
BRAAAAAM!
FRAAAAKOOOM!
I AM GROOT.
YEAH...

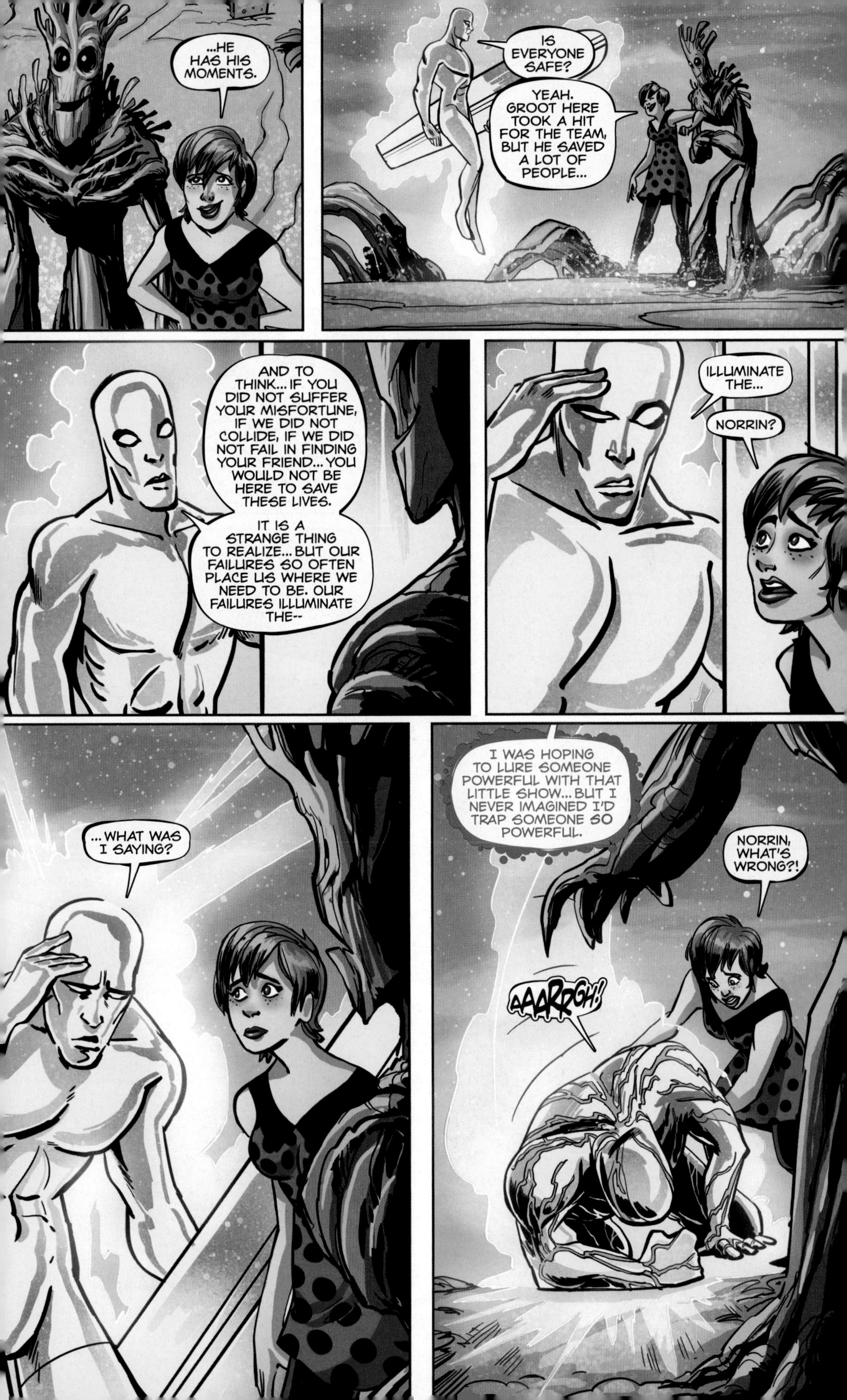
...HE HAS HIS MOMENTS.
IS EVERYONE SAFE?
YEAH. GROOT HERE TOOK A HIT FOR THE TEAM, BUT HE SAVED A LOT OF PEOPLE...
AND TO THINK... IF YOU DID NOT SUFFER YOUR MISFORTUNE, IF WE DID NOT COLLIDE, IF WE DID NOT FAIL IN FINDING YOUR FRIEND... YOU WOULD NOT BE HERE TO SAVE THESE LIVES.
IT IS A STRANGE THING TO REALIZE... BUT OUR FAILURES SO OFTEN PLACE US WHERE WE NEED TO BE. OUR FAILURES ILLUMINATE THE--
ILLUMINATE THE...
NORRIN?
...WHAT WAS I SAYING?
I WAS HOPING TO LURE SOMEONE POWERFUL WITH THAT LITTLE SHOW... BUT I NEVER IMAGINED I'D TRAP SOMEONE SO POWERFUL.
NORRIN, WHAT'S WRONG?!
AAARRGH!

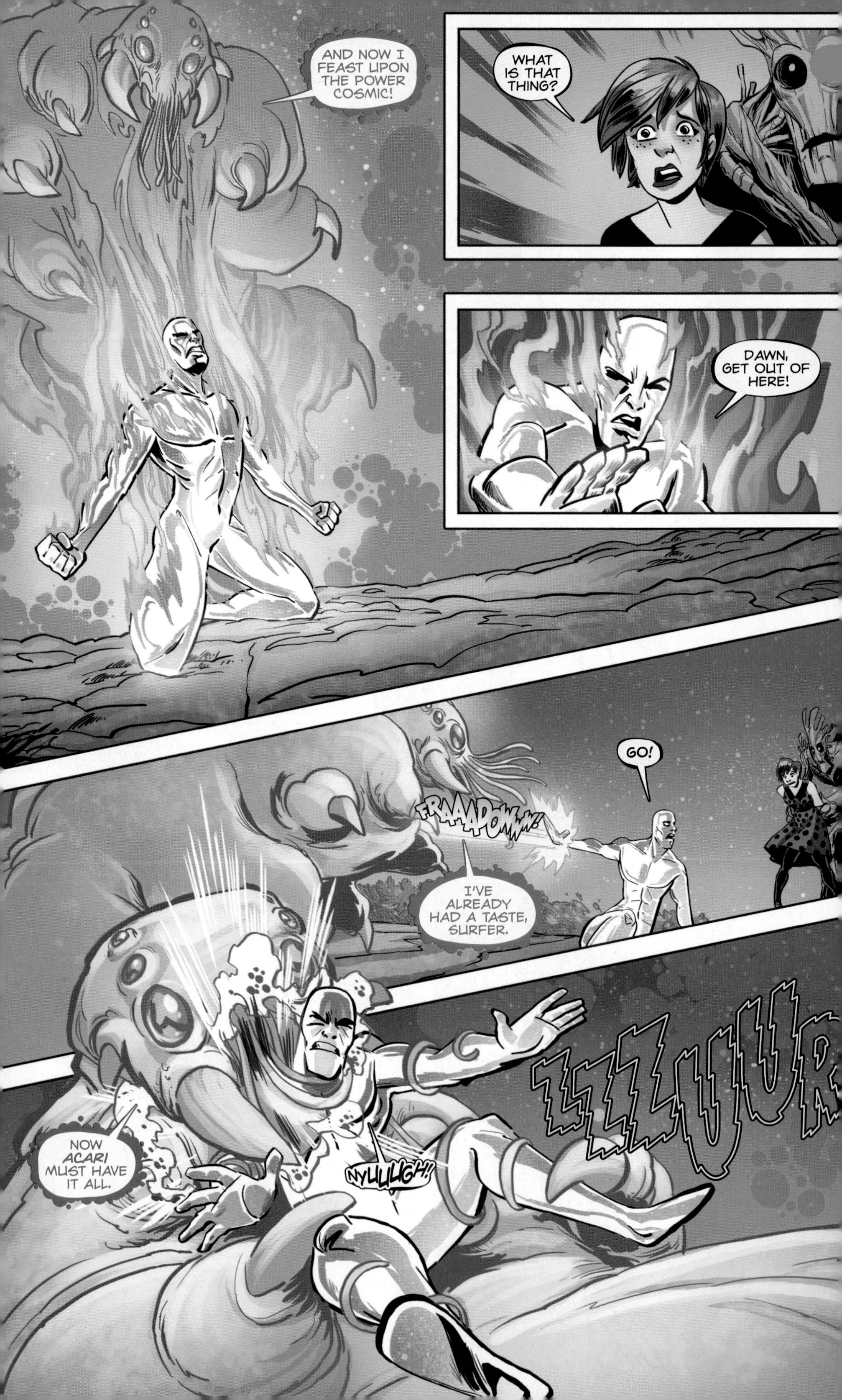
AND NOW I FEAST UPON THE POWER COSMIC!
WHAT IS THAT THING?
DAWN, GET OUT OF HERE!
GO!
FRAAADOWW!
I'VE ALREADY HAD A TASTE, SURFER.
ZZZUUR
NOW ACARI MUST HAVE IT ALL.
NYLLLLIGH!!

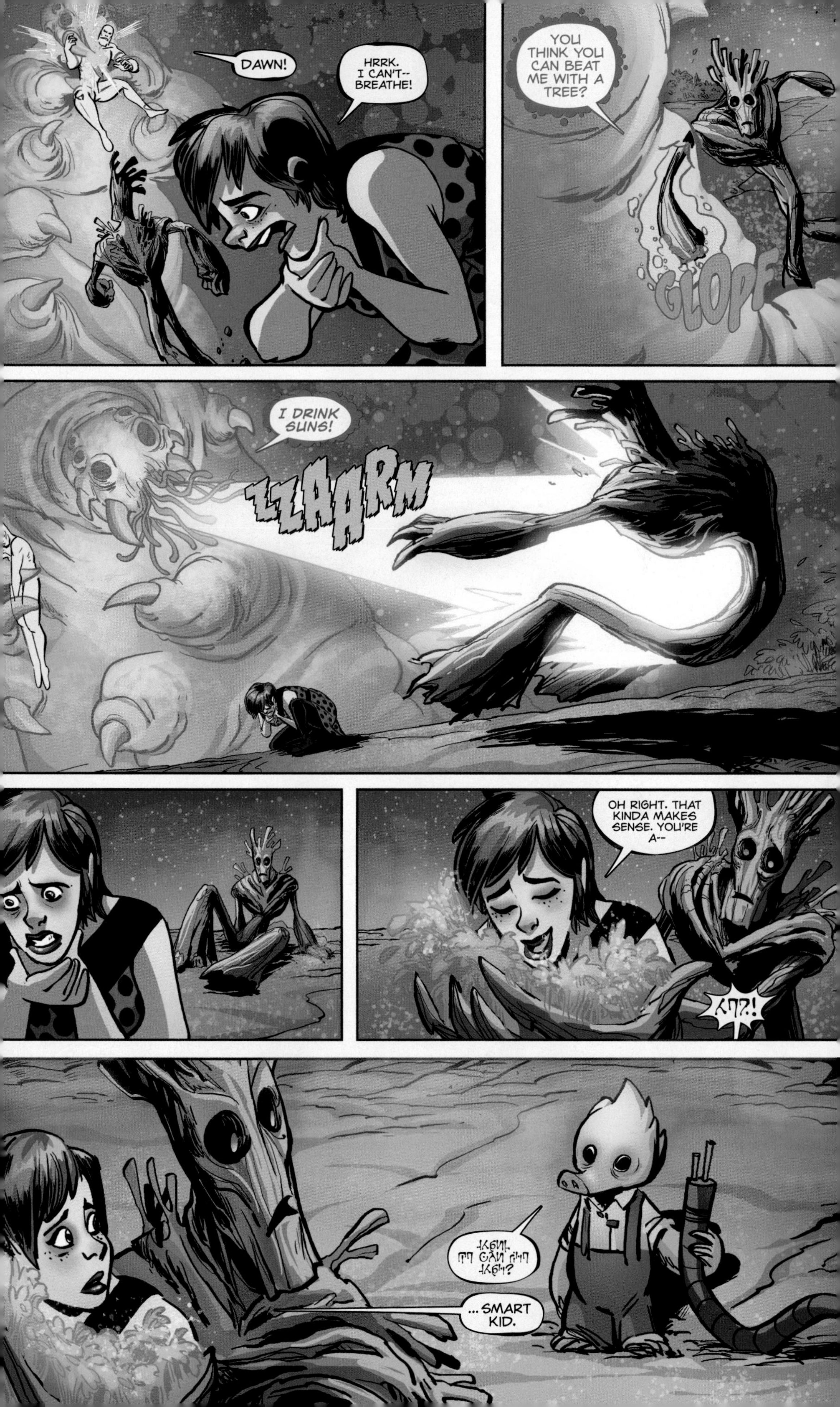
DAWN!
HRRK. I CAN'T-- BREATHE!
YOU THINK YOU CAN BEAT ME WITH A TREE?
GLOPF
I DRINK SUNS!
ZZAARM
OH RIGHT. THAT KINDA MAKES SENSE. YOU'RE A--
... SMART KID.

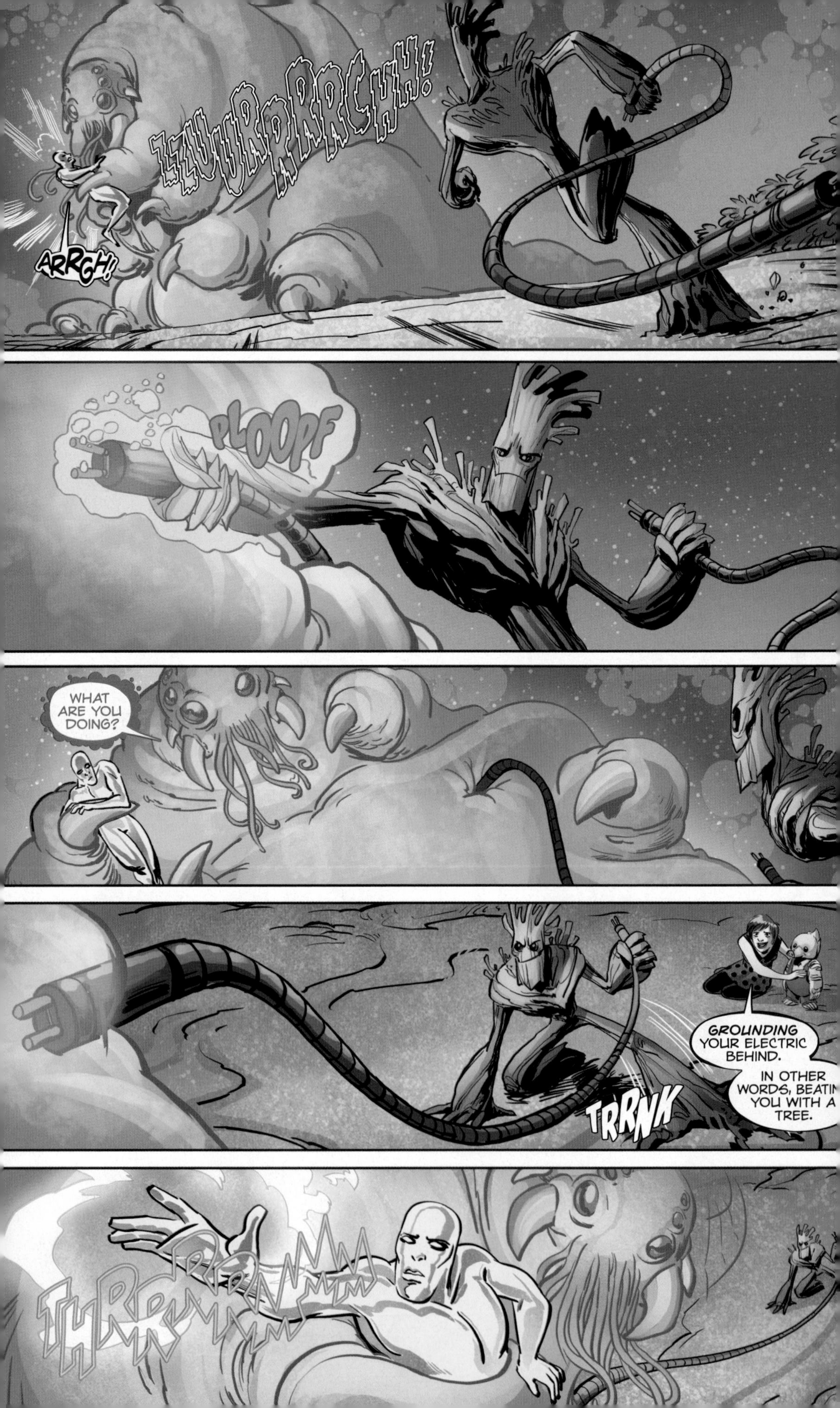
ZZUURRRRCHH!
ARRGH!
PLOOPF
WHAT ARE YOU DOING?
GROUNDING YOUR ELECTRIC BEHIND.
IN OTHER WORDS, BEATIN YOU WITH A TREE.
TRRNK

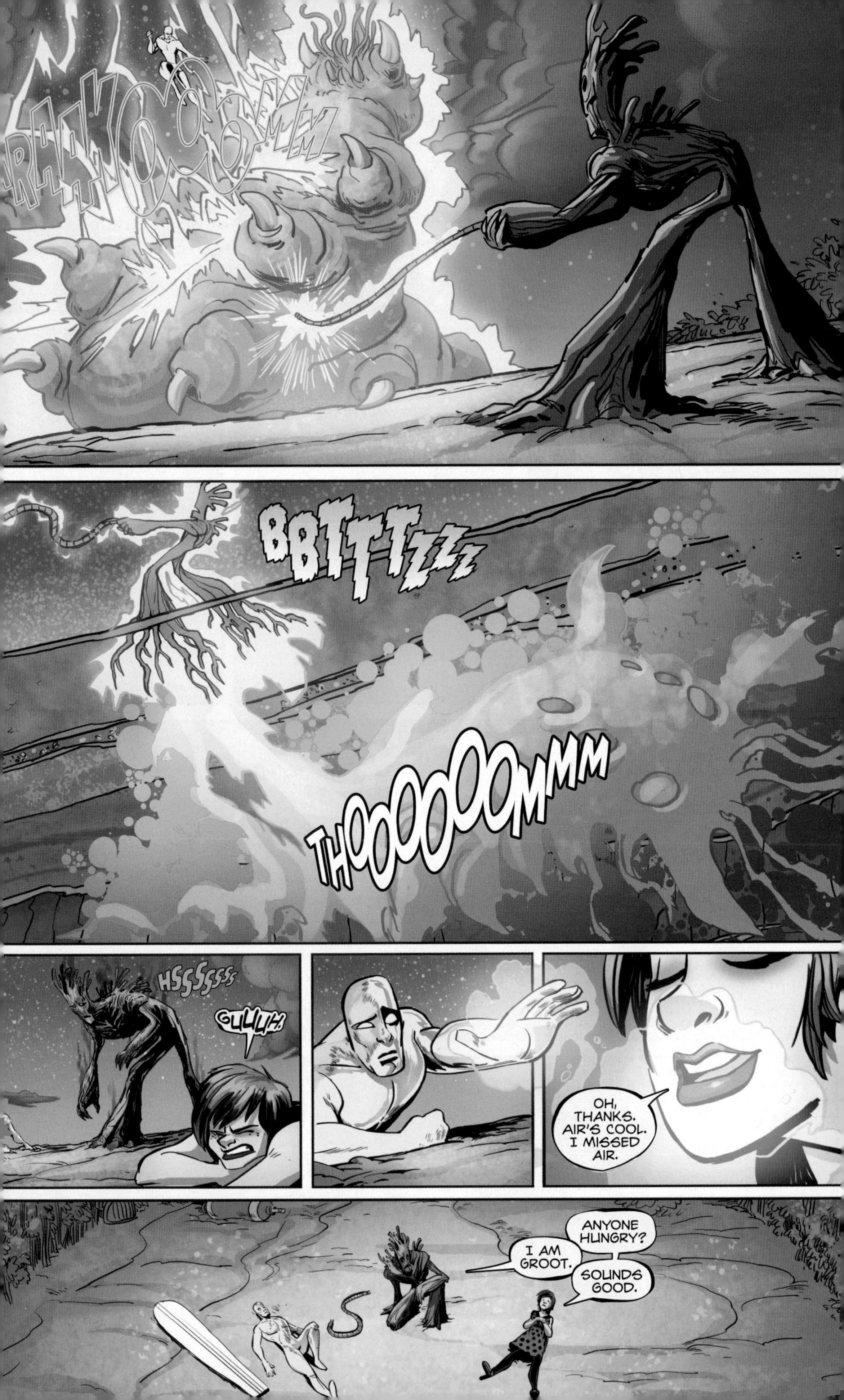
RAAKOOOOOMMM
BBTTTZZZ
THOOOOOOMMM
HSSSSSSS
GUUUH!
OH, THANKS. AIR'S COOL. I MISSED AIR.
ANYONE HUNGRY?
I AM GROOT.
SOUNDS GOOD.

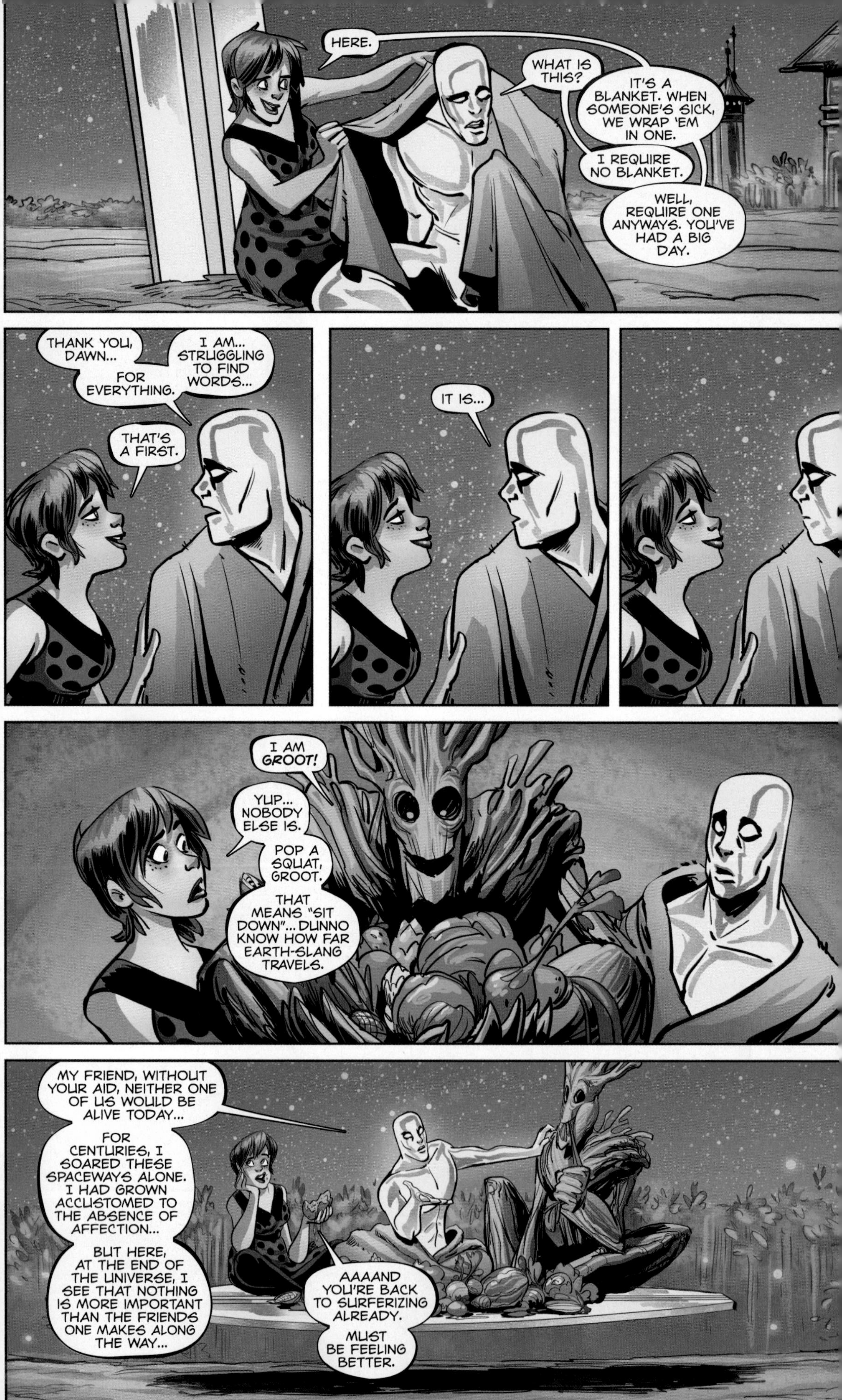
HERE.
WHAT IS THIS?
IT'S A BLANKET. WHEN SOMEONE'S SICK, WE WRAP 'EM IN ONE.
I REQUIRE NO BLANKET.
WELL, REQUIRE ONE ANYWAYS. YOU'VE HAD A BIG DAY.
THANK YOU, DAWN...
FOR EVERYTHING.
I AM... STRUGGLING TO FIND WORDS...
THAT'S A FIRST.
IT IS...
I AM GROOT!
YUP... NOBODY ELSE IS.
POP A SQUAT, GROOT.
THAT MEANS "SIT DOWN"... DUNNO KNOW HOW FAR EARTH-SLANG TRAVELS.
MY FRIEND, WITHOUT YOUR AID, NEITHER ONE OF US WOULD BE ALIVE TODAY...
FOR CENTURIES, I SOARED THESE SPACEWAYS ALONE. I HAD GROWN ACCUSTOMED TO THE ABSENCE OF AFFECTION...
BUT HERE, AT THE END OF THE UNIVERSE, I SEE THAT NOTHING IS MORE IMPORTANT THAN THE FRIENDS ONE MAKES ALONG THE WAY...
AAAAND YOU'RE BACK TO SURFERIZING ALREADY.
MUST BE FEELING BETTER.

FOR THE COSMOS... IS... A COSMIC... CELESTIAL... PORTENT... OF... OF...

I'M [SU]RE YOU [WE]RE GOING [SO]MEWHERE [WI]TH THAT... COSMIC... YUP.

I THINK ALL THAT MEANT "THANK YOU."

AND HE'S RIGHT. IT'S WEIRD TO THINK ABOUT...

...NONE OF THIS WOULD'VE HAPPENED IF WE DIDN'T RUN INTO YOU.

...IF YOU DIDN'T LOSE YOUR FRIEND... IF WE DIDN'T GET LOST, NORRIN WOULDN'T BE HERE TO SAVE THE PLANET. YOU WOULDN'T BE HERE TO SAVE THOSE PEOPLE. TO SAVE ALL OF US.

SOMETIMES OUR MISTAKES PUT US EXACTLY WHERE WE NEED TO BE...

I GUESS THAT'S WHAT I'VE LEARNED TO LOVE ABOUT TRAVEL...

YOU MEET SO MANY RANDOM PEOPLE. YOU'RE NOT SO CLOSED OFF. YOU'RE MORE OPEN TO YOURSELF...

EVERYTHING'S NEW AGAIN.

I DON'T KNOW A BETTER WAY TO BE.

ᕋᒪᐃᐅᒋᐳ ᑦᐃ ᕲᒼᗻ ᖰᐅᑫᑌ ᓳᗺᗺ···ᑫᐃᕲ!

I AM GROOT.

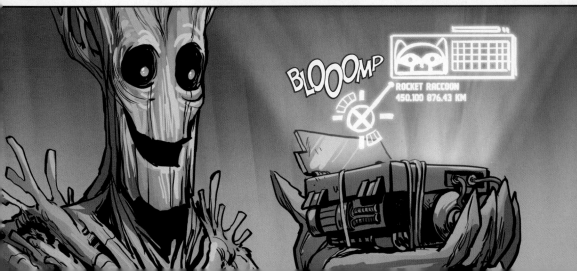

BLOOOMP

ROCKET RACCOON
450.100 876.43 KM

?2d CAN dyn T267 T0 QdME ?2dU QUQm7e!

DON'T WORRY... TOOMIE AND I'LL TAKE CARE OF HIM.

I... LIKE SPACE...

I KNOW YOU DO, NORRIN.

HOPE YOU FIND WHAT YOU'RE LOOKING FOR.

IF YOU'RE EVER IN MASSACHUSETTS, LEMME KNOW. I CAN RECOMMEND A GREAT BED 'N' BREAKFAST.

NOW GET BACK OUT THERE.

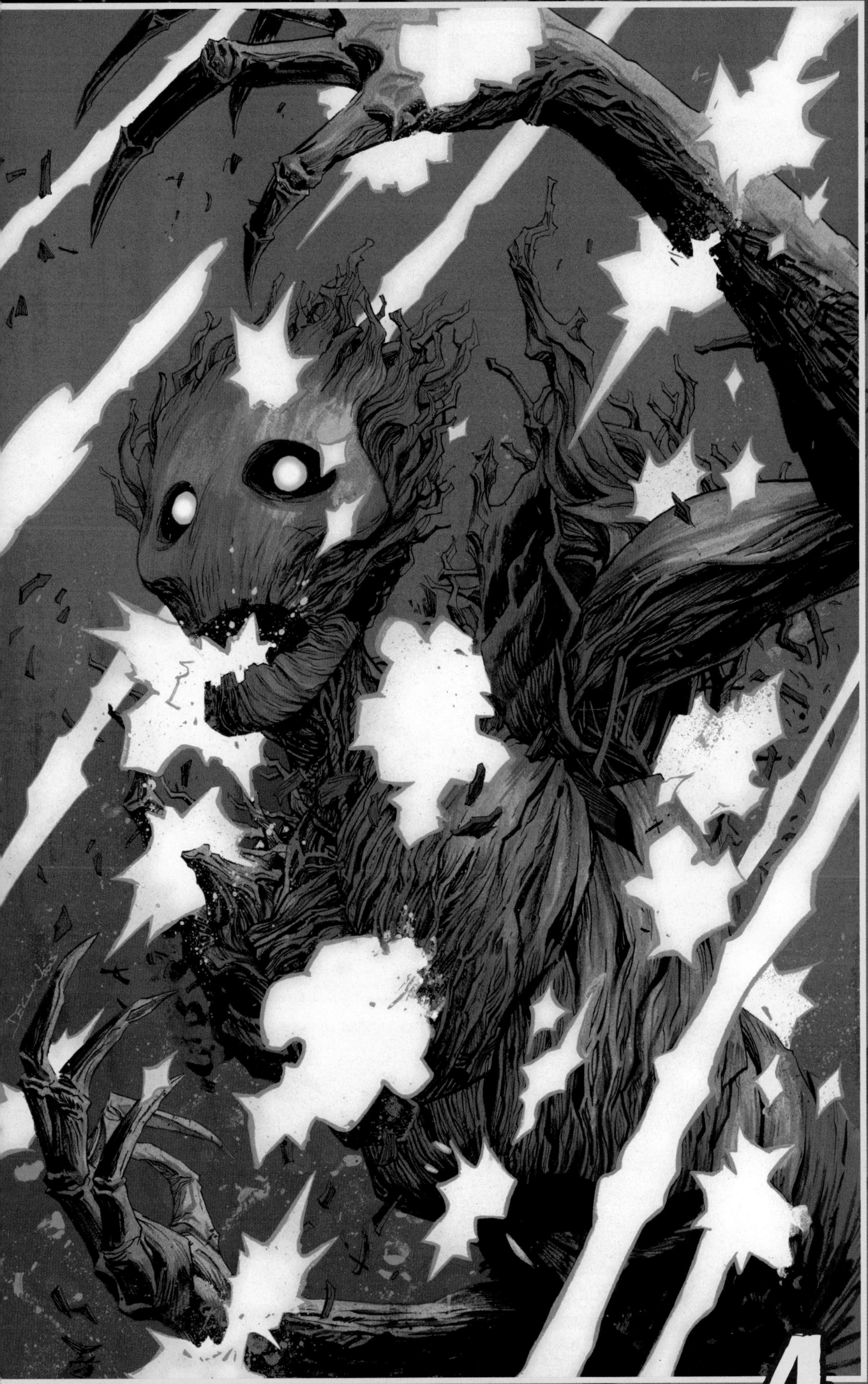

4

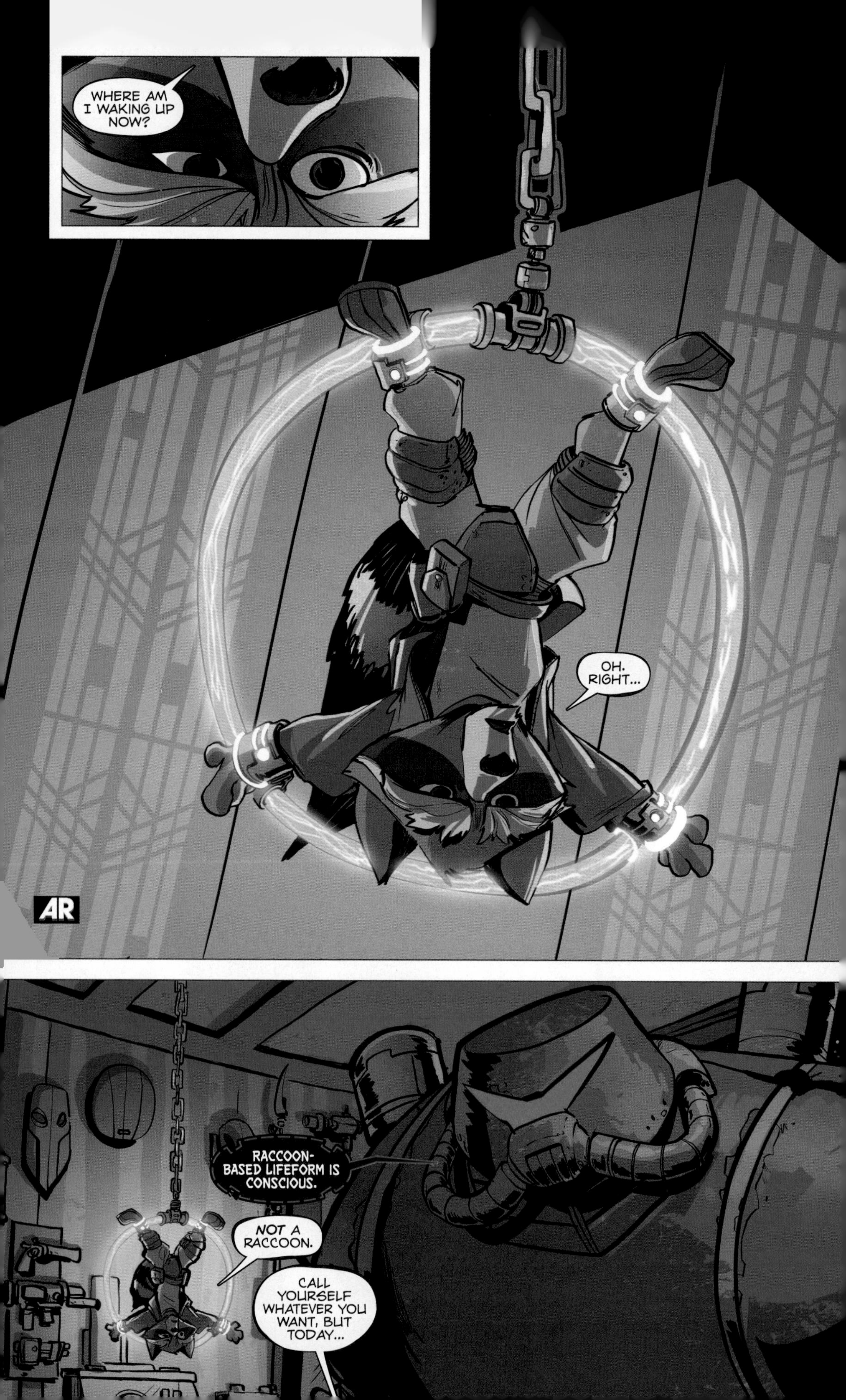

WHERE AM I WAKING UP NOW?
OH. RIGHT...
AR
RACCOON-BASED LIFEFORM IS CONSCIOUS.
NOT A RACCOON.
CALL YOURSELF WHATEVER YOU WANT, BUT TODAY...

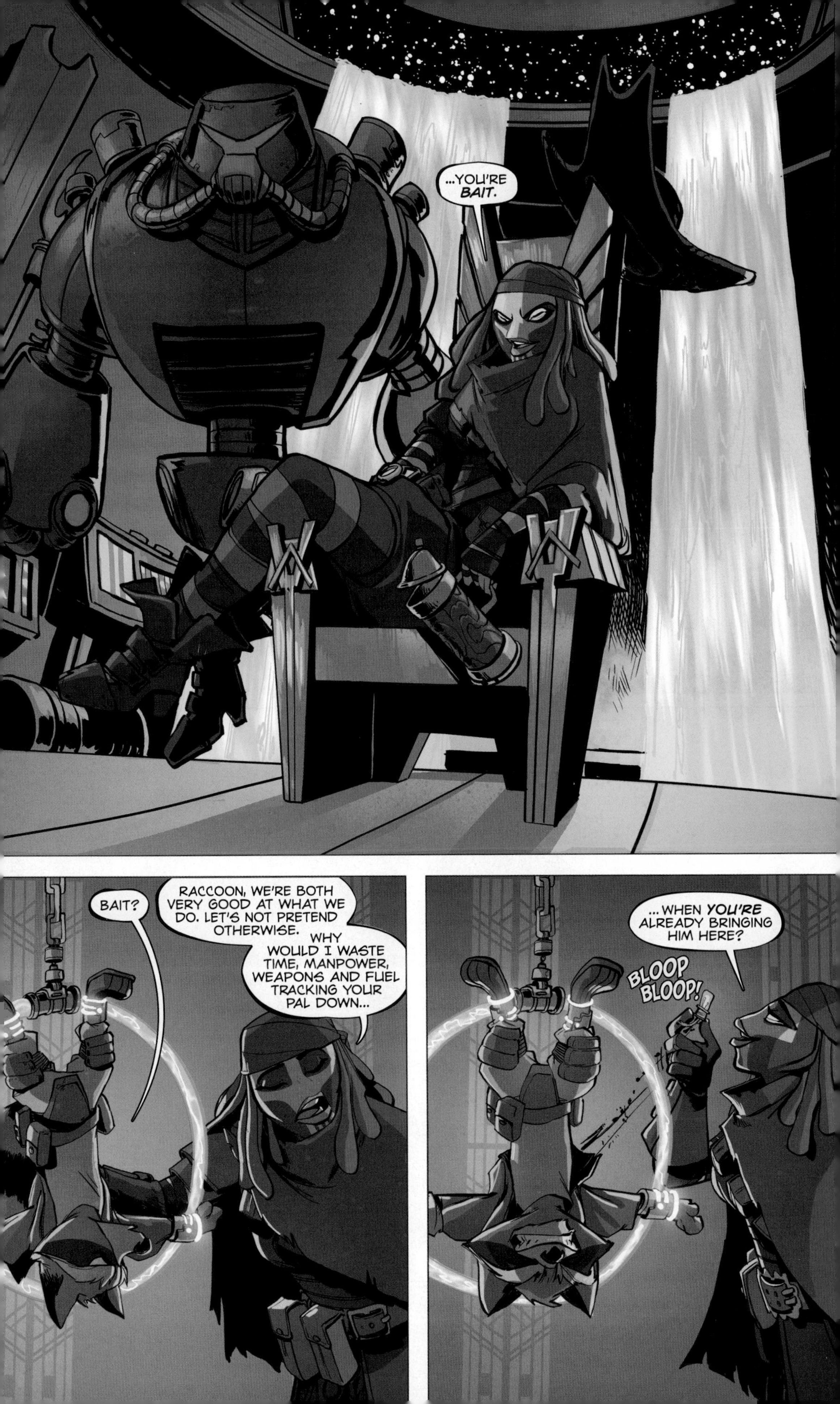
...YOU'RE BAIT.
BAIT?
RACCOON, WE'RE BOTH VERY GOOD AT WHAT WE DO. LET'S NOT PRETEND OTHERWISE.
WHY WOULD I WASTE TIME, MANPOWER, WEAPONS AND FUEL TRACKING YOUR PAL DOWN...
...WHEN YOU'RE ALREADY BRINGING HIM HERE?
BLOOP BLOOP!

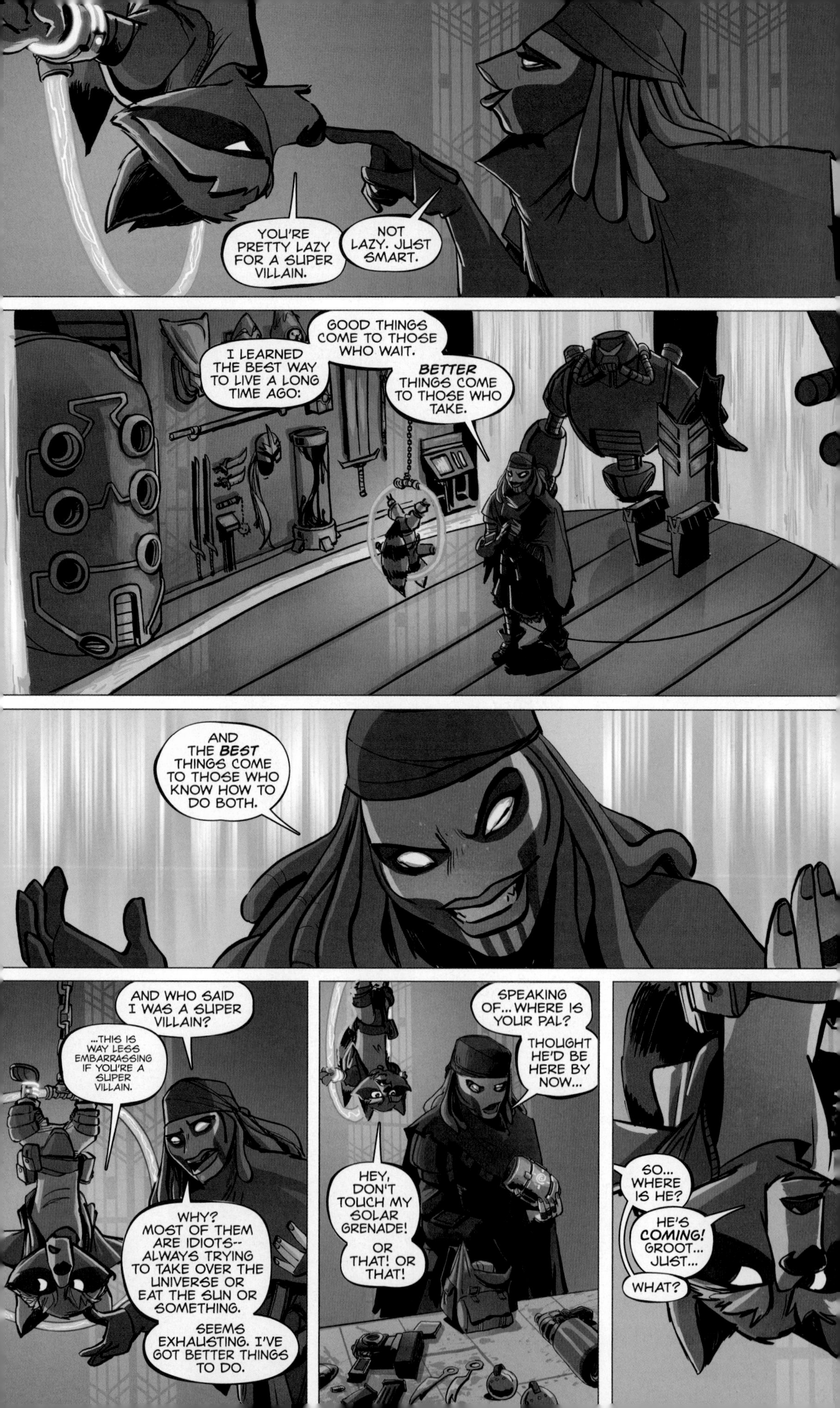

YOU'RE PRETTY LAZY FOR A SUPER VILLAIN.
NOT LAZY. JUST SMART.
I LEARNED THE BEST WAY TO LIVE A LONG TIME AGO:
GOOD THINGS COME TO THOSE WHO WAIT.
BETTER THINGS COME TO THOSE WHO TAKE.
AND THE BEST THINGS COME TO THOSE WHO KNOW HOW TO DO BOTH.
AND WHO SAID I WAS A SUPER VILLAIN?
...THIS IS WAY LESS EMBARRASSING IF YOU'RE A SUPER VILLAIN.
WHY? MOST OF THEM ARE IDIOTS-- ALWAYS TRYING TO TAKE OVER THE UNIVERSE OR EAT THE SUN OR SOMETHING.
SEEMS EXHAUSTING. I'VE GOT BETTER THINGS TO DO.
SPEAKING OF... WHERE IS YOUR PAL?
THOUGHT HE'D BE HERE BY NOW...
HEY, DON'T TOUCH MY SOLAR GRENADE!
OR THAT! OR THAT!
SO... WHERE IS HE?
HE'S COMING! GROOT... JUST...
WHAT?

"GROOT TAKES HIS TIME..."

I AM GROOT.

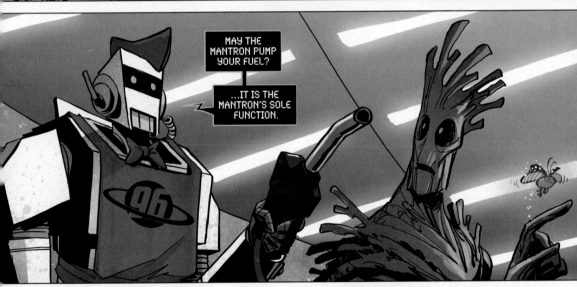

MAY THE MANTRON PUMP YOUR FUEL?

...IT IS THE MANTRON'S SOLE FUNCTION.

YET...THE MANTRON DREAMS OF GREATER THINGS.

THE MANTRON DREAMS OF SEEING THE STARS.

I AM GROO--

THE MANTRON WAS BUILT TO THE PINNACLE OF EARTHDATE 1996 TECHNOLOGY...

BUT THE MANTRON WAS JETTISONED BY HIS MAKERS.

...TIME HAS FORGOTTEN THE MANTRON.

YET THE MANTRON FEELS HE WAS BUILT FOR SO MUCH MORE.

WE WERE BUILT FOR ONLY ONE THING...

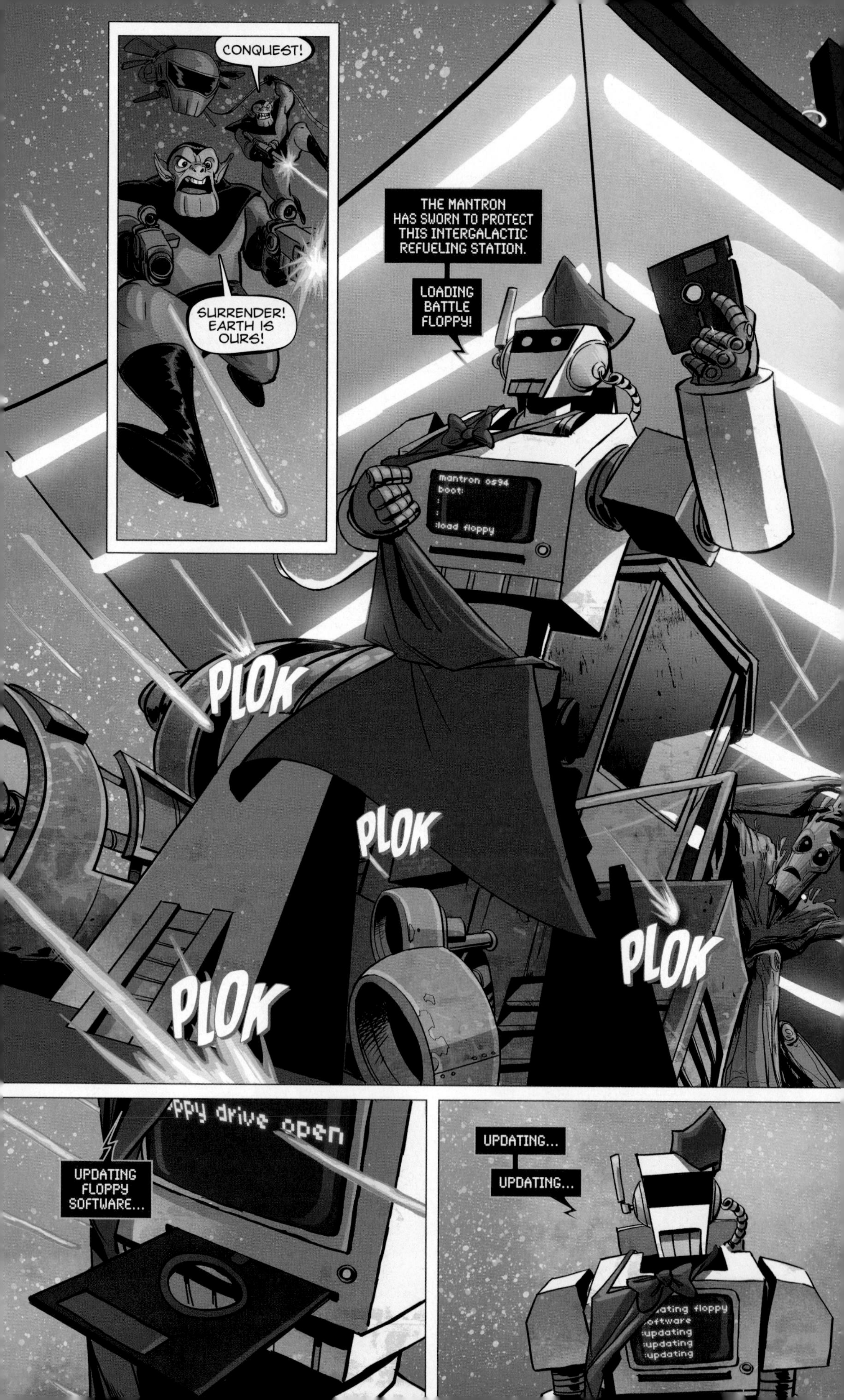

CONQUEST!
SURRENDER! EARTH IS OURS!
THE MANTRON HAS SWORN TO PROTECT THIS INTERGALACTIC REFUELING STATION.
LOADING BATTLE FLOPPY!
mantron os94
boot:
:
:
:load floppy
PLOK
PLOK
PLOK
PLOK
UPDATING FLOPPY SOFTWARE...
UPDATING...
UPDATING...
:updating
:updating
:updating

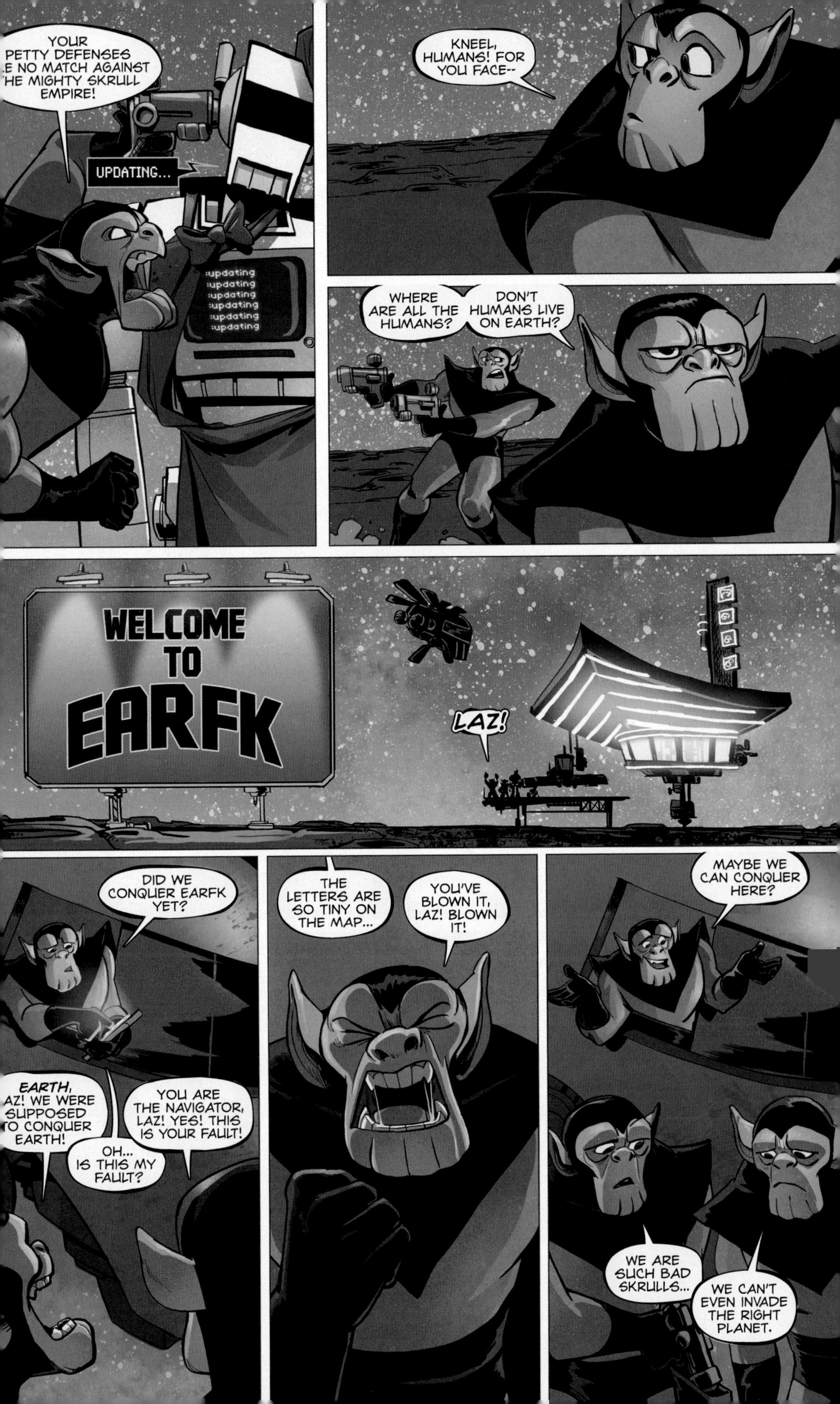
YOUR PETTY DEFENSES E NO MATCH AGAINST HE MIGHTY SKRULL EMPIRE!
UPDATING...
:updating
:updating
:updating
:updating
:updating
:updating
KNEEL, HUMANS! FOR YOU FACE--
WHERE ARE ALL THE HUMANS?
DON'T HUMANS LIVE ON EARTH?
WELCOME TO EARFK
LAZ!
DID WE CONQUER EARFK YET?
EARTH, AZ! WE WERE SUPPOSED TO CONQUER EARTH!
OH... IS THIS MY FAULT?
YOU ARE THE NAVIGATOR, LAZ! YES! THIS IS YOUR FAULT!
THE LETTERS ARE SO TINY ON THE MAP...
YOU'VE BLOWN IT, LAZ! BLOWN IT!
MAYBE WE CAN CONQUER HERE?
WE ARE SUCH BAD SKRULLS...
WE CAN'T EVEN INVADE THE RIGHT PLANET.

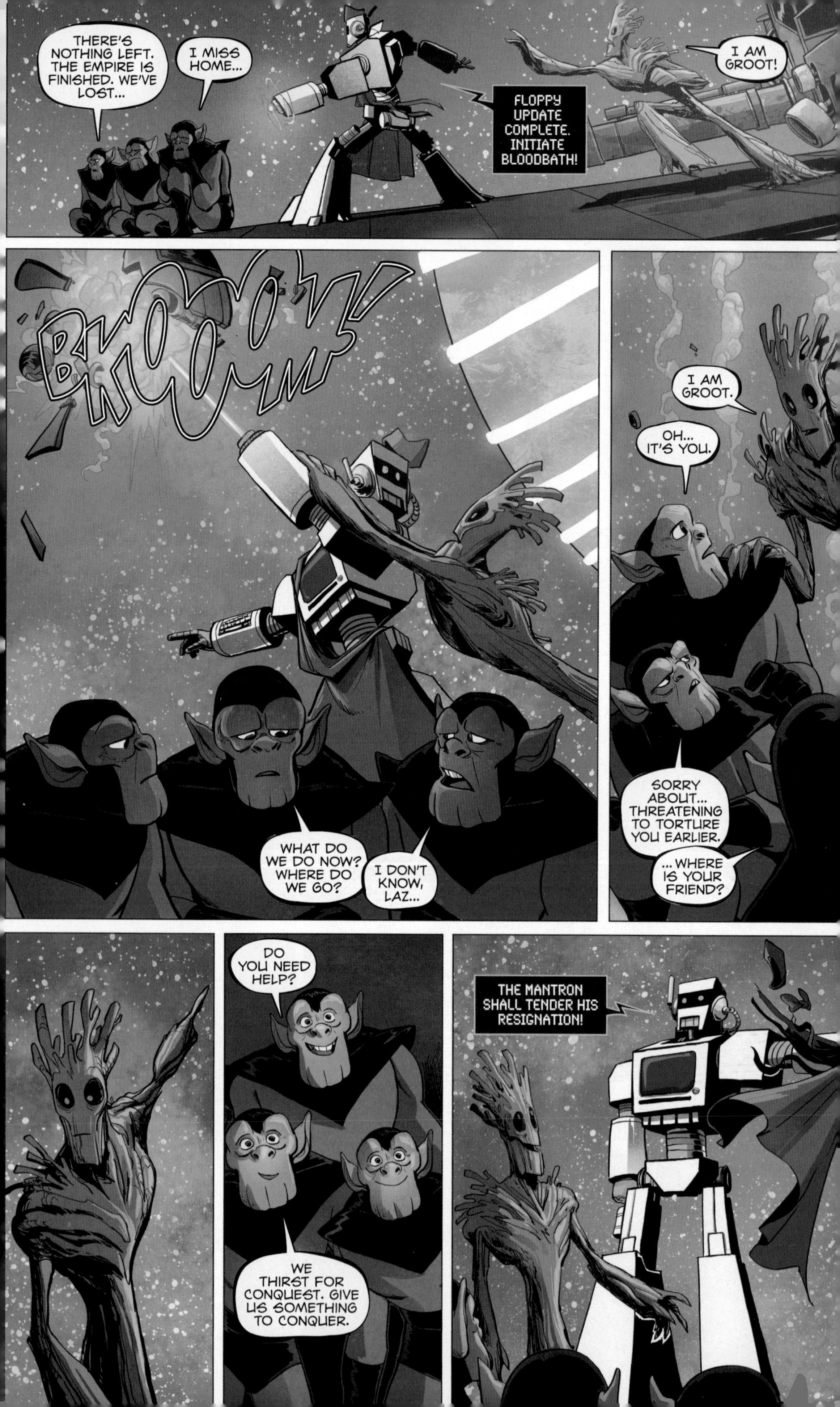
THERE'S NOTHING LEFT. THE EMPIRE IS FINISHED. WE'VE LOST...
I MISS HOME...
FLOPPY UPDATE COMPLETE. INITIATE BLOODBATH!
I AM GROOT!
BKOOOOM
WHAT DO WE DO NOW? WHERE DO WE GO?
I DON'T KNOW, LAZ...
I AM GROOT.
OH... IT'S YOU.
SORRY ABOUT... THREATENING TO TORTURE YOU EARLIER.
...WHERE IS YOUR FRIEND?
DO YOU NEED HELP?
WE THIRST FOR CONQUEST. GIVE US SOMETHING TO CONQUER.
THE MANTRON SHALL TENDER HIS RESIGNATION!

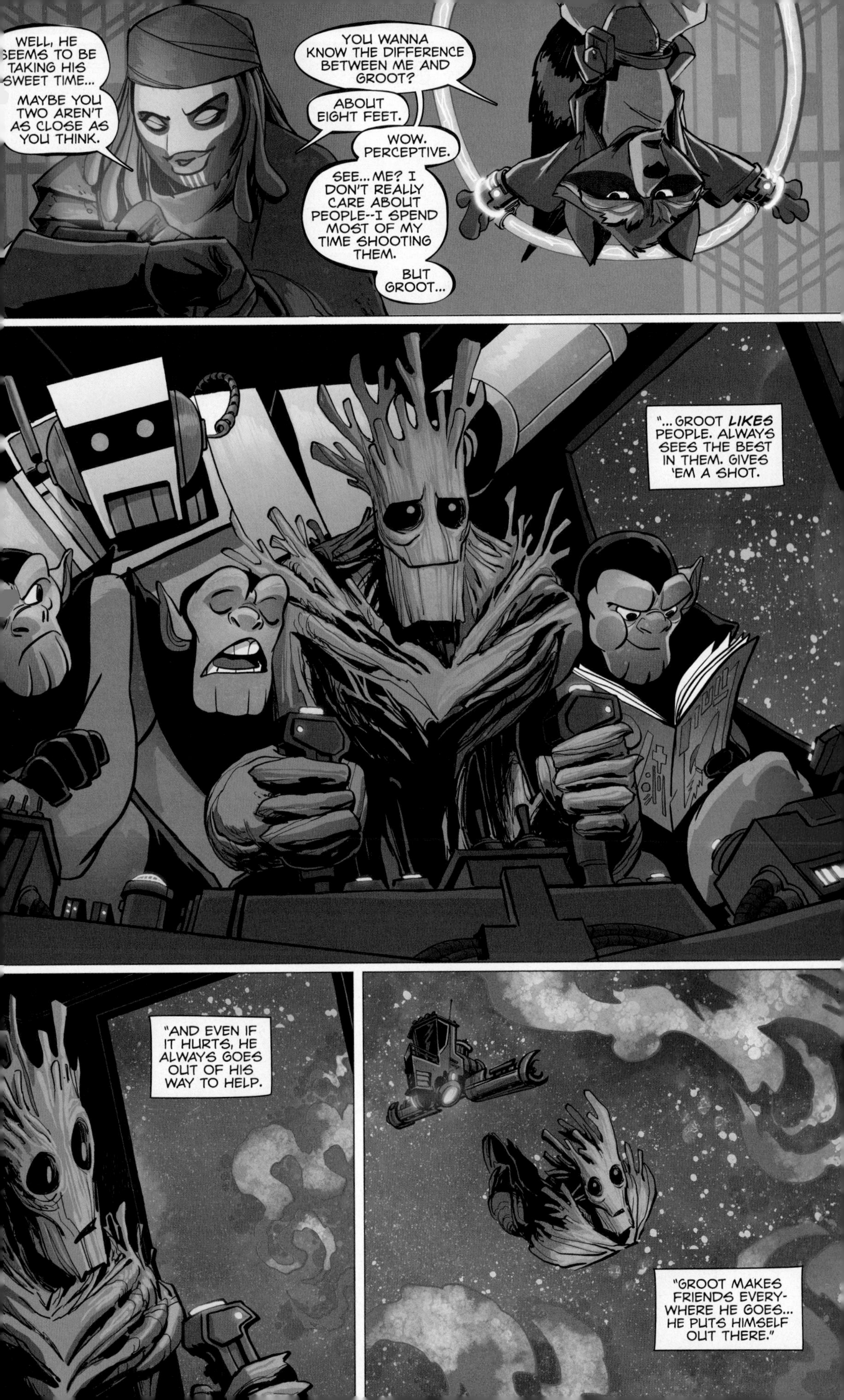
WELL, HE SEEMS TO BE TAKING HIS SWEET TIME...
MAYBE YOU TWO AREN'T AS CLOSE AS YOU THINK.
YOU WANNA KNOW THE DIFFERENCE BETWEEN ME AND GROOT?
ABOUT EIGHT FEET.
WOW. PERCEPTIVE.
SEE... ME? I DON'T REALLY CARE ABOUT PEOPLE--I SPEND MOST OF MY TIME SHOOTING THEM.
BUT GROOT...
"...GROOT LIKES PEOPLE. ALWAYS SEES THE BEST IN THEM. GIVES 'EM A SHOT.
"AND EVEN IF IT HURTS, HE ALWAYS GOES OUT OF HIS WAY TO HELP.
"GROOT MAKES FRIENDS EVERY-WHERE HE GOES... HE PUTS HIMSELF OUT THERE."

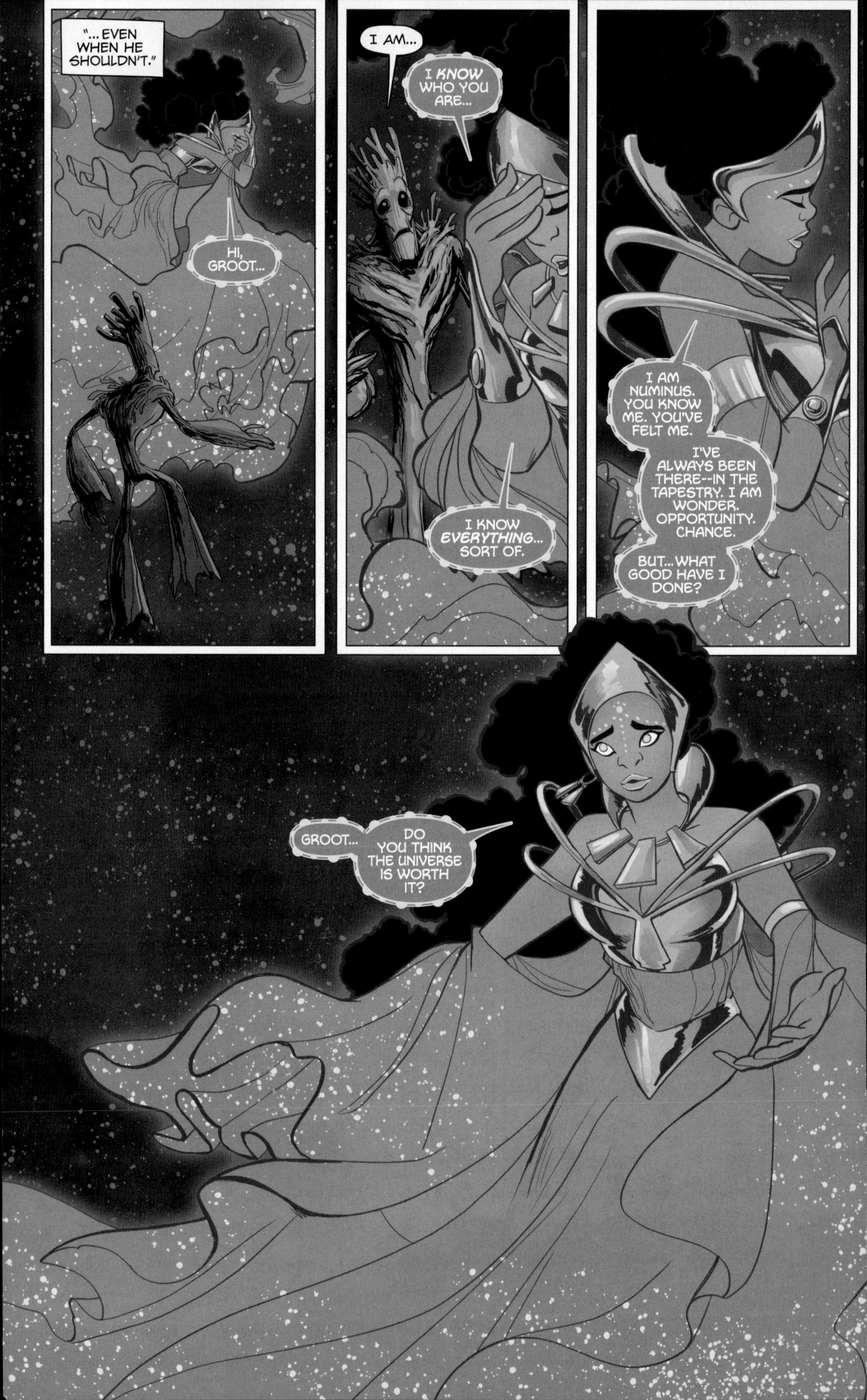
"... EVEN WHEN HE SHOULDN'T."
HI, GROOT...
I AM...
I *KNOW* WHO YOU ARE...
I KNOW *EVERYTHING*... SORT OF.
I AM NUMINUS. YOU KNOW ME. YOU'VE FELT ME.
I'VE ALWAYS BEEN THERE--IN THE TAPESTRY. I AM WONDER. OPPORTUNITY. CHANCE.
BUT... WHAT GOOD HAVE I DONE?
GROOT...
DO YOU THINK THE UNIVERSE IS WORTH IT?

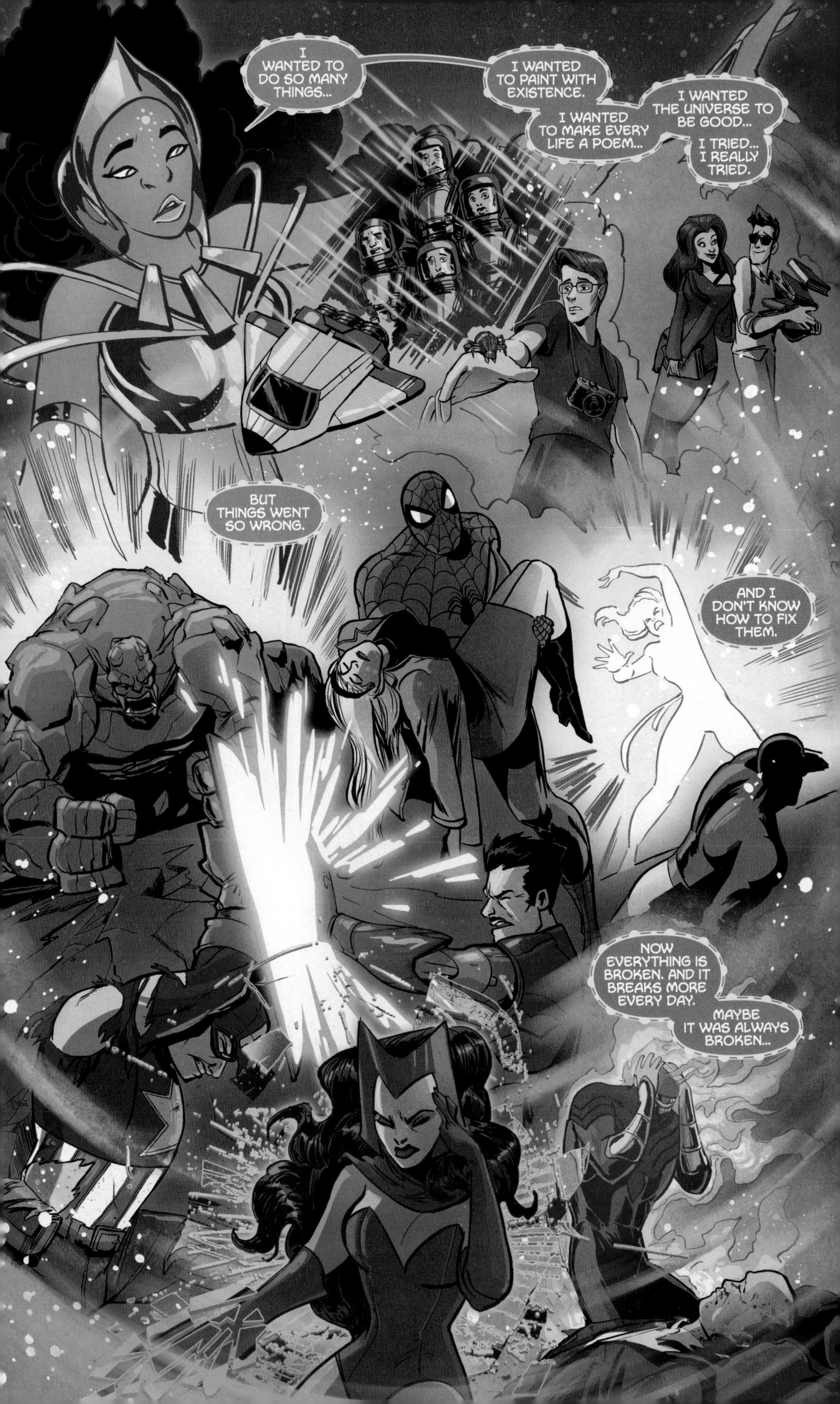

I WANTED TO DO SO MANY THINGS...
I WANTED TO PAINT WITH EXISTENCE.
I WANTED TO MAKE EVERY LIFE A POEM...
I WANTED THE UNIVERSE TO BE GOOD...
I TRIED... I REALLY TRIED.
BUT THINGS WENT SO WRONG.
AND I DON'T KNOW HOW TO FIX THEM.
NOW EVERYTHING IS BROKEN. AND IT BREAKS MORE EVERY DAY.
MAYBE IT WAS ALWAYS BROKEN...

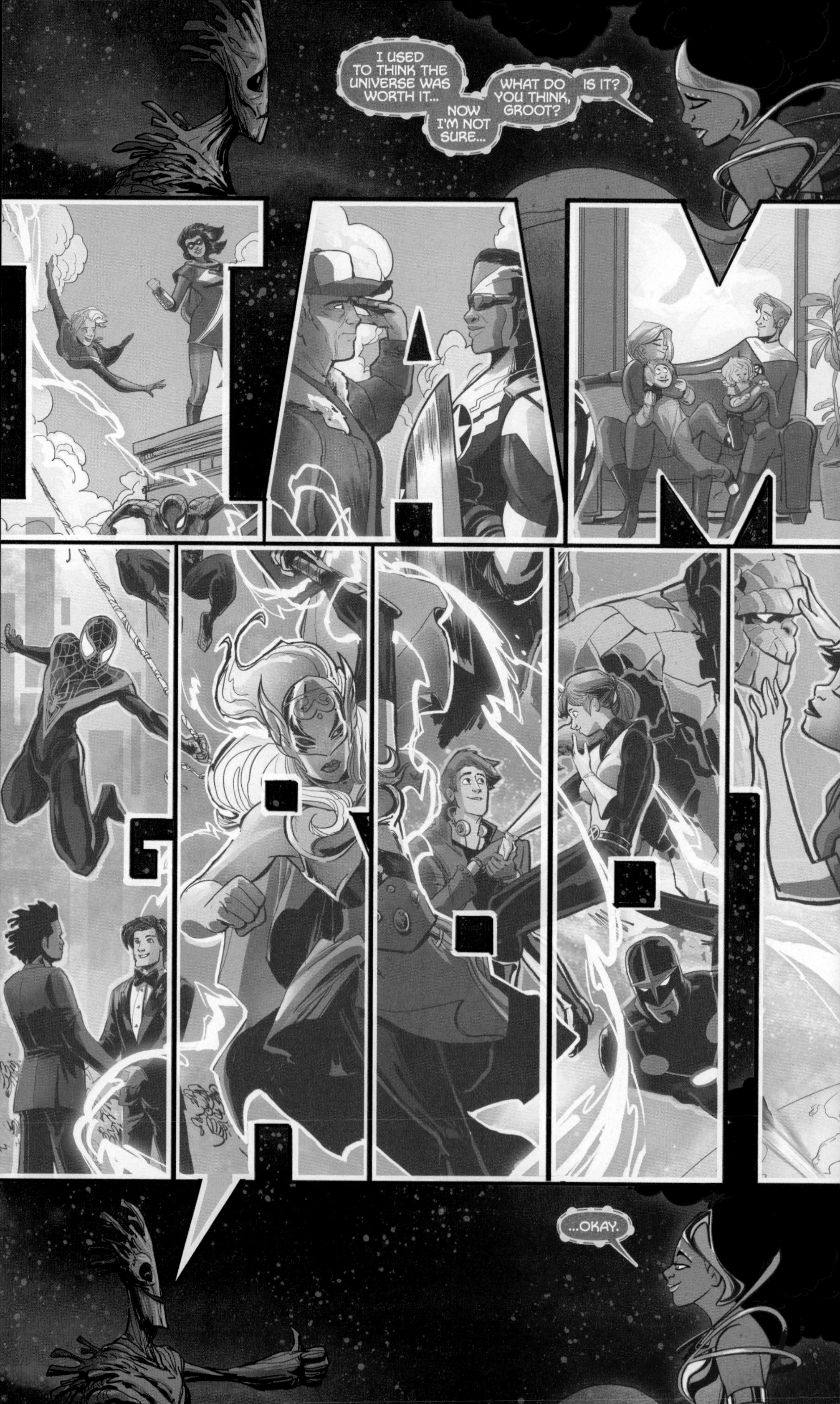
I USED TO THINK THE UNIVERSE WAS WORTH IT...
NOW I'M NOT SURE...
WHAT DO YOU THINK, GROOT?
IS IT?
I AM
...OKAY.

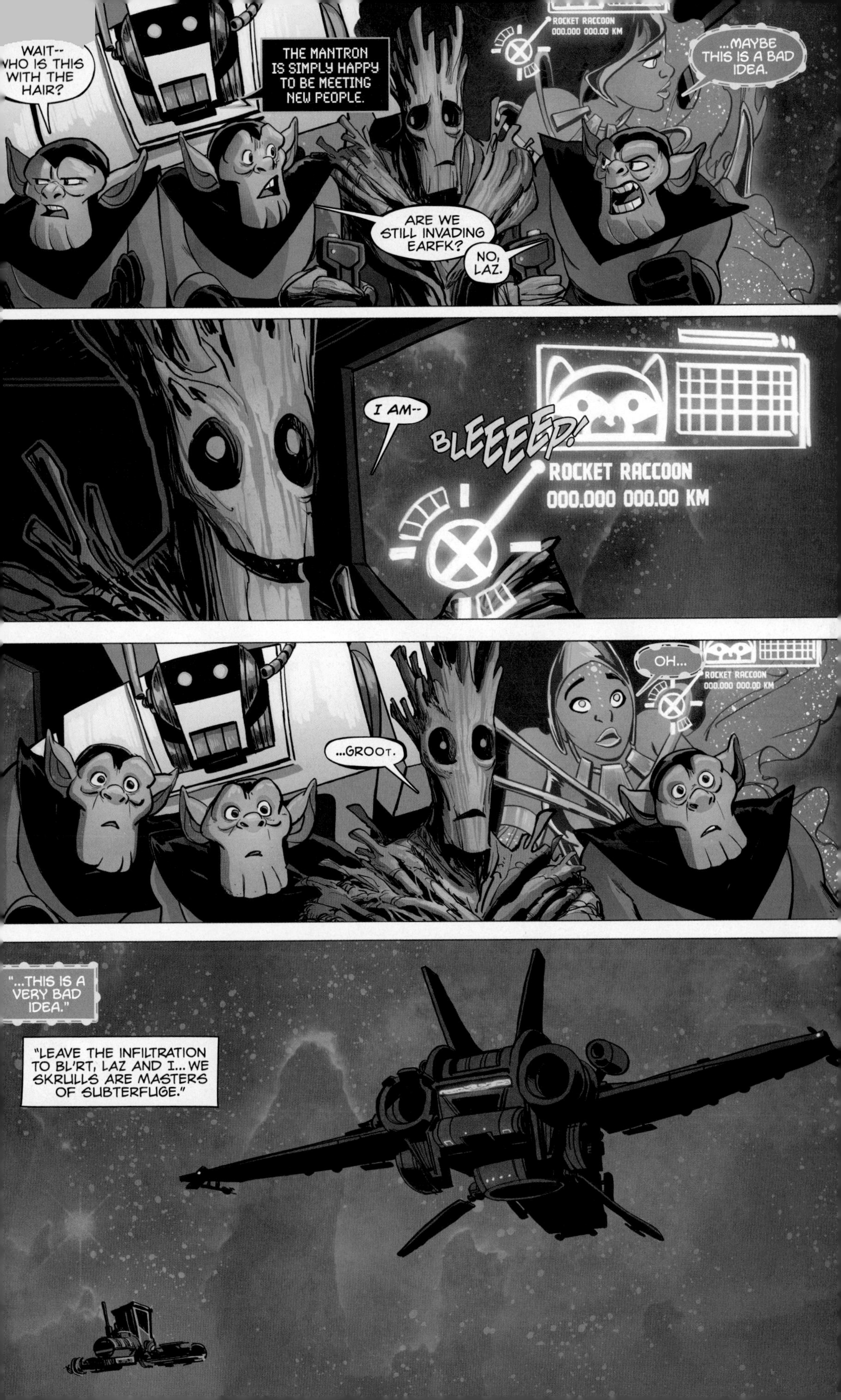
WAIT-- WHO IS THIS WITH THE HAIR?
THE MANTRON IS SIMPLY HAPPY TO BE MEETING NEW PEOPLE.
ROCKET RACCOON 000.000 000.00 KM
...MAYBE THIS IS A BAD IDEA.
ARE WE STILL INVADING EARFK?
NO, LAZ.
I AM--
BLEEEEP!
ROCKET RACCOON
000.000 000.00 KM
OH...
ROCKET RACCOON 000.000 000.00 KM
...GROOT.
"...THIS IS A VERY BAD IDEA."
"LEAVE THE INFILTRATION TO BL'RT, LAZ AND I... WE SKRULLS ARE MASTERS OF SUBTERFUGE."

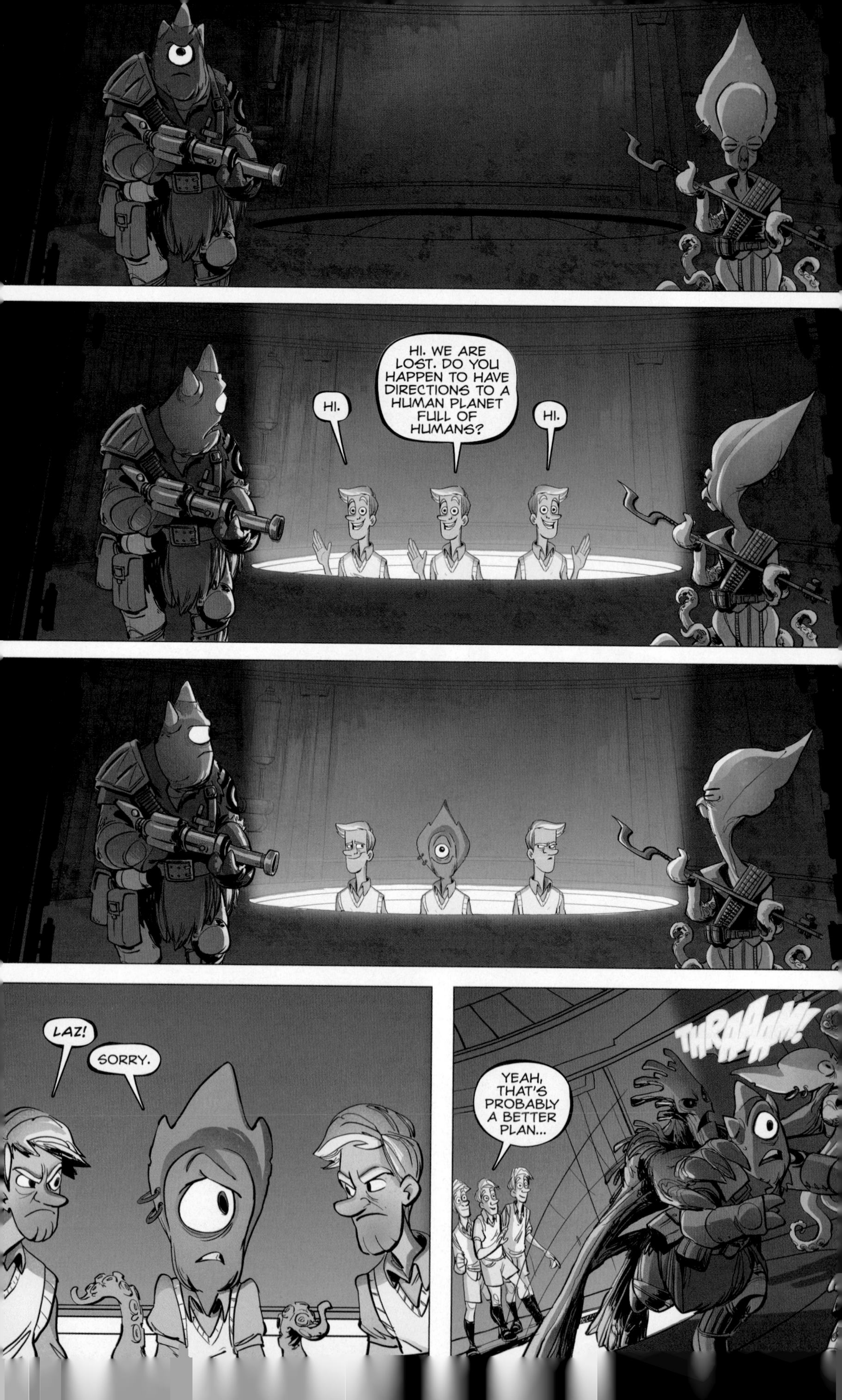
HI.
HI. WE ARE LOST. DO YOU HAPPEN TO HAVE DIRECTIONS TO A HUMAN PLANET FULL OF HUMANS?
HI.
LAZ!
SORRY.
THRAAAM!
YEAH, THAT'S PROBABLY A BETTER PLAN...

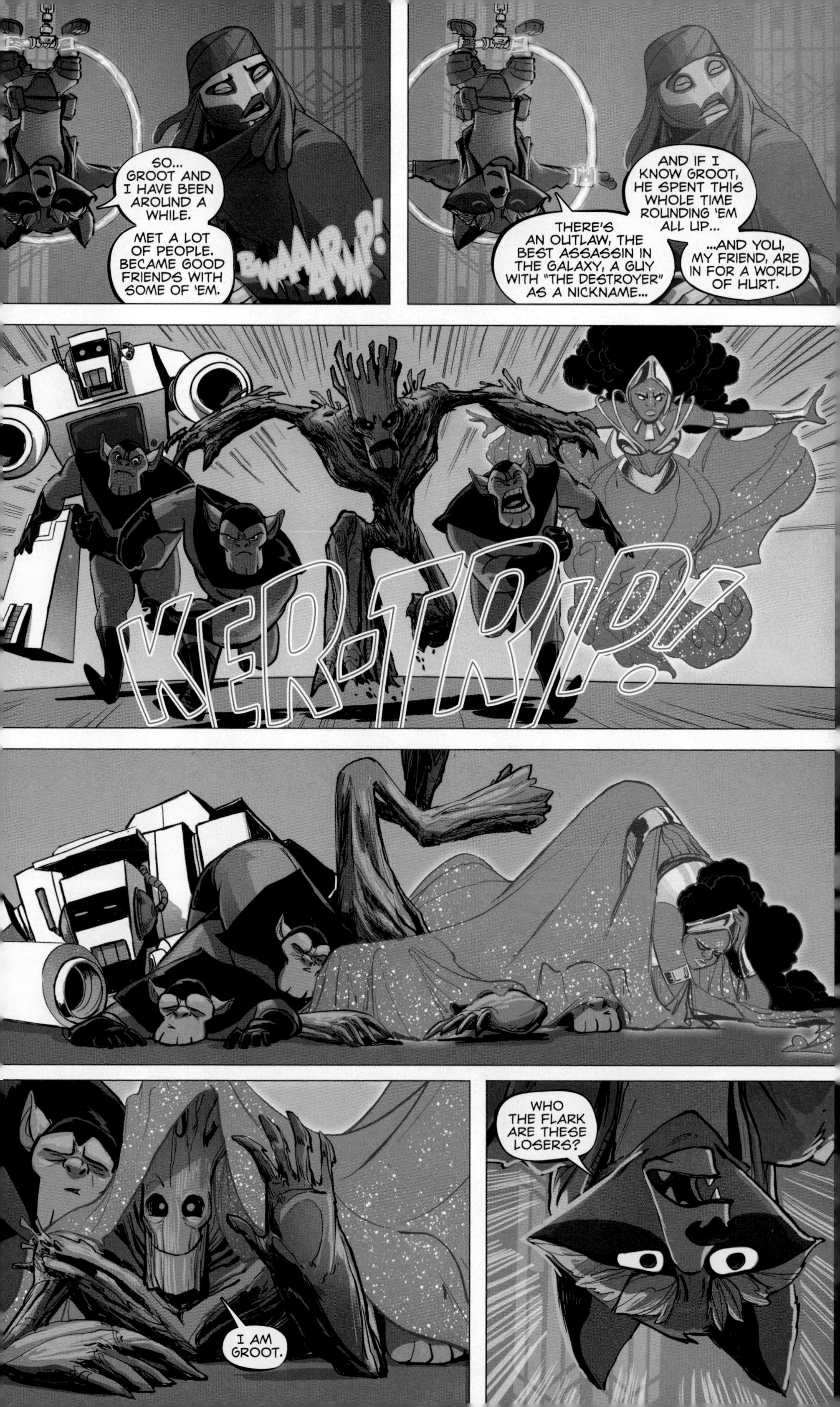
SO... GROOT AND I HAVE BEEN AROUND A WHILE.
MET A LOT OF PEOPLE. BECAME GOOD FRIENDS WITH SOME OF 'EM.
BWAAARMP!
THERE'S AN OUTLAW, THE BEST ASSASSIN IN THE GALAXY, A GUY WITH "THE DESTROYER" AS A NICKNAME...
AND IF I KNOW GROOT, HE SPENT THIS WHOLE TIME ROUNDING 'EM ALL UP...
...AND YOU, MY FRIEND, ARE IN FOR A WORLD OF HURT.
KER-TRIPP!
I AM GROOT.
WHO THE FLARK ARE THESE LOSERS?

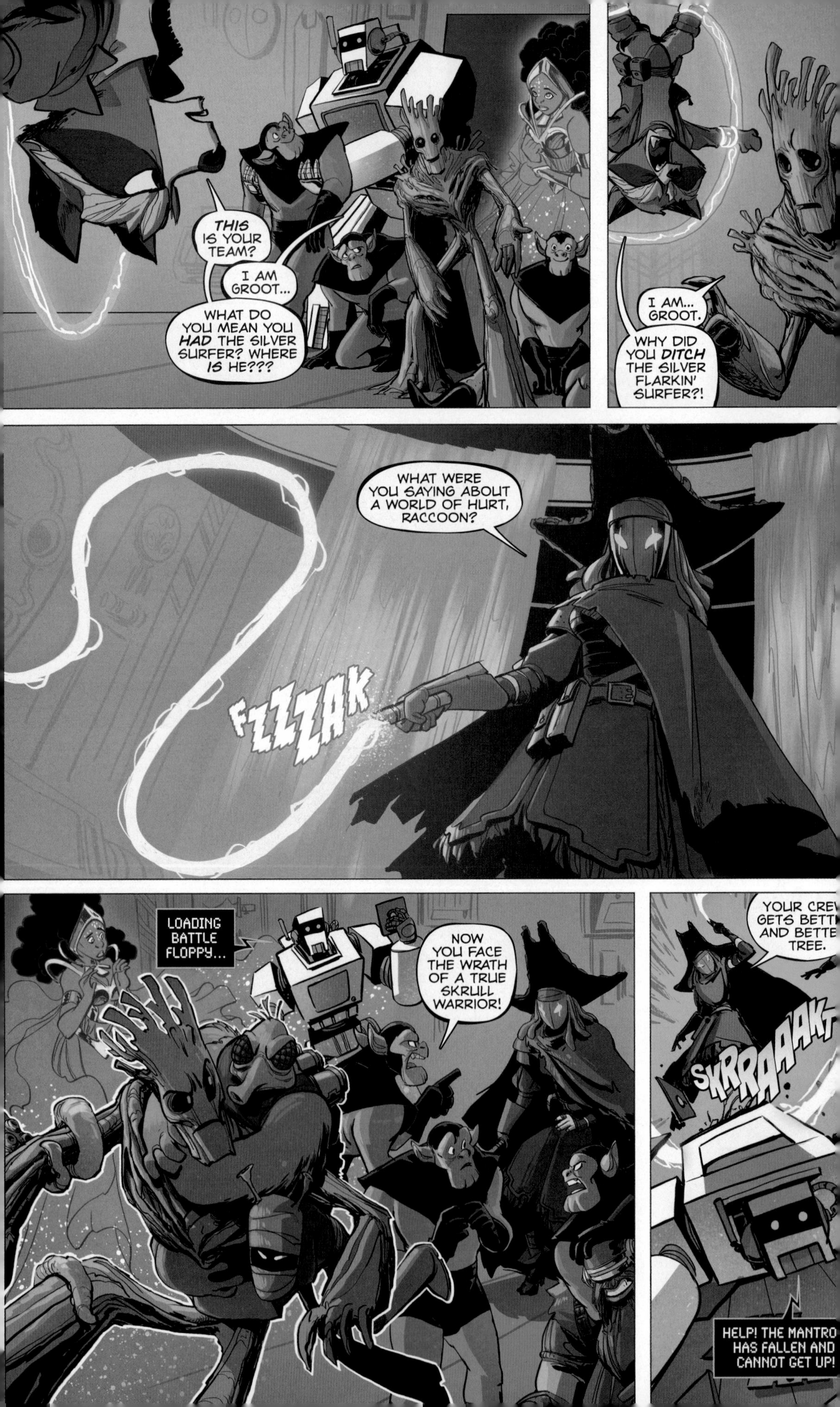

THIS IS YOUR TEAM?
I AM GROOT...
WHAT DO YOU MEAN YOU HAD THE SILVER SURFER? WHERE IS HE???
I AM... GROOT.
WHY DID YOU DITCH THE SILVER FLARKIN' SURFER?!
WHAT WERE YOU SAYING ABOUT A WORLD OF HURT, RACCOON?
FZZZAK
LOADING BATTLE FLOPPY...
NOW YOU FACE THE WRATH OF A TRUE SKRULL WARRIOR!
YOUR CREW GETS BETT AND BETTE TREE.
SKRRAAAKT
HELP! THE MANTRO HAS FALLEN AND CANNOT GET UP!

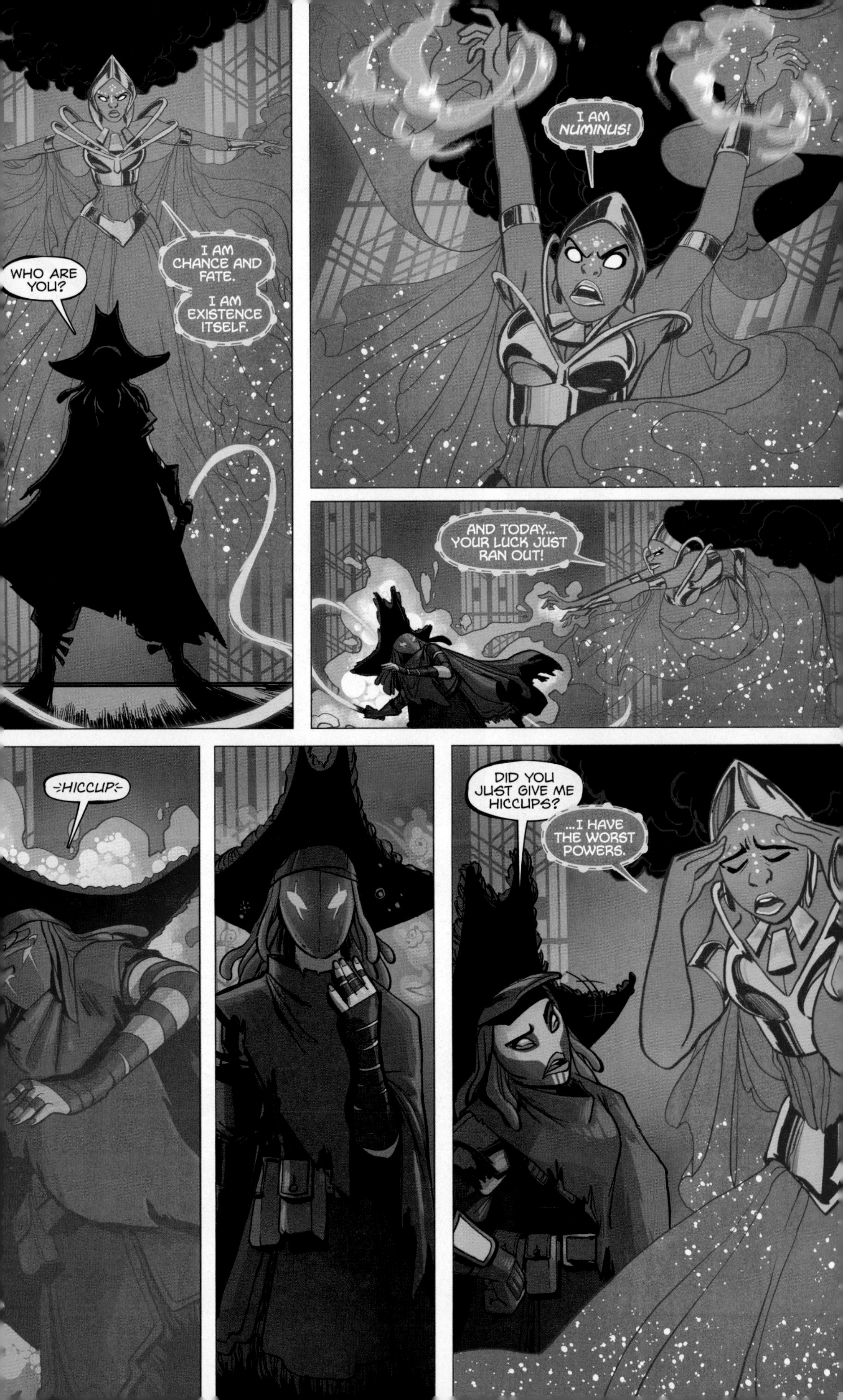
WHO ARE YOU?
I AM CHANCE AND FATE.
I AM EXISTENCE ITSELF.
I AM NUMINUS!
AND TODAY... YOUR LUCK JUST RAN OUT!
HICCUP
DID YOU JUST GIVE ME HICCUPS?
...I HAVE THE WORST POWERS.

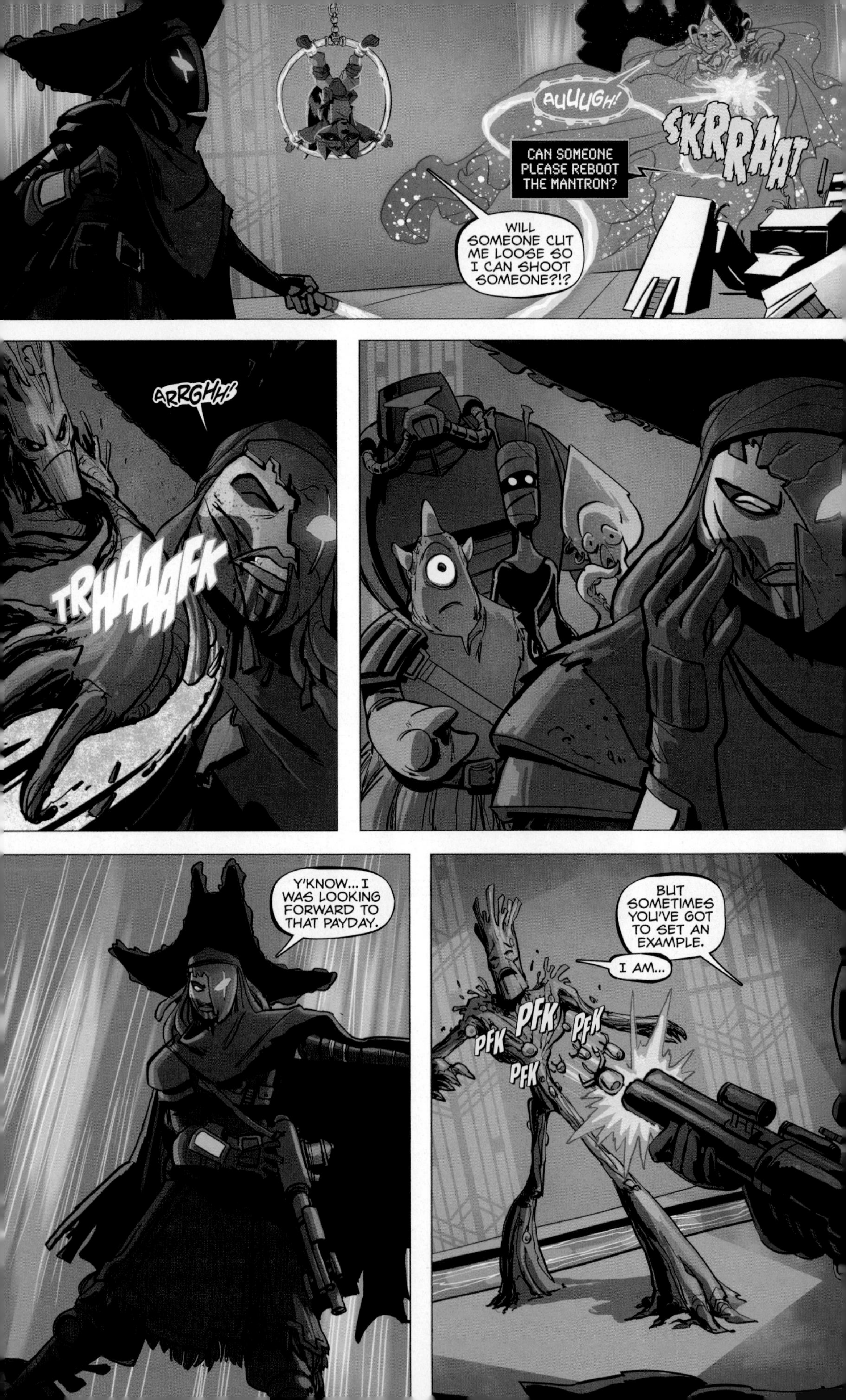
AUUUGH!
SKRRAAT
CAN SOMEONE PLEASE REBOOT THE MANTRON?
WILL SOMEONE CUT ME LOOSE SO I CAN SHOOT SOMEONE?!?
ARRGHH!
TRHAAAAFK
Y'KNOW... I WAS LOOKING FORWARD TO THAT PAYDAY.
BUT SOMETIMES YOU'VE GOT TO SET AN EXAMPLE.
I AM...
PFK
PFK
PFK
PFK

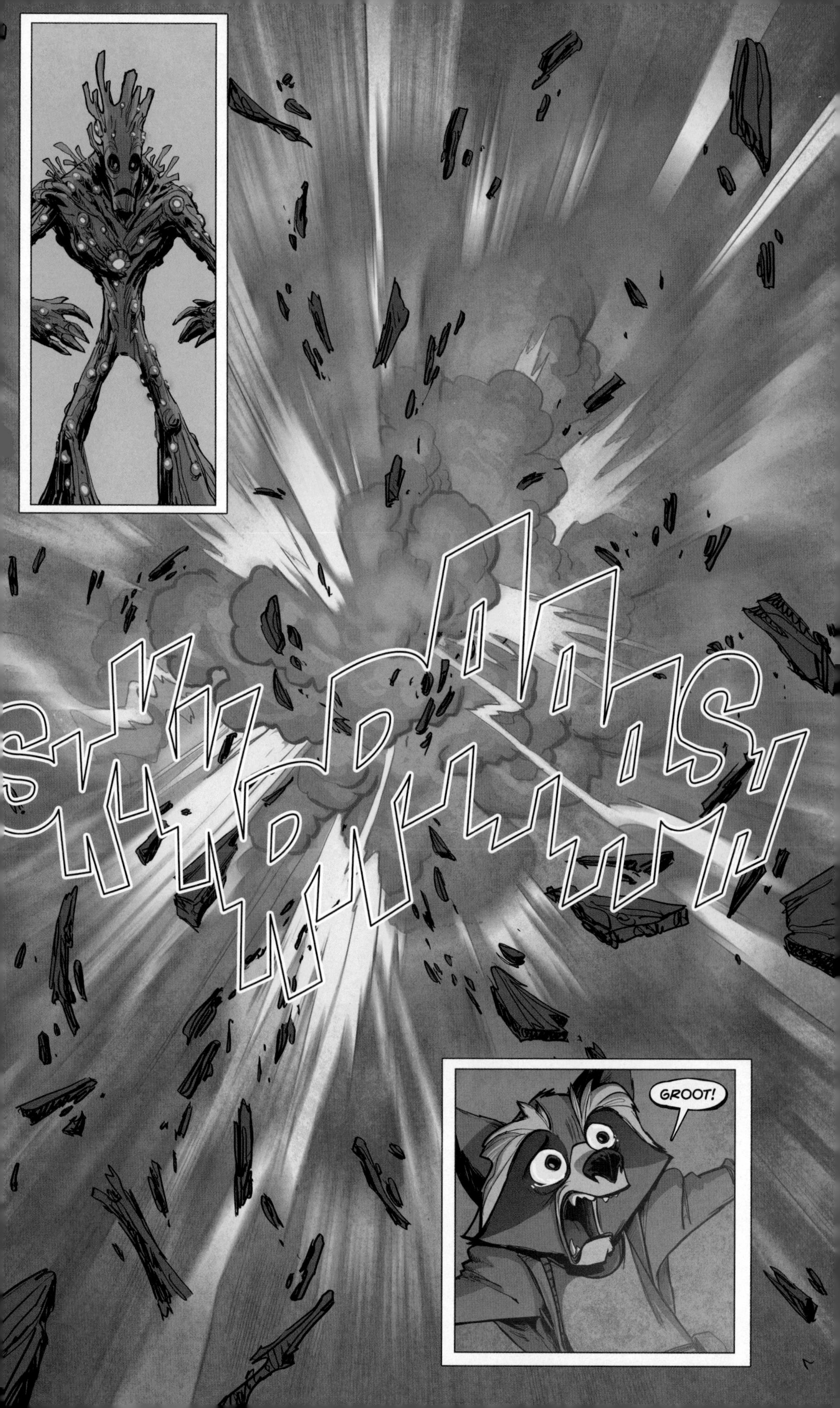
GROOT!

FWOOOOOSH

TORCH EVERY-THING.

HE GROWS BACK FAST. I DON'T WANT A SPLINTER LEFT!

AND SHOW HIS FRIENDS THE AIRLOCK. THEY'RE NOT WORTH ANY-THING.

WHAT ARE YOU DOING?

THE ONLY THING I CAN DO...

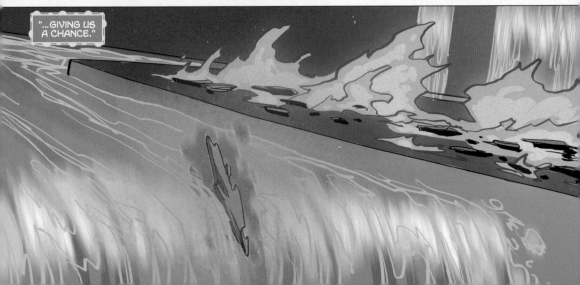

"...GIVING US A CHANCE."

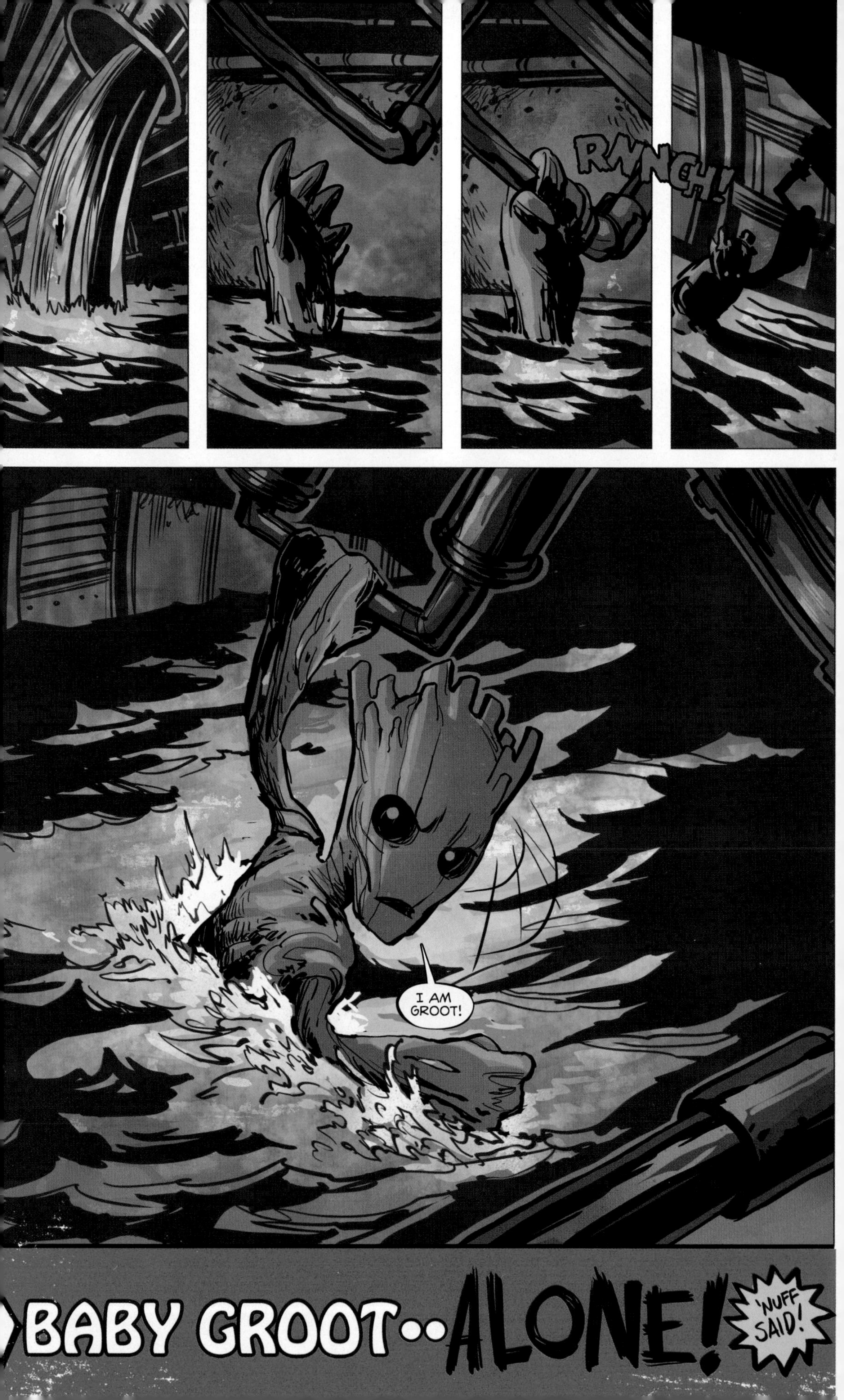
RANCH!
I AM GROOT!
BABY GROOT··ALONE!
'NUFF SAID!

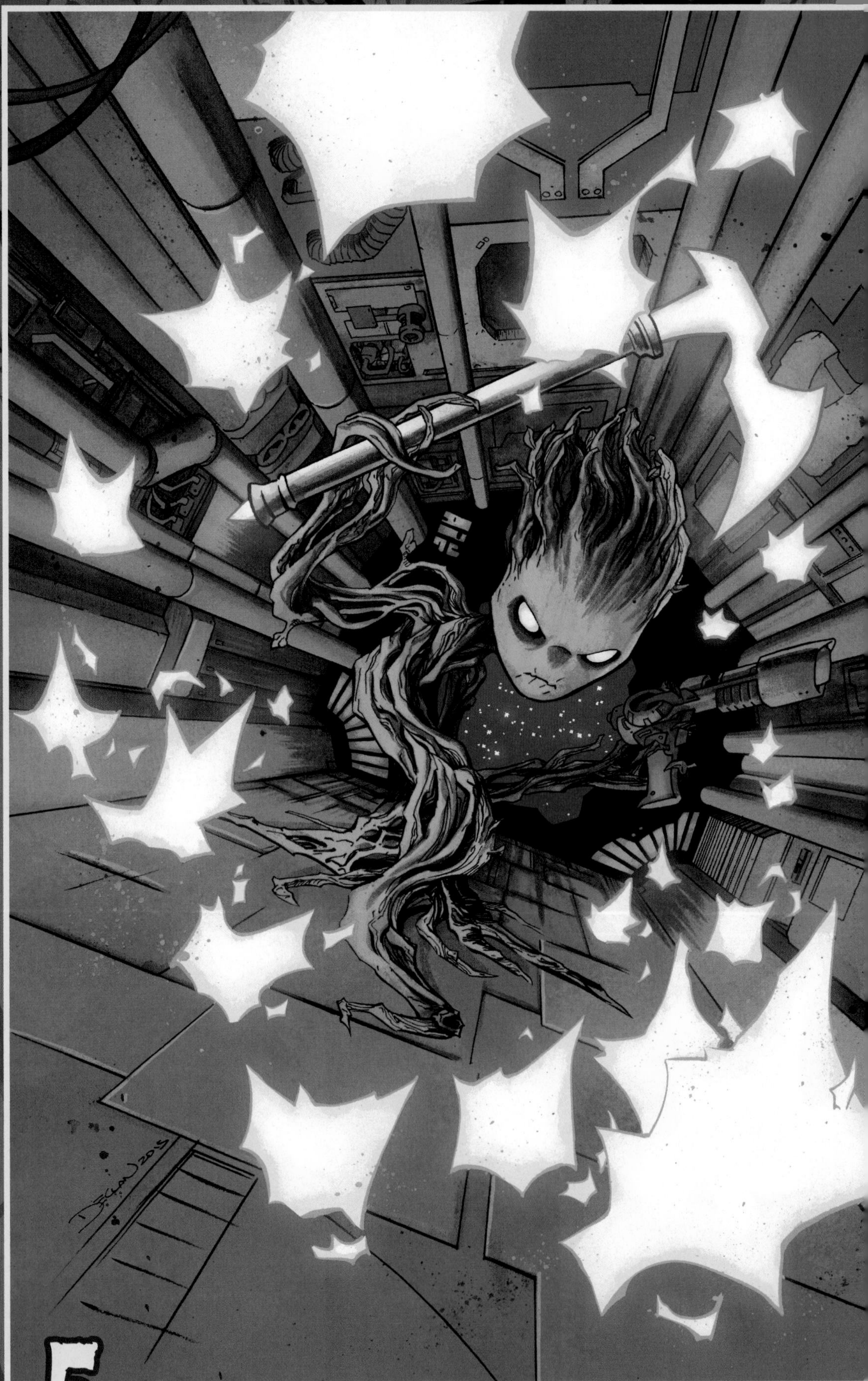

5

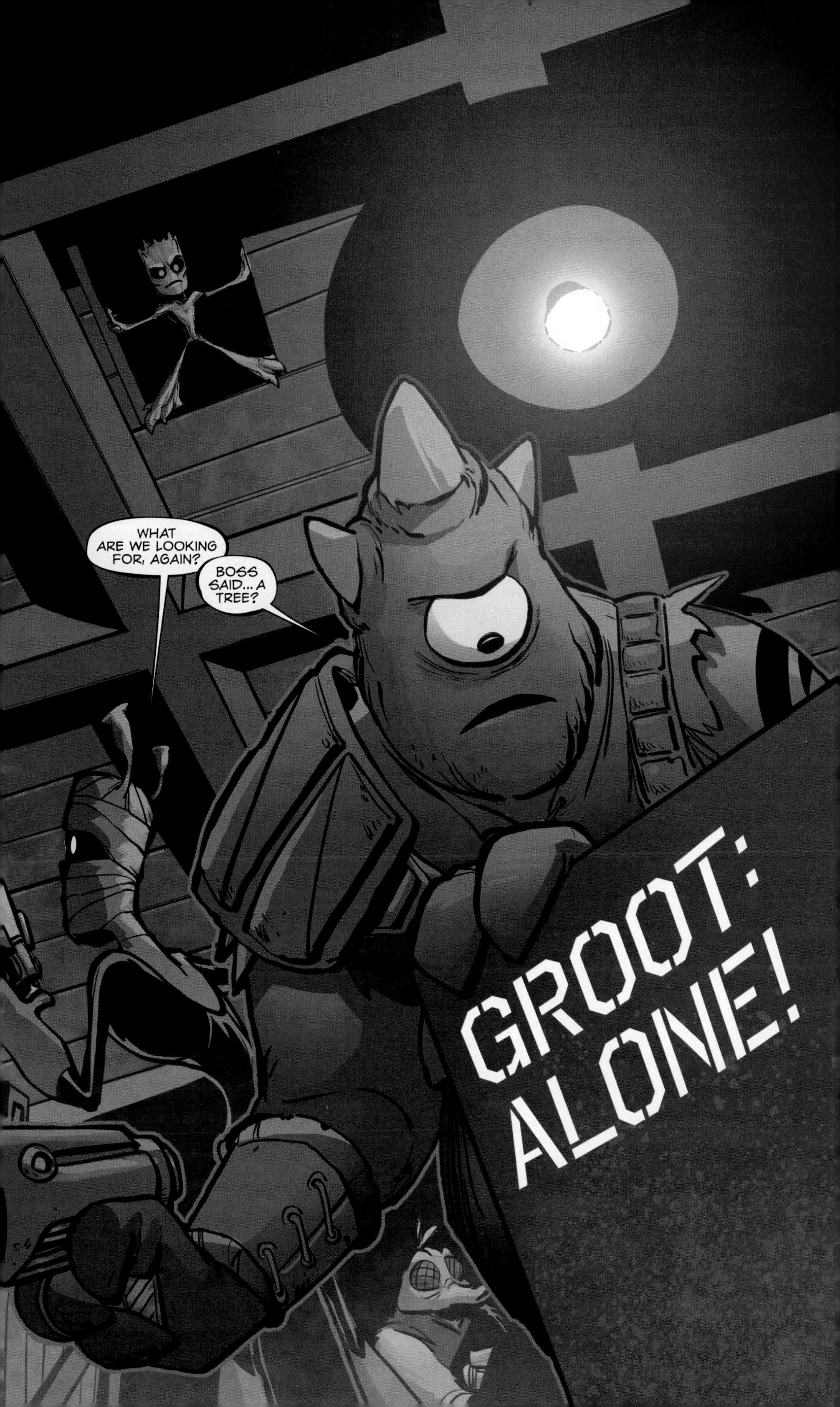

WHAT ARE WE LOOKING FOR, AGAIN?
BOSS SAID... A TREE?
GROOT: ALONE!

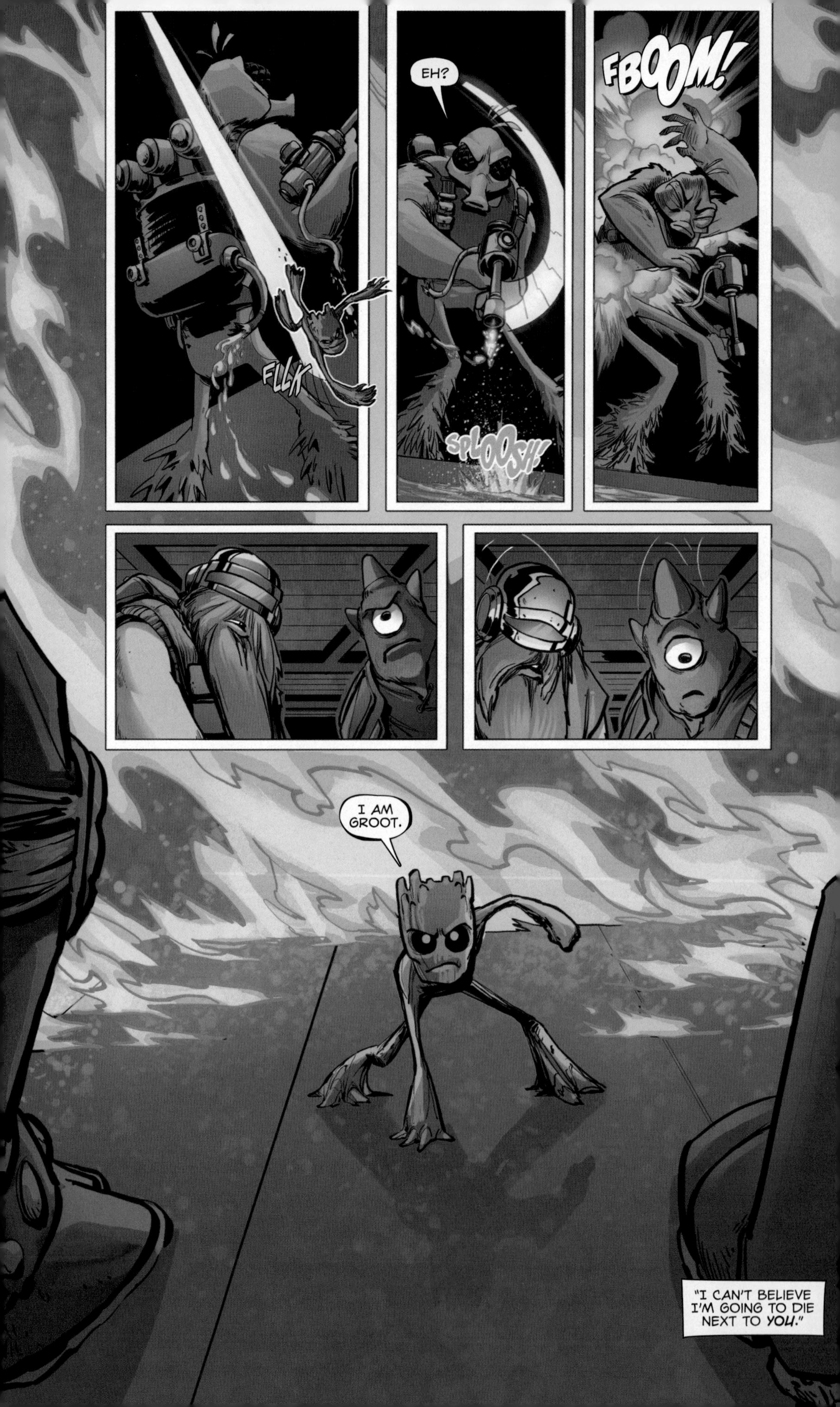
FLLK
EH?
SPLOOSH!
FBOOM!
I AM GROOT.
"I CAN'T BELIEVE I'M GOING TO DIE NEXT TO *YOU*."

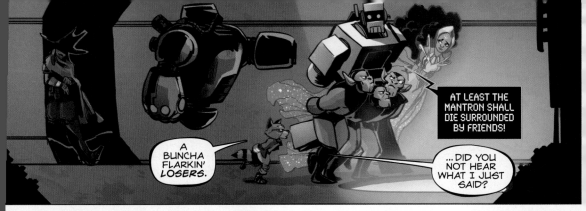

AT LEAST THE MANTRON SHALL DIE SURROUNDED BY FRIENDS!

A BUNCHA FLARKIN' **LOSERS**.

...DID YOU **NOT** HEAR WHAT I JUST SAID?

NO.

THE MANTRON WAS...DISTRACTED.

SO... UH... ARE THEY GOING TO **KILL US** NOW? IS THAT WHAT'S HAPPENING?

LAZ, AT LEAST PAY ATTENTION TO YOUR OWN EXECUTION. DIE WITH HONOR.

AREN'T YOU SOME SORT OF GLOWING SPACE **GOD**? FREE US!

IT **DOESN'T** WORK THAT WAY. I EMPOWER OPPORTUNITY. WONDER. CHANCE. BUT...

...I THINK WE'RE OUT OF LUCK.

YOU GONNA GIVE ME HICCUPS AGAIN?

WHAT HAPPENED TO JUST TAKING **BOUNTIES**?

HATE TO BREAK IT TO YA, BUT YOU AIN'T WORTH AS MUCH AS YOU THINK.

AND HONESTLY, I'D **PAY** MONEY TO KILL YOU.

I'VE GOT FRIENDS. THEY'LL COME LOOKING FOR--

DON'T COUNT GROOT OUT...

YEAH, YOUR TREE PAL TURNED OUT TO BE A WINNER.

OH, I'M NOT... I KNOW HIS LITTLE TRICK. I'VE GOT MY BOYS DOWN THERE BURNING EVERYTHING. TRUST ME...

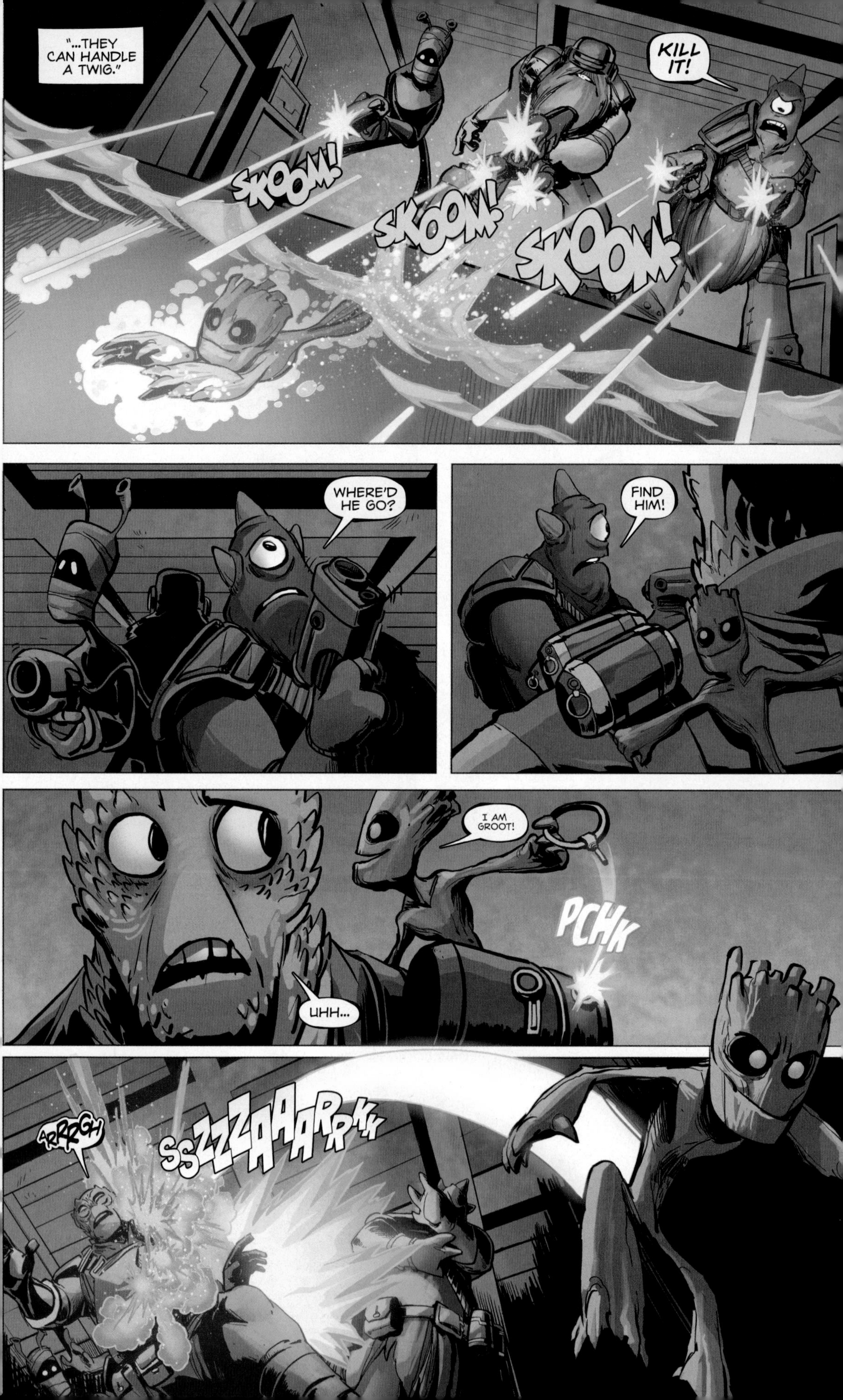
"...THEY CAN HANDLE A TWIG."
KILL IT!
SKOOM!
SKOOM!
SKOOM!
WHERE'D HE GO?
FIND HIM!
I AM GROOT!
PCHK
UHH...
ARRRGH
SSZZZAAARRKK

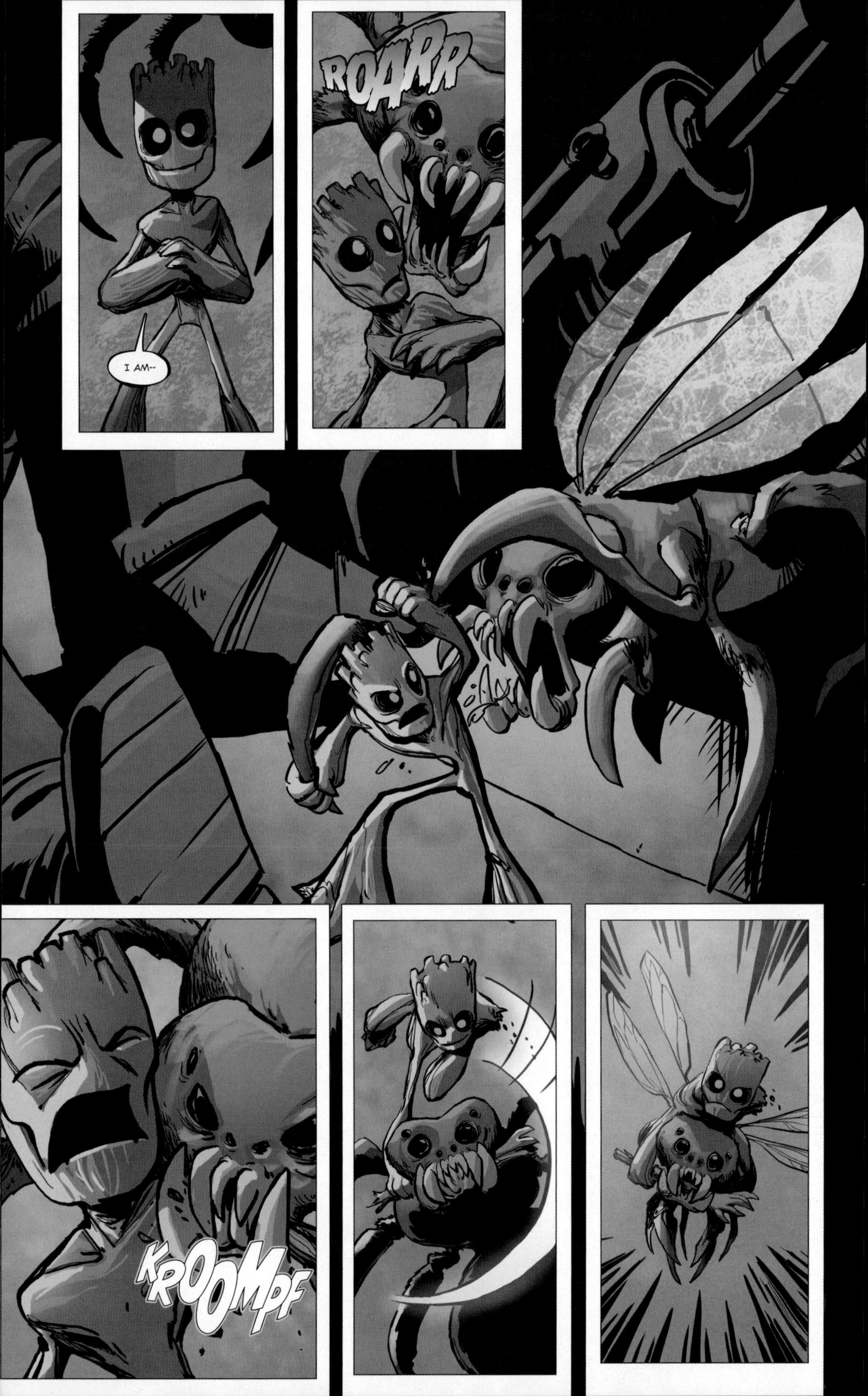
I AM--
ROARR
KROOMPF

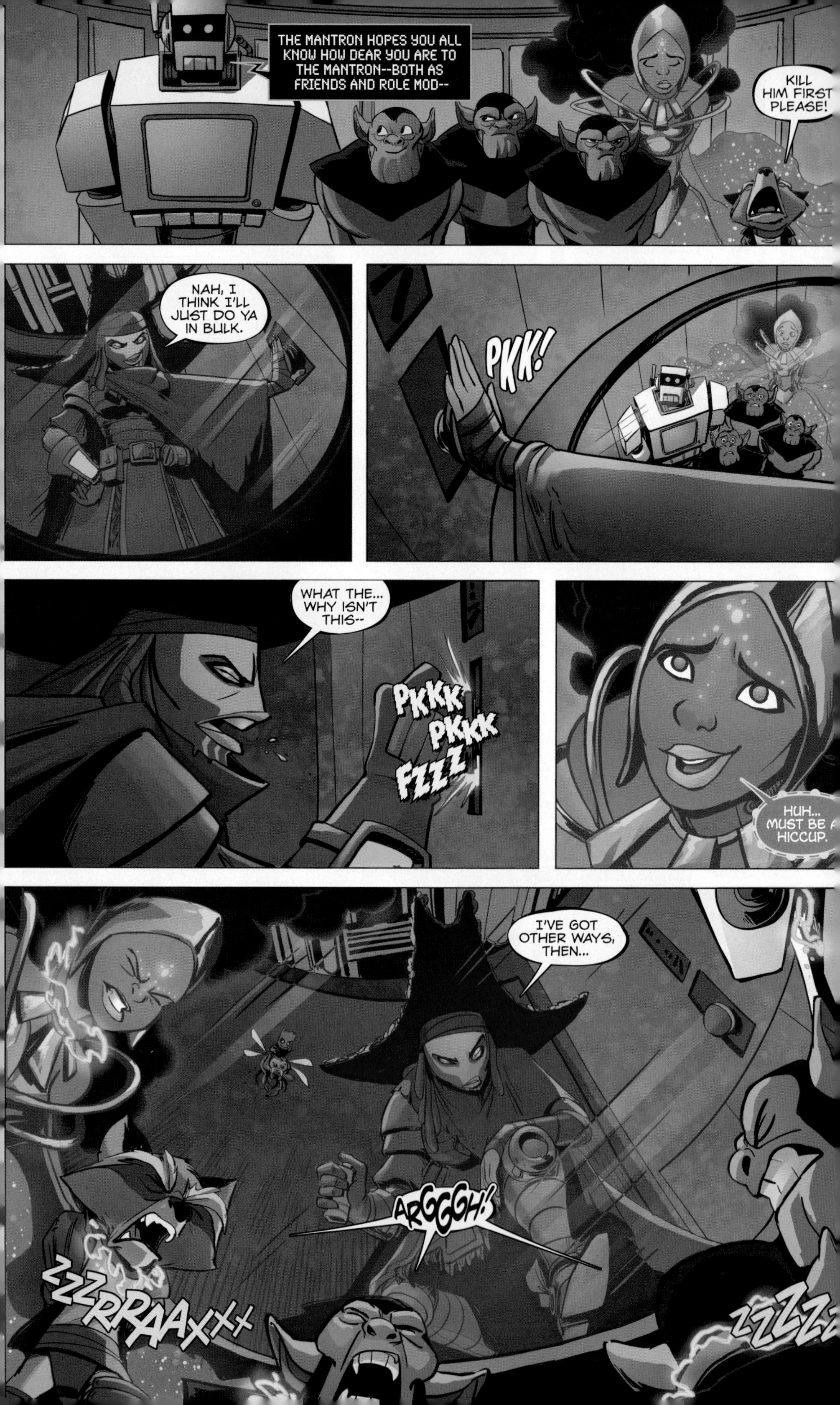

THE MANTRON HOPES YOU ALL KNOW HOW DEAR YOU ARE TO THE MANTRON--BOTH AS FRIENDS AND ROLE MOD--
KILL HIM FIRST PLEASE!
NAH, I THINK I'LL JUST DO YA IN BULK.
PKK!
WHAT THE... WHY ISN'T THIS--
PKKK
PKKK
FZZZ
HUH... MUST BE A HICCUP.
I'VE GOT OTHER WAYS, THEN...
ARGGGH!
ZZZRRAAXXX

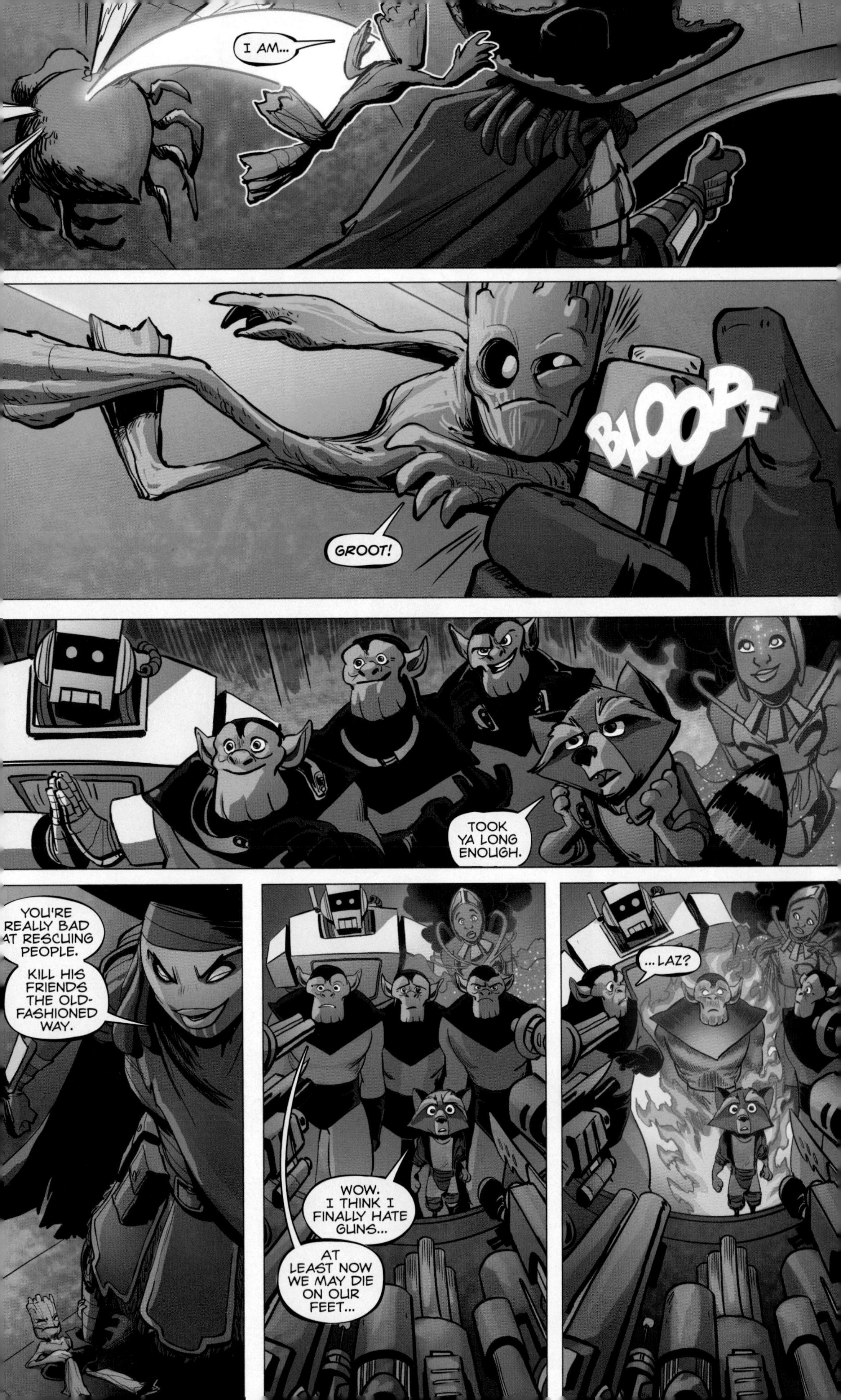

I AM...
BLOOPF
GROOT!
TOOK YA LONG ENOUGH.
YOU'RE REALLY BAD AT RESCUING PEOPLE.
KILL HIS FRIENDS THE OLD-FASHIONED WAY.
WOW. I THINK I FINALLY HATE GUNS...
AT LEAST NOW WE MAY DIE ON OUR FEET...
...LAZ?

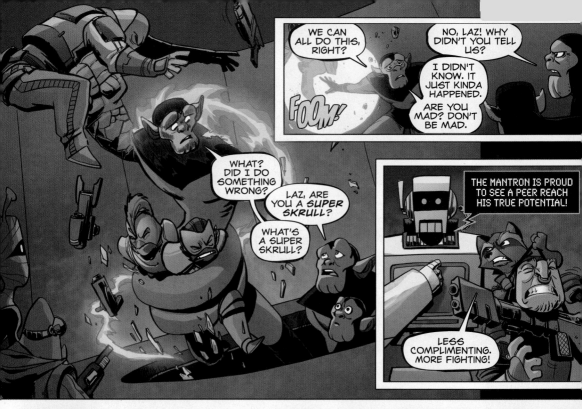

WE CAN ALL DO THIS, RIGHT?

NO, LAZ! WHY DIDN'T YOU TELL US?

I DIDN'T KNOW. IT JUST KINDA HAPPENED.

ARE YOU MAD? DON'T BE MAD.

FOOM!

WHAT? DID I DO SOMETHING WRONG?

LAZ, ARE YOU A *SUPER SKRULL?*

WHAT'S A SUPER SKRULL?

THE MANTRON IS PROUD TO SEE A PEER REACH HIS TRUE POTENTIAL!

LESS COMPLIMENTING. MORE FIGHTING!

OH HEY. I MISSED SHOOTING YOU.

BLAFF! BLAFF!

A.P.E.-- DEAL WITH 'EM.

YOUR NEW FRIENDS ARE WEIRD...

YOU READY FOR THIS?

I AM GROOT.

BEST IDEA I'VE HEARD ALL DAY, PAL...

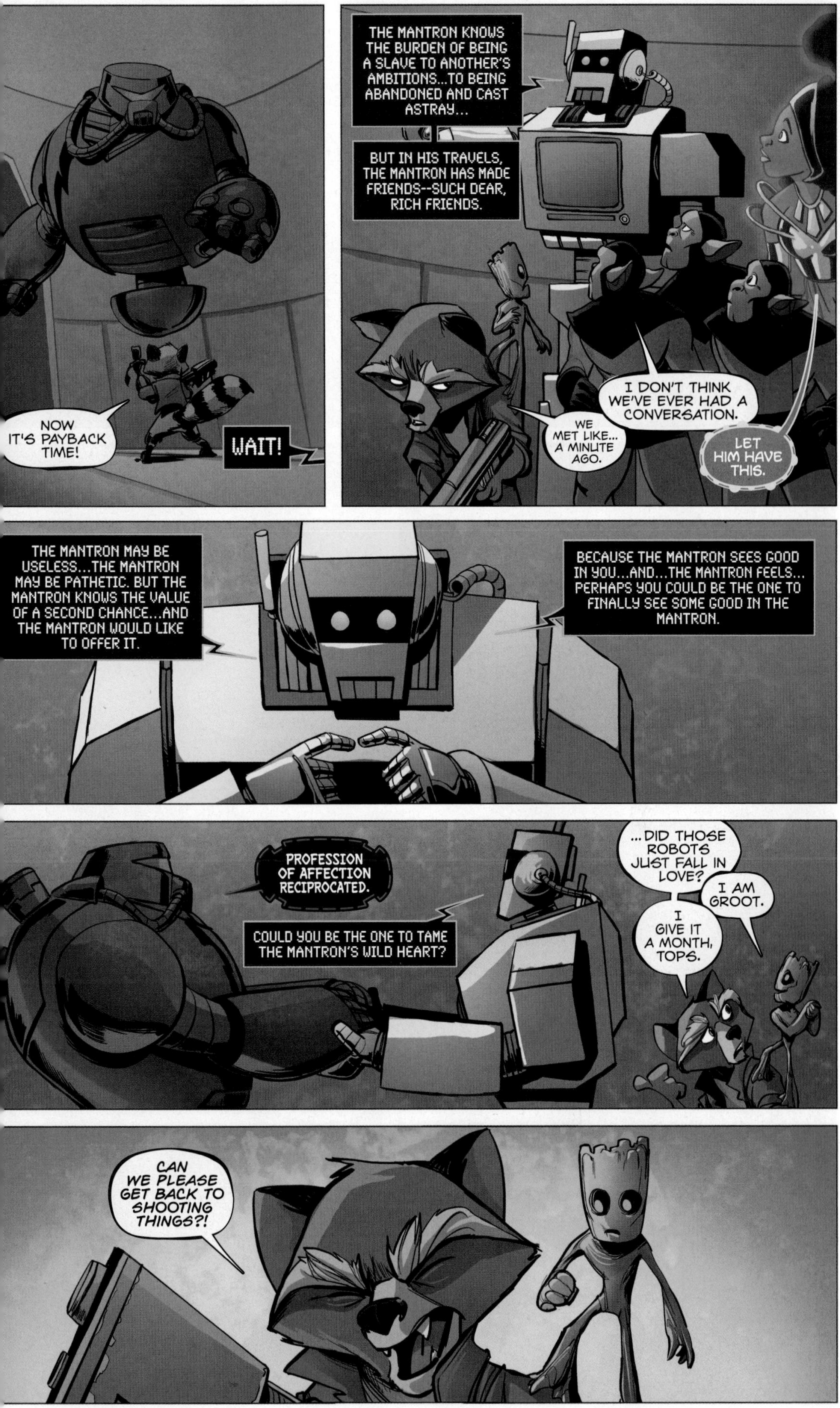
NOW IT'S PAYBACK TIME!
WAIT!
THE MANTRON KNOWS THE BURDEN OF BEING A SLAVE TO ANOTHER'S AMBITIONS...TO BEING ABANDONED AND CAST ASTRAY...
BUT IN HIS TRAVELS, THE MANTRON HAS MADE FRIENDS--SUCH DEAR, RICH FRIENDS.
WE MET LIKE... A MINUTE AGO.
I DON'T THINK WE'VE EVER HAD A CONVERSATION.
LET HIM HAVE THIS.
THE MANTRON MAY BE USELESS...THE MANTRON MAY BE PATHETIC. BUT THE MANTRON KNOWS THE VALUE OF A SECOND CHANCE...AND THE MANTRON WOULD LIKE TO OFFER IT.
BECAUSE THE MANTRON SEES GOOD IN YOU...AND...THE MANTRON FEELS... PERHAPS YOU COULD BE THE ONE TO FINALLY SEE SOME GOOD IN THE MANTRON.
PROFESSION OF AFFECTION RECIPROCATED.
COULD YOU BE THE ONE TO TAME THE MANTRON'S WILD HEART?
...DID THOSE ROBOTS JUST FALL IN LOVE?
I AM GROOT.
I GIVE IT A MONTH, TOPS.
CAN WE PLEASE GET BACK TO SHOOTING THINGS?!

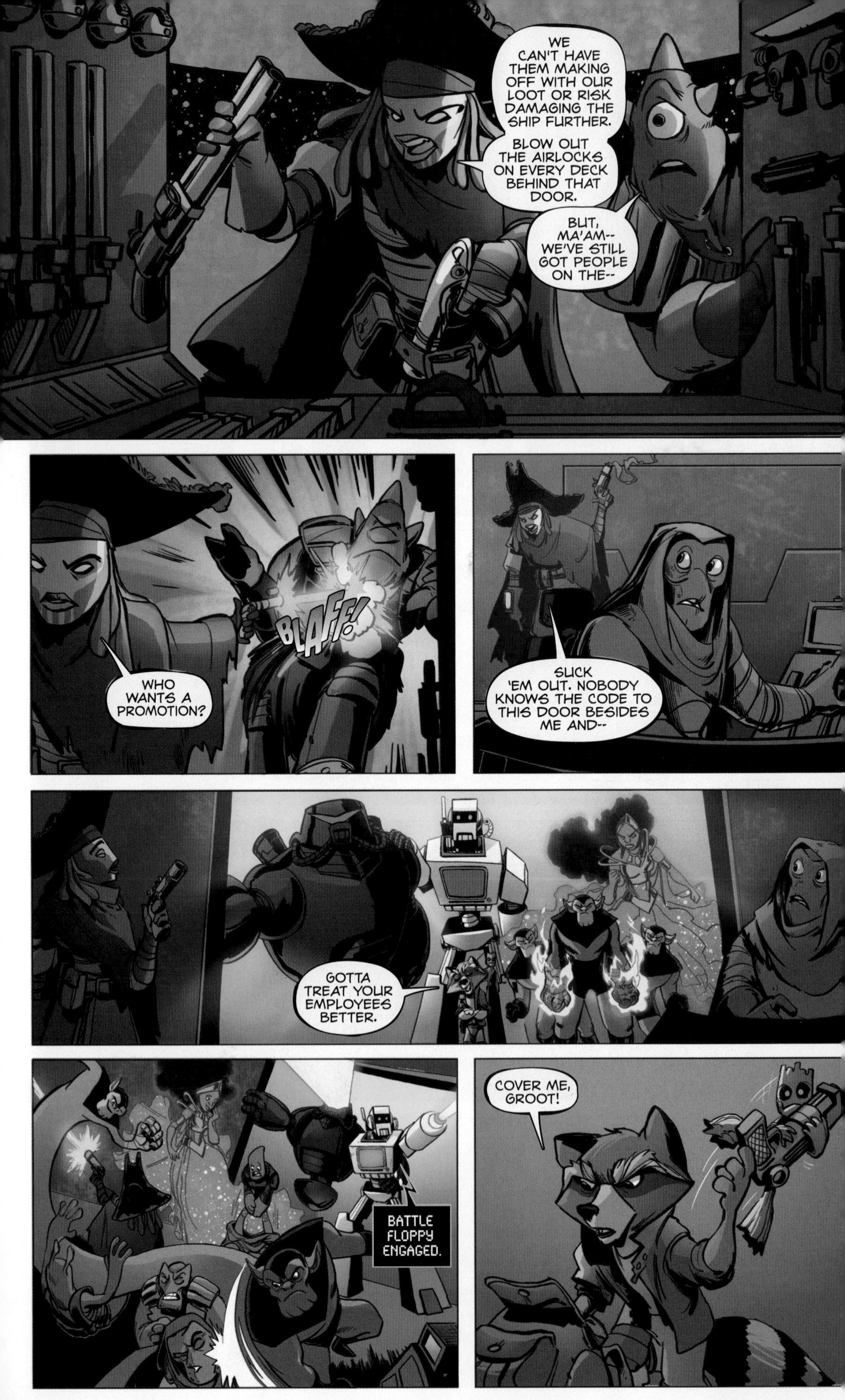
WE CAN'T HAVE THEM MAKING OFF WITH OUR LOOT OR RISK DAMAGING THE SHIP FURTHER.
BLOW OUT THE AIRLOCKS ON EVERY DECK BEHIND THAT DOOR.
BUT, MA'AM-- WE'VE STILL GOT PEOPLE ON THE--
BLAFF!
WHO WANTS A PROMOTION?
SUCK 'EM OUT. NOBODY KNOWS THE CODE TO THIS DOOR BESIDES ME AND--
GOTTA TREAT YOUR EMPLOYEES BETTER.
BATTLE FLOPPY ENGAGED.
COVER ME, GROOT!

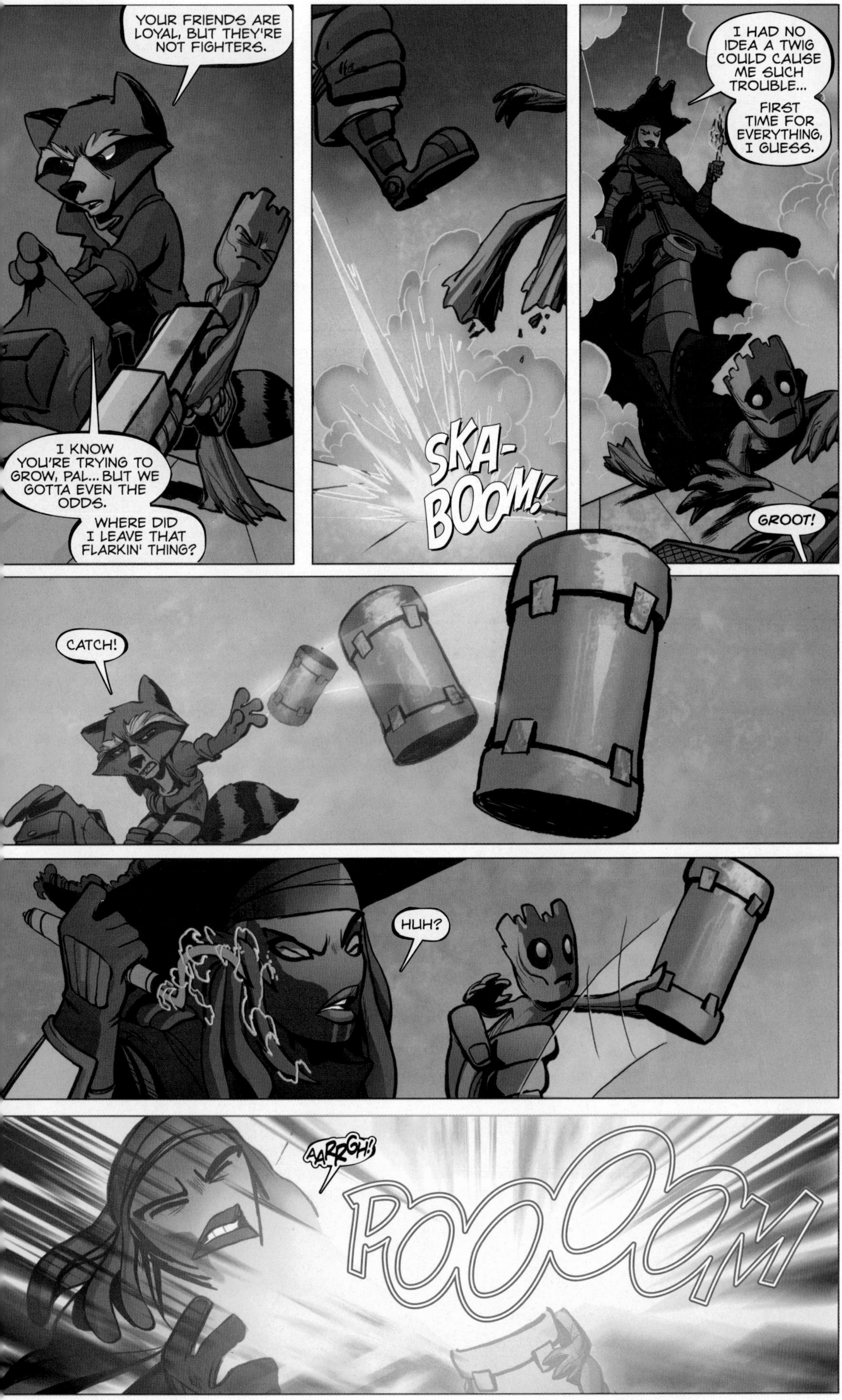
YOUR FRIENDS ARE LOYAL, BUT THEY'RE NOT FIGHTERS.
I KNOW YOU'RE TRYING TO GROW, PAL... BUT WE GOTTA EVEN THE ODDS.
WHERE DID I LEAVE THAT FLARKIN' THING?
SKA-BOOM!
I HAD NO IDEA A TWIG COULD CAUSE ME SUCH TROUBLE...
FIRST TIME FOR EVERYTHING, I GUESS.
GROOT!
CATCH!
HUH?
AARRGH!
POOOOOM

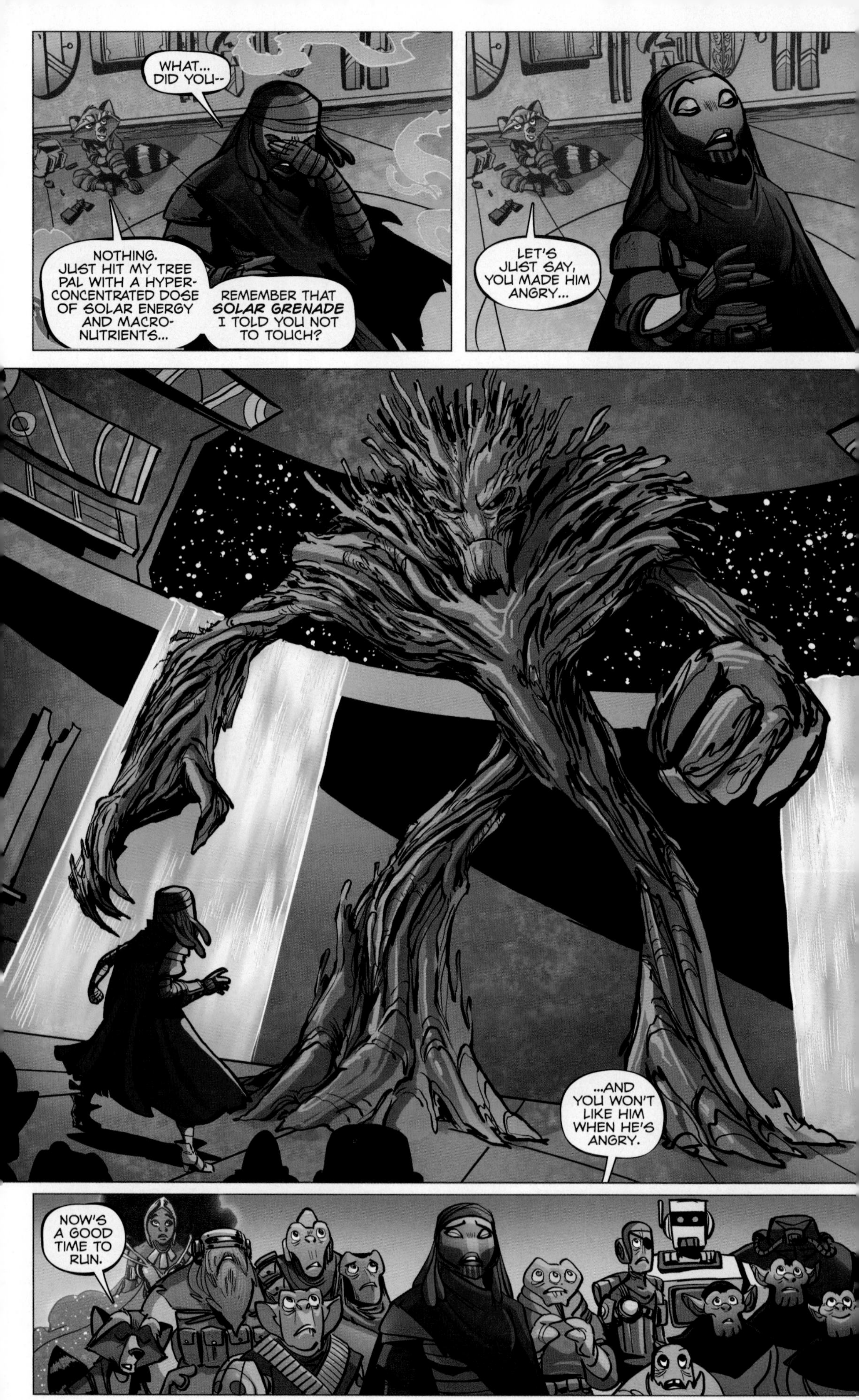
WHAT... DID YOU--
NOTHING. JUST HIT MY TREE PAL WITH A HYPER-CONCENTRATED DOSE OF SOLAR ENERGY AND MACRO-NUTRIENTS...
REMEMBER THAT SOLAR GRENADE I TOLD YOU NOT TO TOUCH?
LET'S JUST SAY, YOU MADE HIM ANGRY...
...AND YOU WON'T LIKE HIM WHEN HE'S ANGRY.
NOW'S A GOOD TIME TO RUN.

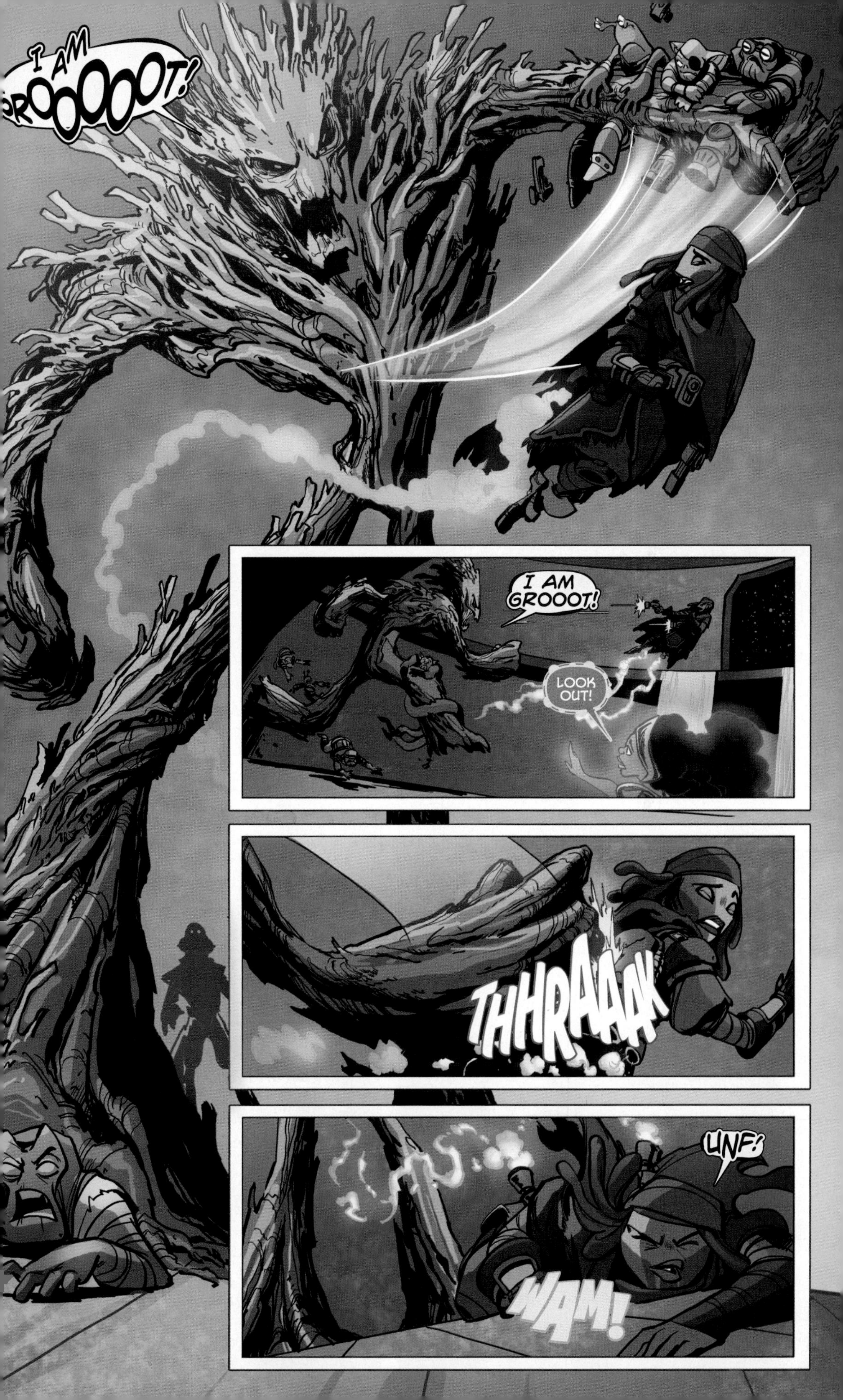

I AM GROOOOOOT!
I AM GROOOT!
LOOK OUT!
THHRAAAK
UNF!
WAM!

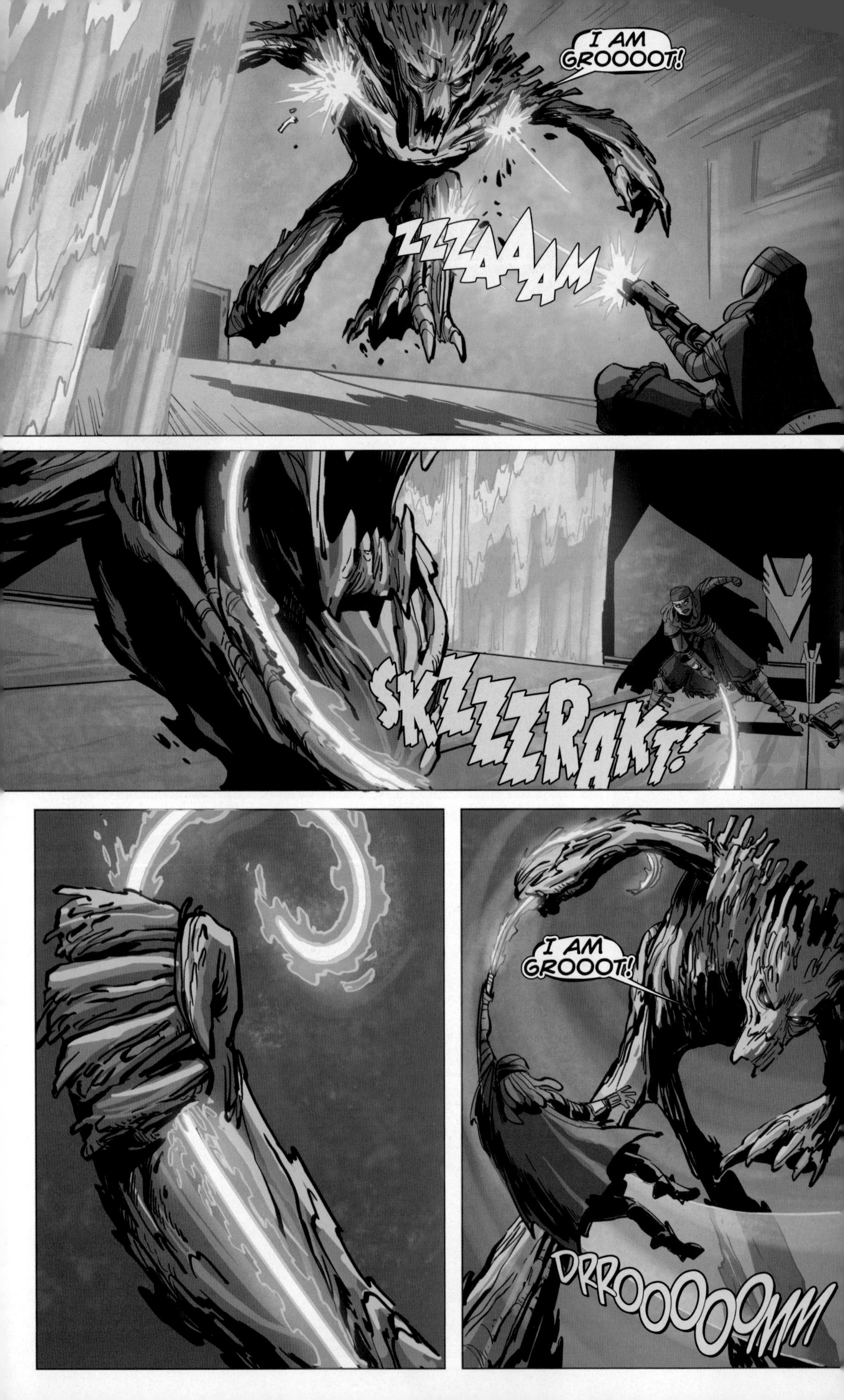
I AM GROOOOT!
ZZZAAAAM
SKZZZZRAKT!
I AM GROOOT!
DRROOOOOOMM

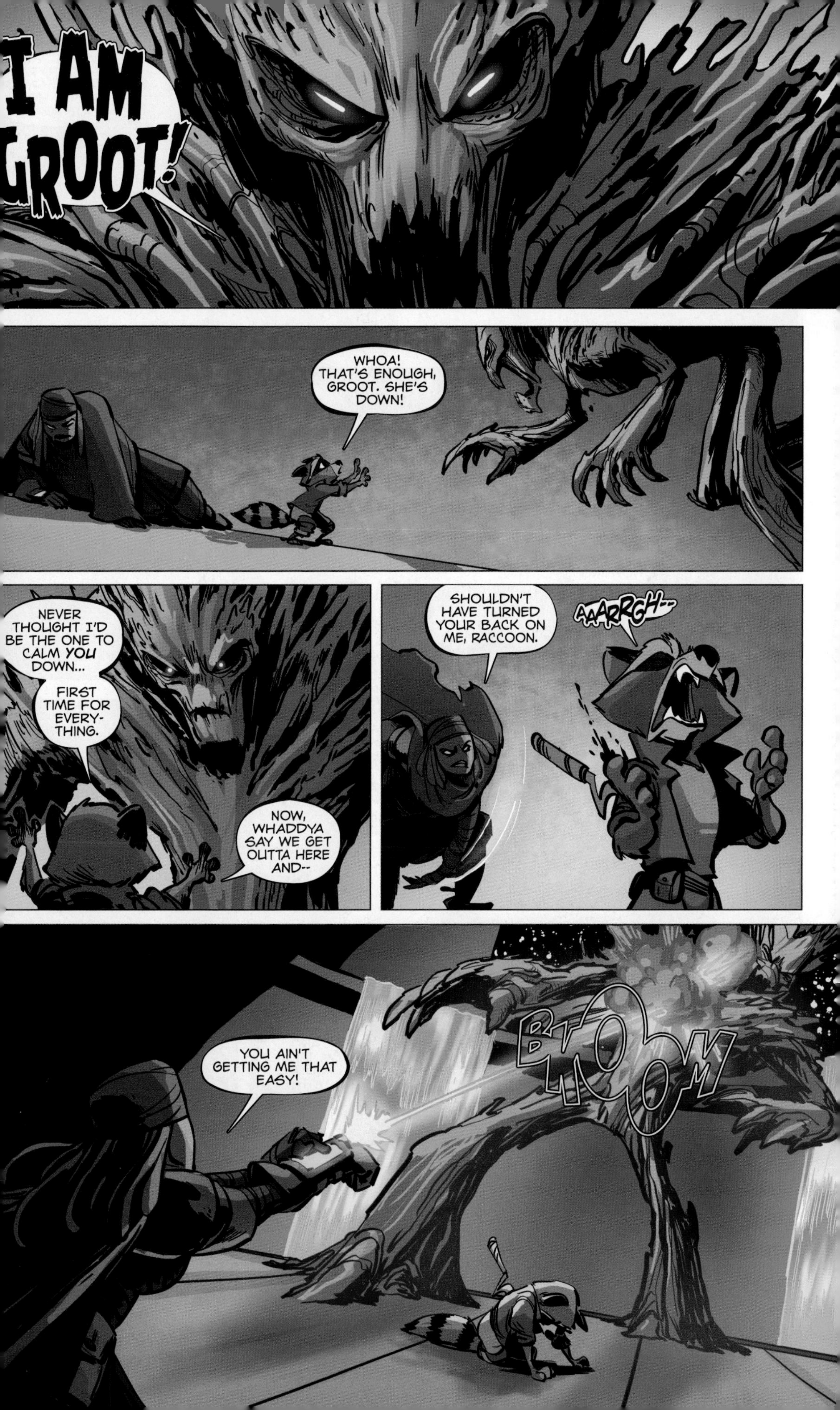
I AM GROOT!
WHOA! THAT'S ENOUGH, GROOT. SHE'S DOWN!
NEVER THOUGHT I'D BE THE ONE TO CALM *YOU* DOWN...
FIRST TIME FOR EVERY-THING.
NOW, WHADDYA SAY WE GET OUTTA HERE AND--
SHOULDN'T HAVE TURNED YOUR BACK ON ME, RACCOON.
AAARRGH--
YOU AIN'T GETTING ME THAT EASY!
BLOOOM

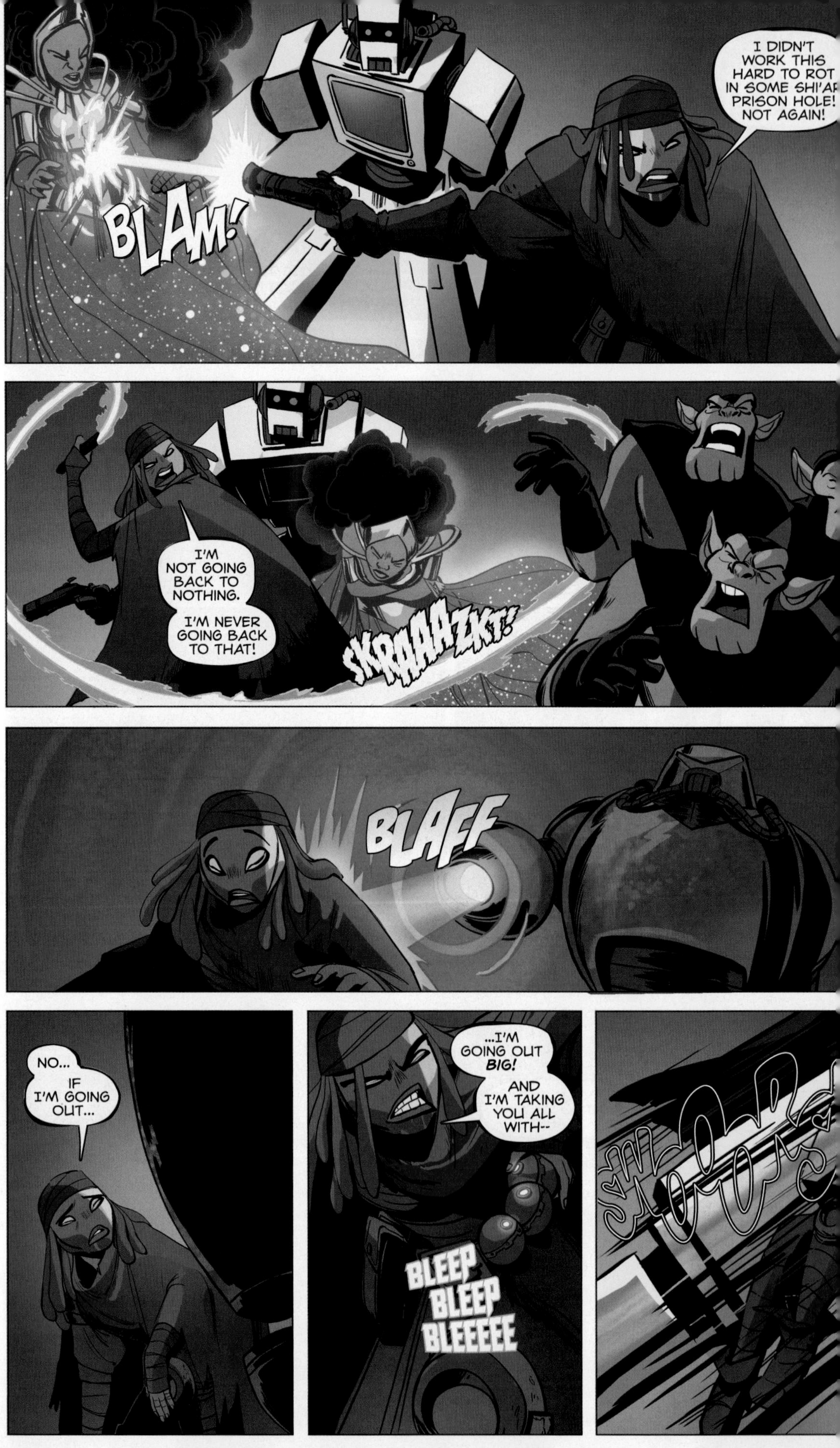
I DIDN'T WORK THIS HARD TO ROT IN SOME SHI'AR PRISON HOLE! NOT AGAIN!
BLAM!
I'M NOT GOING BACK TO NOTHING.
I'M NEVER GOING BACK TO THAT!
SKRAAAZKT!
BLAFF
NO...
IF I'M GOING OUT...
...I'M GOING OUT *BIG!*
AND I'M TAKING YOU ALL WITH--
BLEEP
BLEEP
BLEEEEE

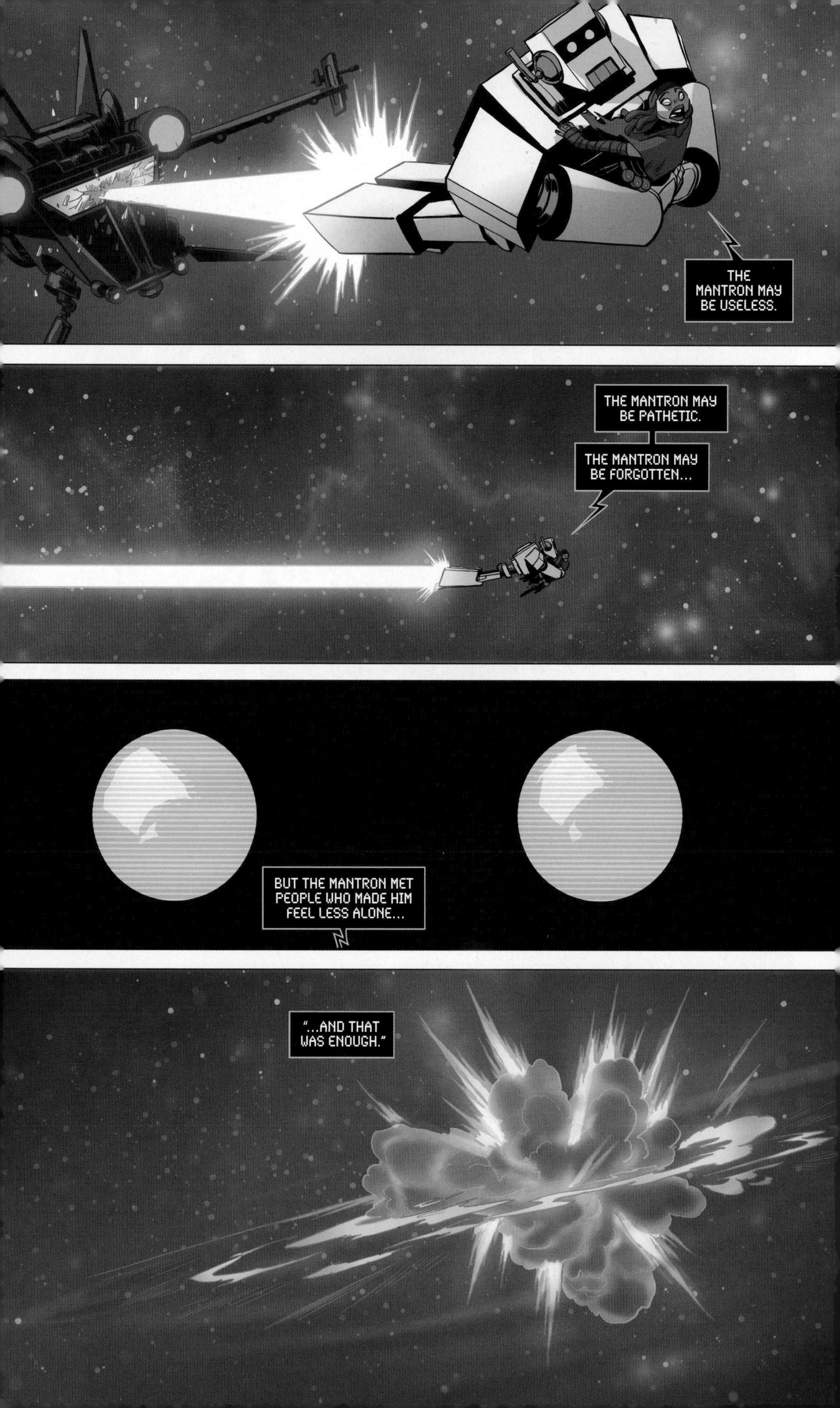
THE MANTRON MAY BE USELESS.
THE MANTRON MAY BE PATHETIC.
THE MANTRON MAY BE FORGOTTEN...
BUT THE MANTRON MET PEOPLE WHO MADE HIM FEEL LESS ALONE...
"...AND THAT WAS ENOUGH."

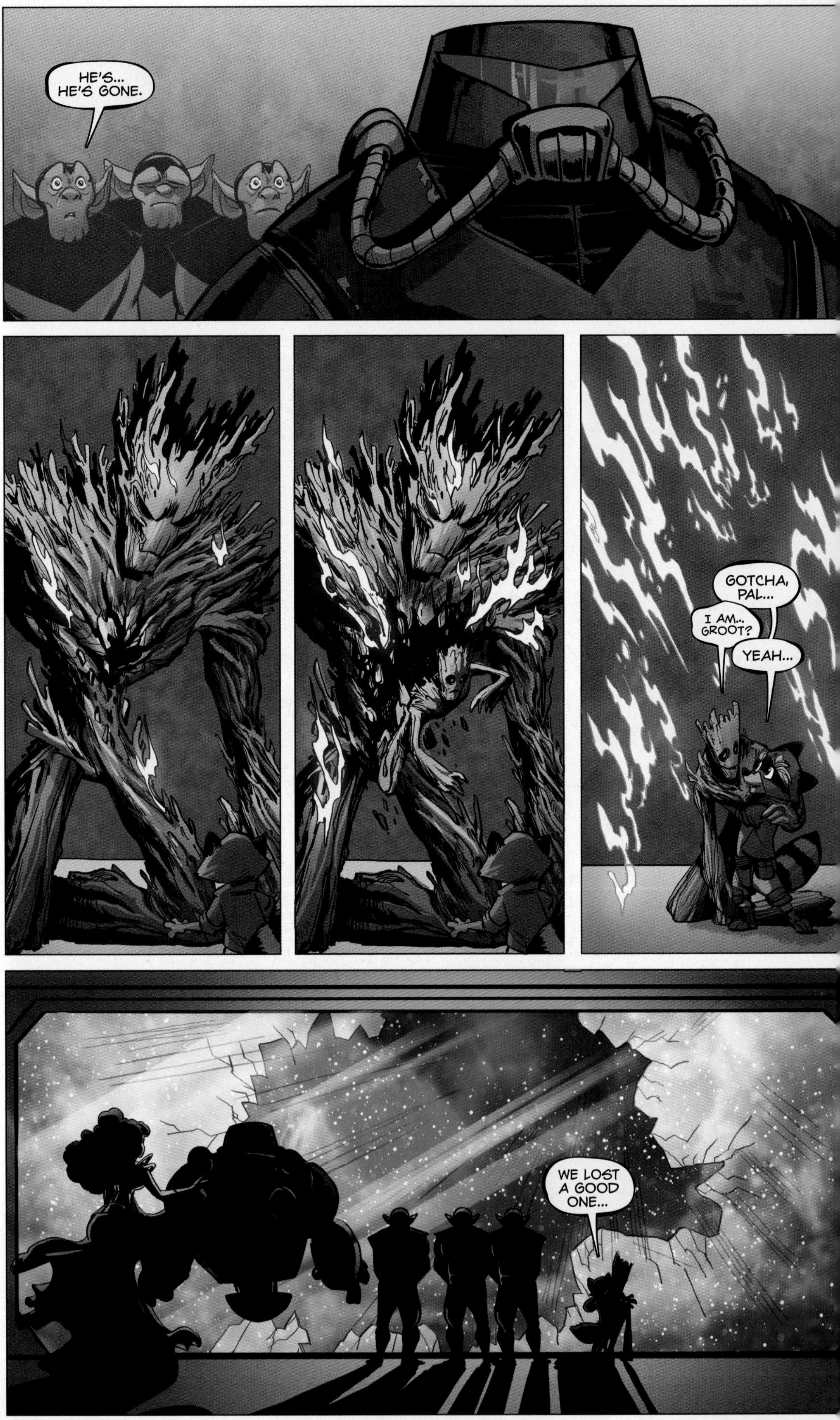
HE'S... HE'S GONE.
GOTCHA, PAL...
I AM... GROOT?
YEAH...
WE LOST A GOOD ONE...

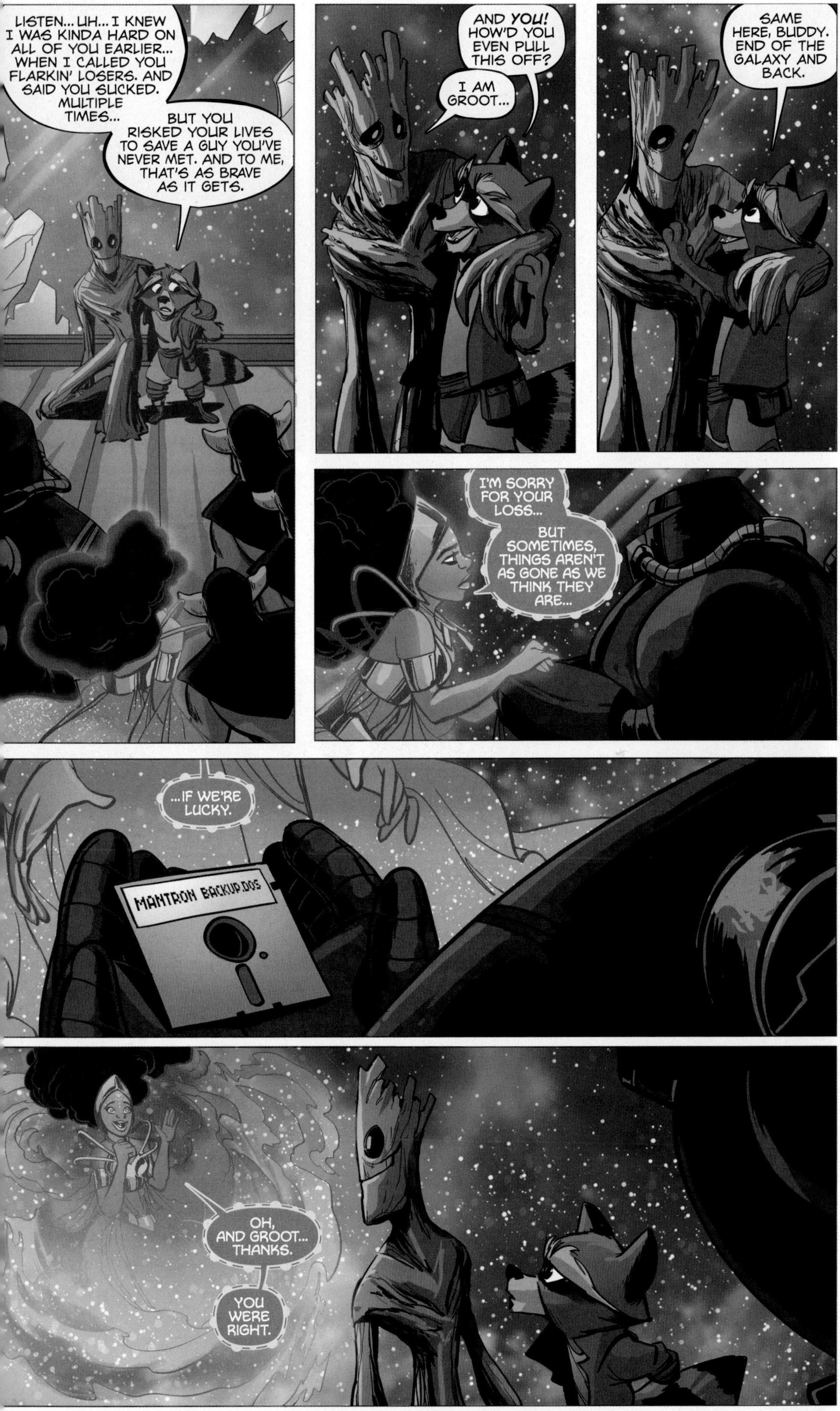
LISTEN... UH... I KNEW I WAS KINDA HARD ON ALL OF YOU EARLIER... WHEN I CALLED YOU FLARKIN' LOSERS. AND SAID YOU SUCKED. MULTIPLE TIMES...
BUT YOU RISKED YOUR LIVES TO SAVE A GUY YOU'VE NEVER MET. AND TO ME, THAT'S AS BRAVE AS IT GETS.
AND YOU! HOW'D YOU EVEN PULL THIS OFF?
I AM GROOT...
SAME HERE, BUDDY. END OF THE GALAXY AND BACK.
I'M SORRY FOR YOUR LOSS...
BUT SOMETIMES, THINGS AREN'T AS GONE AS WE THINK THEY ARE...
...IF WE'RE LUCKY.
MANTRON BACKUP.DOS
OH, AND GROOT... THANKS.
YOU WERE RIGHT.

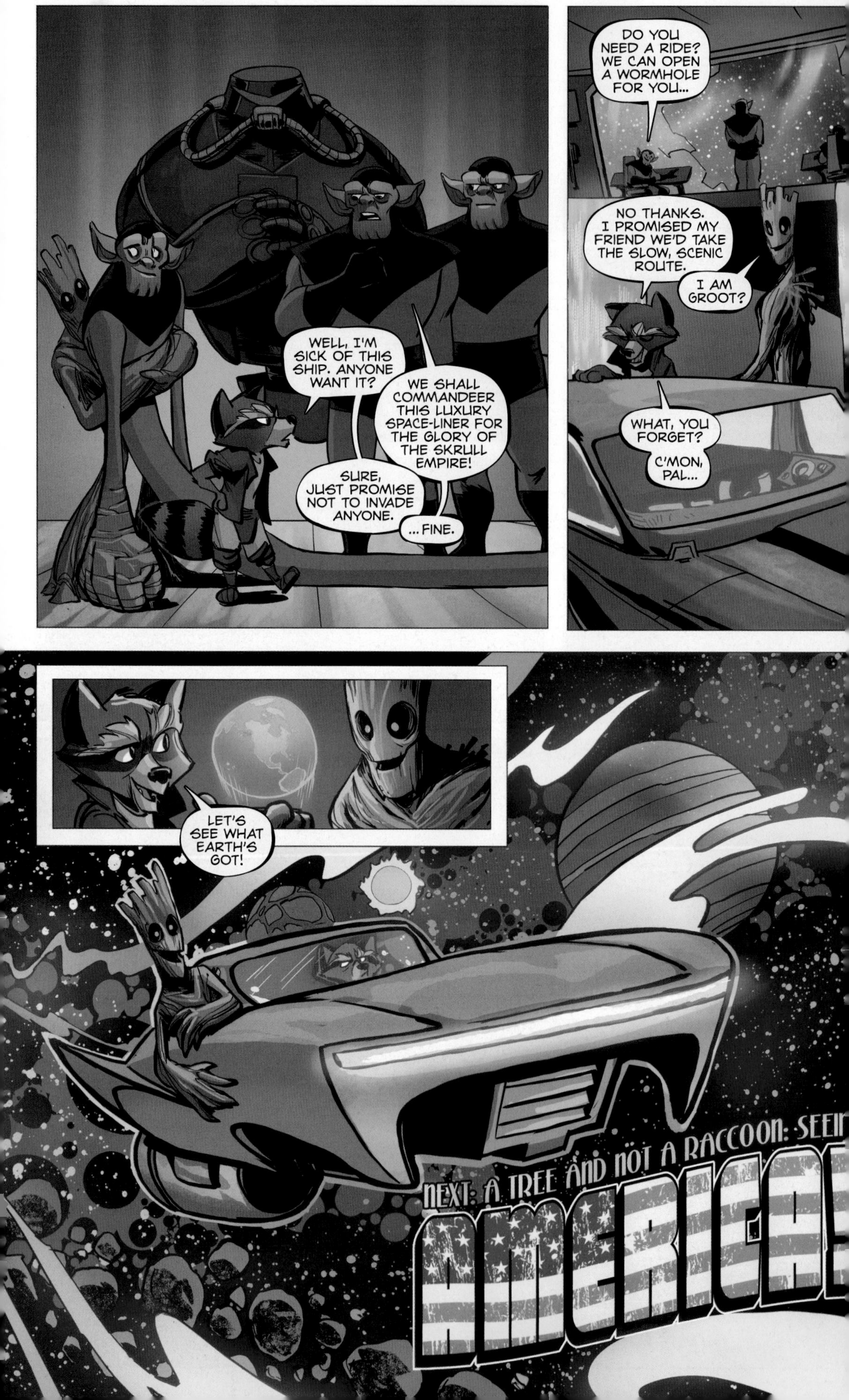

WELL, I'M SICK OF THIS SHIP. ANYONE WANT IT?
WE SHALL COMMANDEER THIS LUXURY SPACE-LINER FOR THE GLORY OF THE SKRULL EMPIRE!
SURE, JUST PROMISE NOT TO INVADE ANYONE.
...FINE.
DO YOU NEED A RIDE? WE CAN OPEN A WORMHOLE FOR YOU...
NO THANKS. I PROMISED MY FRIEND WE'D TAKE THE SLOW, SCENIC ROUTE.
I AM GROOT?
WHAT, YOU FORGET?
C'MON, PAL...
LET'S SEE WHAT EARTH'S GOT!
NEXT: A TREE AND NOT A RACCOON: SEEIN

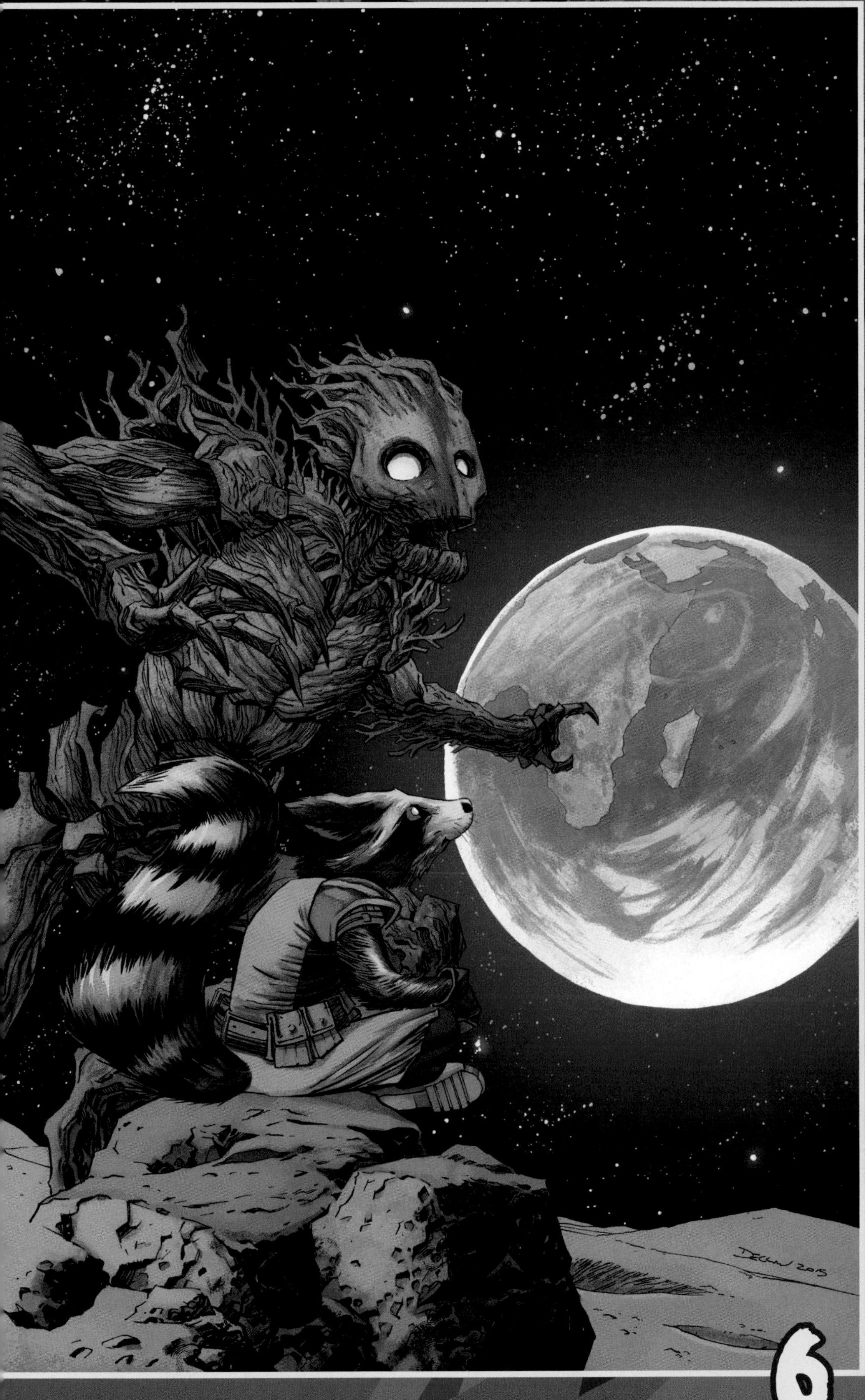
DECLAN 2015

6

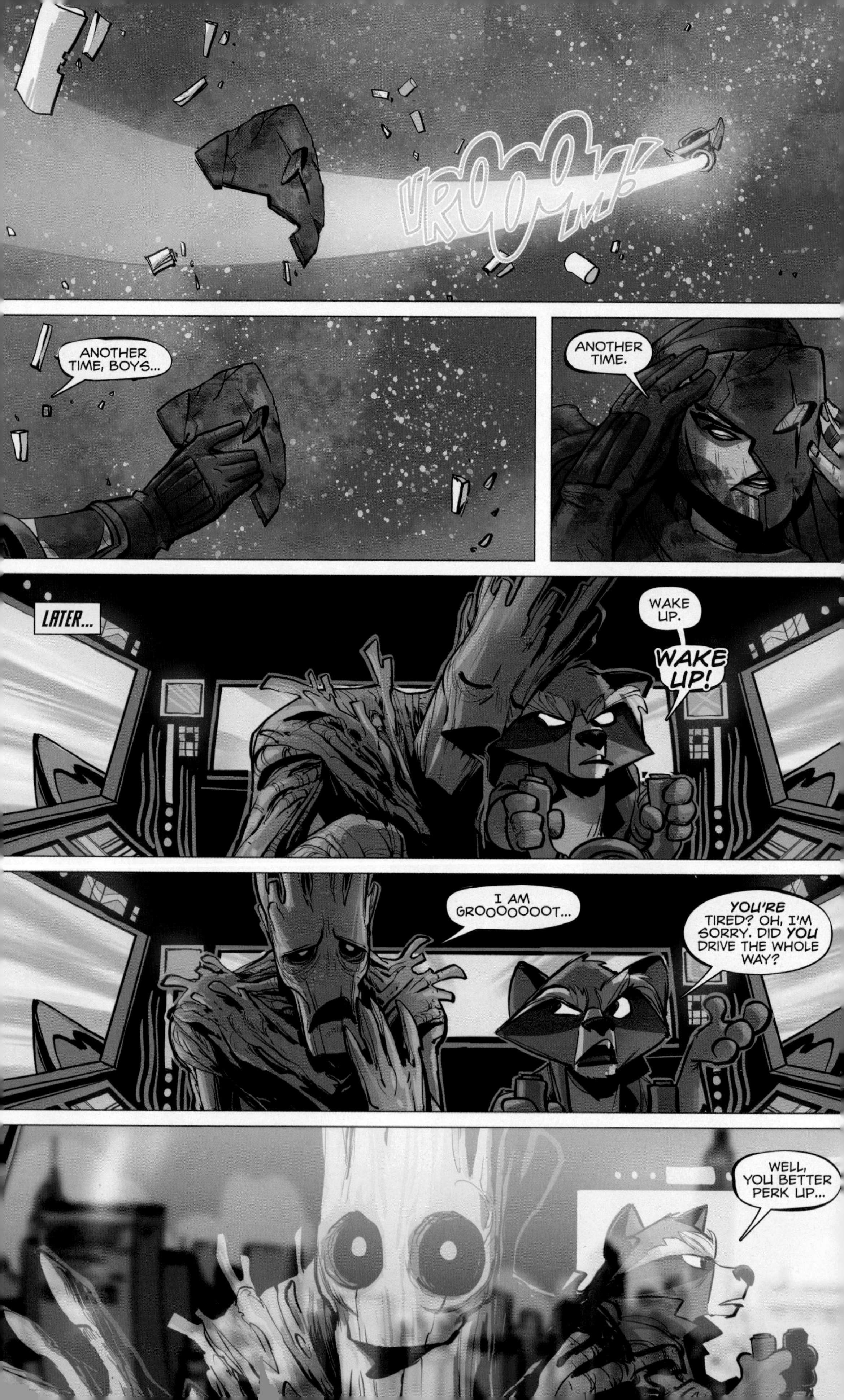
VROOOOM!
ANOTHER TIME, BOYS...
ANOTHER TIME.
LATER...
WAKE UP.
WAKE UP!
I AM GROOOOOOOT...
YOU'RE TIRED? OH, I'M SORRY. DID YOU DRIVE THE WHOLE WAY?
WELL, YOU BETTER PERK UP...

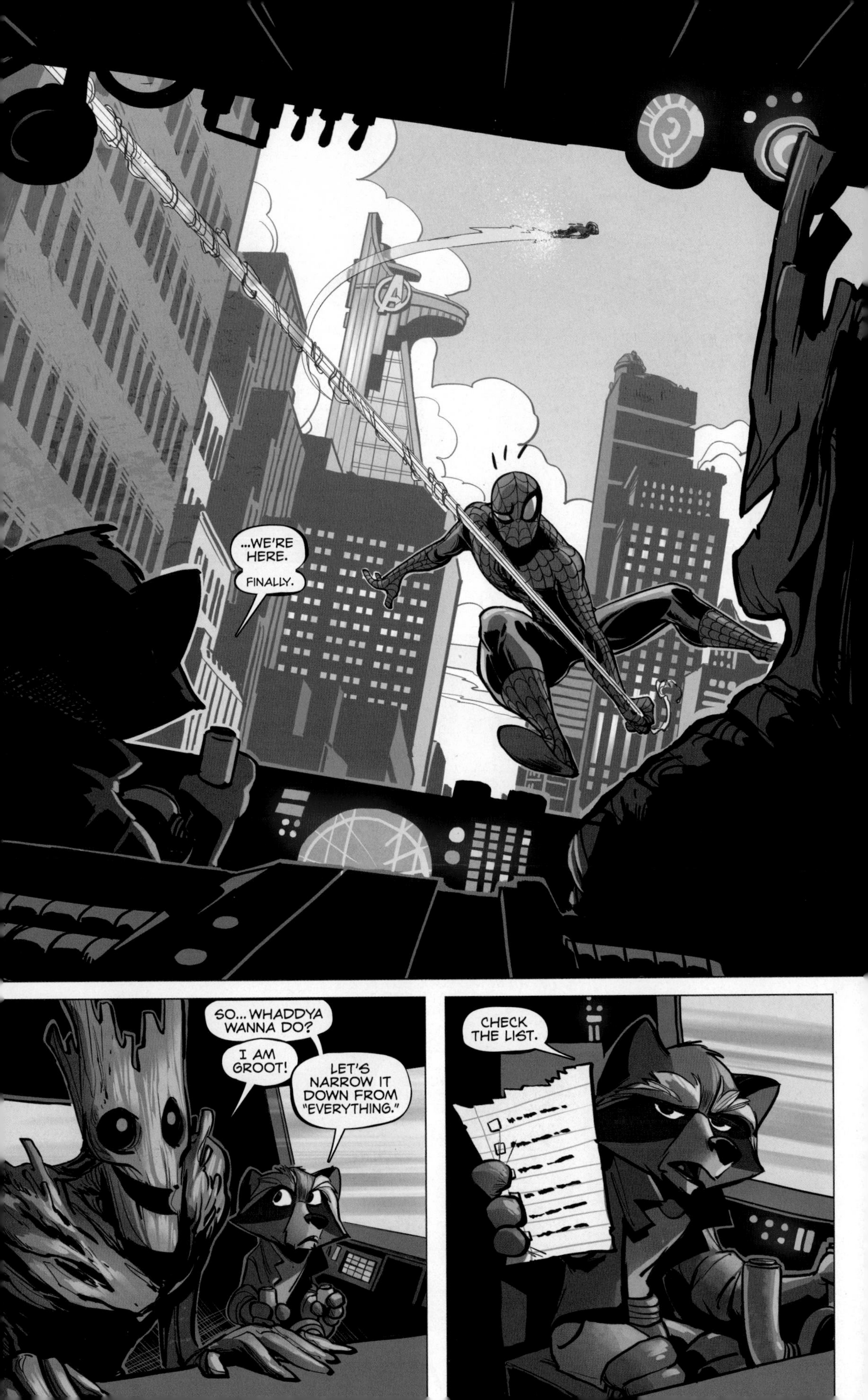
...WE'RE HERE.
FINALLY.
SO... WHADDYA WANNA DO?
I AM GROOT!
LET'S NARROW IT DOWN FROM "EVERYTHING."
CHECK THE LIST.

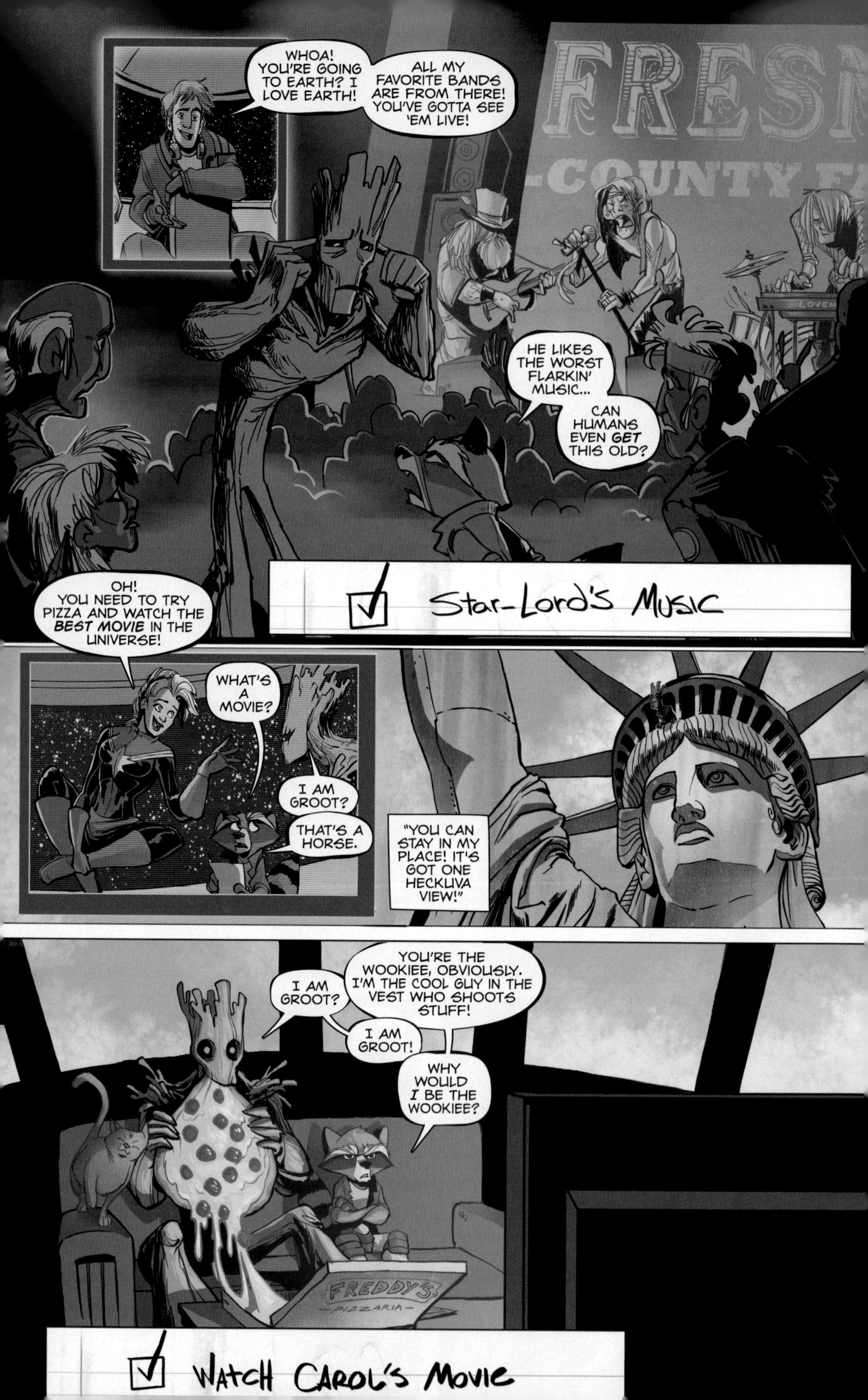
WHOA! YOU'RE GOING TO EARTH? I LOVE EARTH!
ALL MY FAVORITE BANDS ARE FROM THERE! YOU'VE GOTTA SEE 'EM LIVE!
FRESN
-COUNTY FA
HE LIKES THE WORST FLARKIN' MUSIC...
CAN HUMANS EVEN *GET* THIS OLD?
☑ Star-Lord's Music
OH! YOU NEED TO TRY PIZZA AND WATCH THE *BEST MOVIE* IN THE UNIVERSE!
WHAT'S A MOVIE?
I AM GROOT?
THAT'S A HORSE.
"YOU CAN STAY IN MY PLACE! IT'S GOT ONE HECKUVA VIEW!"
I AM GROOT?
YOU'RE THE WOOKIEE, OBVIOUSLY. I'M THE COOL GUY IN THE VEST WHO SHOOTS STUFF!
I AM GROOT!
WHY WOULD *I* BE THE WOOKIEE?
FREDDY'S PIZZARIA
☑ Watch Carol's Movie

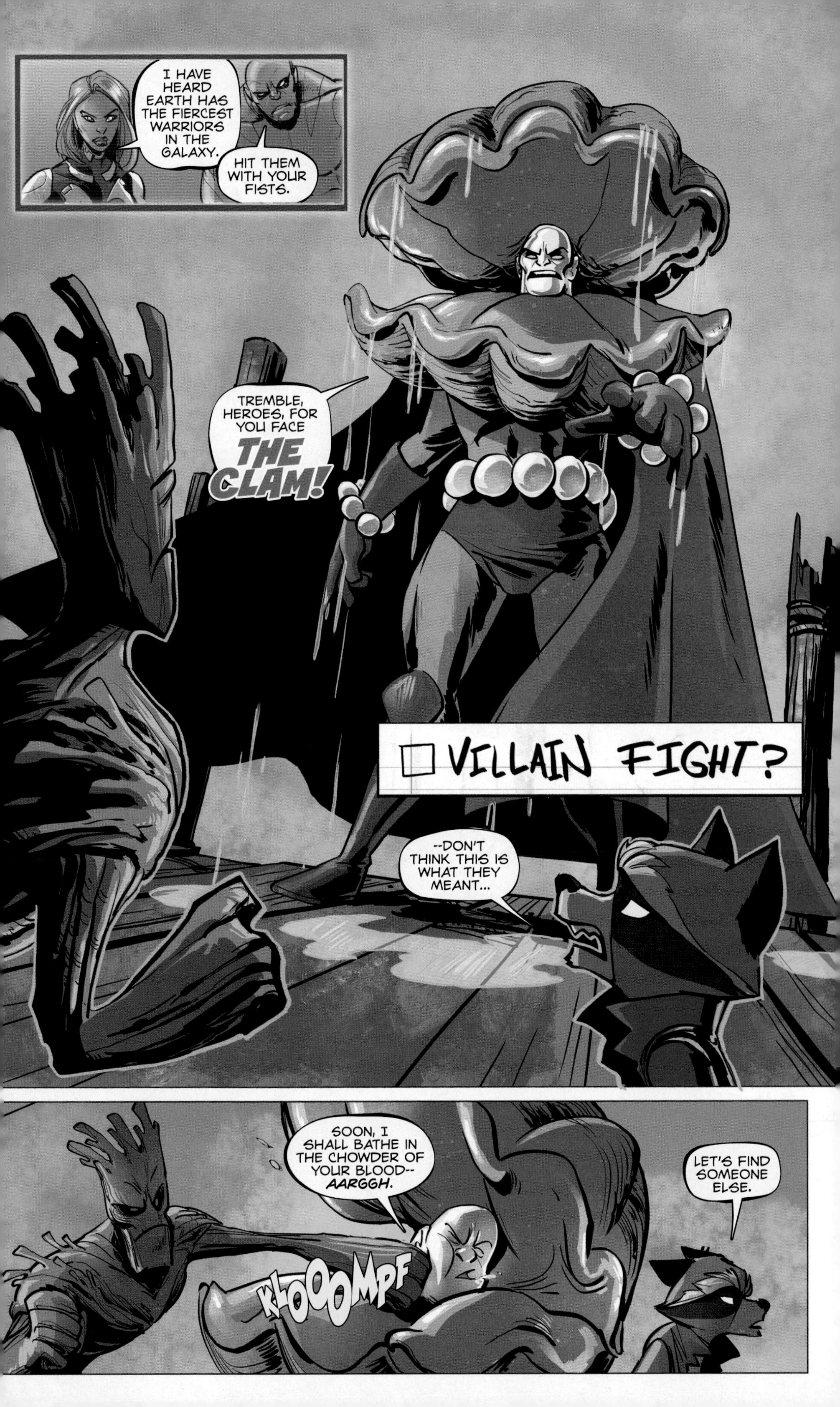
I HAVE HEARD EARTH HAS THE FIERCEST WARRIORS IN THE GALAXY.
HIT THEM WITH YOUR FISTS.
TREMBLE, HEROES, FOR YOU FACE THE CLAM!
☐ VILLAIN FIGHT?
--DON'T THINK THIS IS WHAT THEY MEANT...
SOON, I SHALL BATHE IN THE CHOWDER OF YOUR BLOOD-- AARGGH.
KLOOOOMPF
LET'S FIND SOMEONE ELSE.

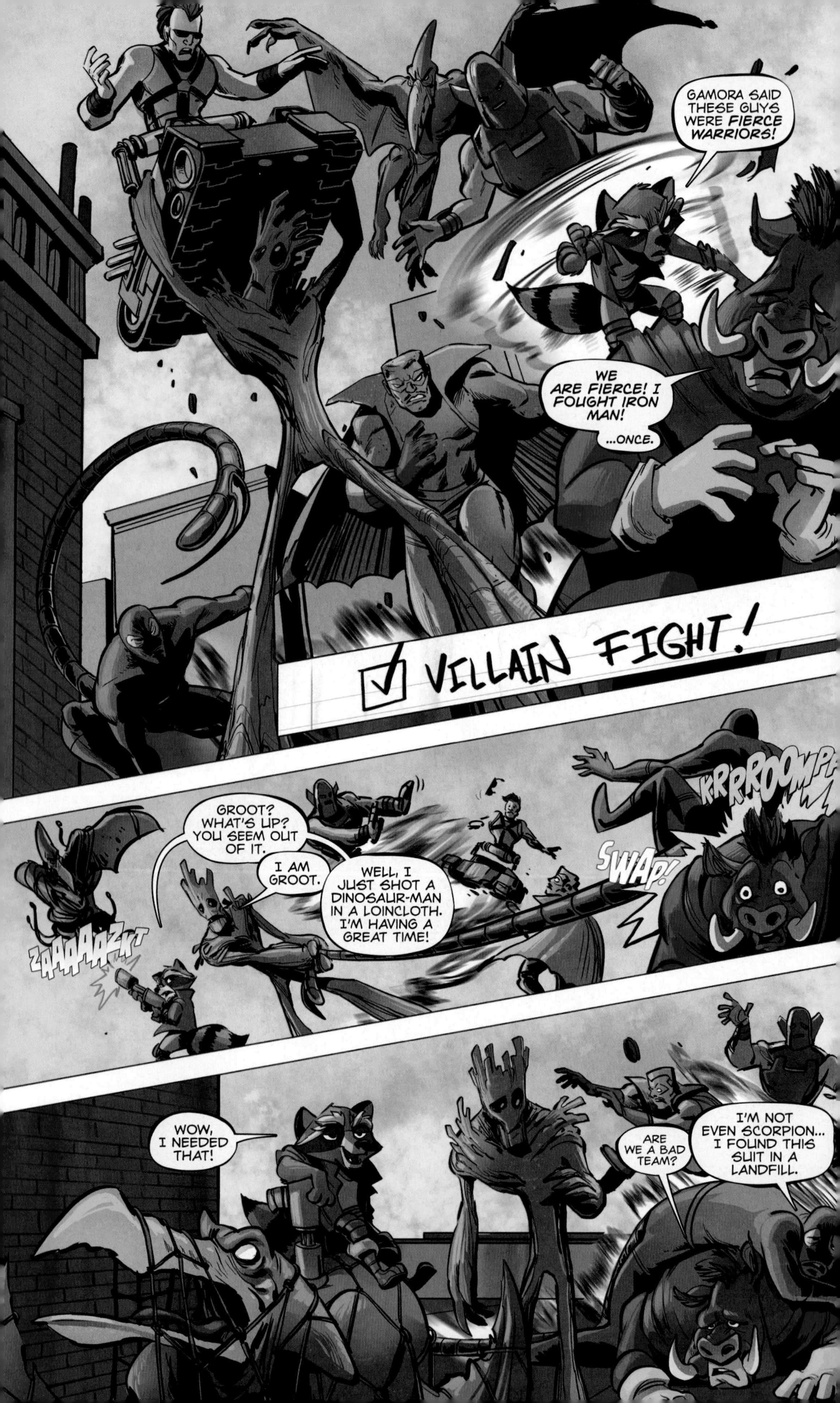
GAMORA SAID THESE GUYS WERE FIERCE WARRIORS!
WE ARE FIERCE! I FOUGHT IRON MAN!
...ONCE.
☑ VILLAIN FIGHT!
KRRROOMP!
GROOT? WHAT'S UP? YOU SEEM OUT OF IT.
I AM GROOT.
WELL, I JUST SHOT A DINOSAUR-MAN IN A LOINCLOTH. I'M HAVING A GREAT TIME!
SWAP!
ZAAAAAAZKT
WOW, I NEEDED THAT!
ARE WE A BAD TEAM?
I'M NOT EVEN SCORPION... I FOUND THIS SUIT IN A LANDFILL.

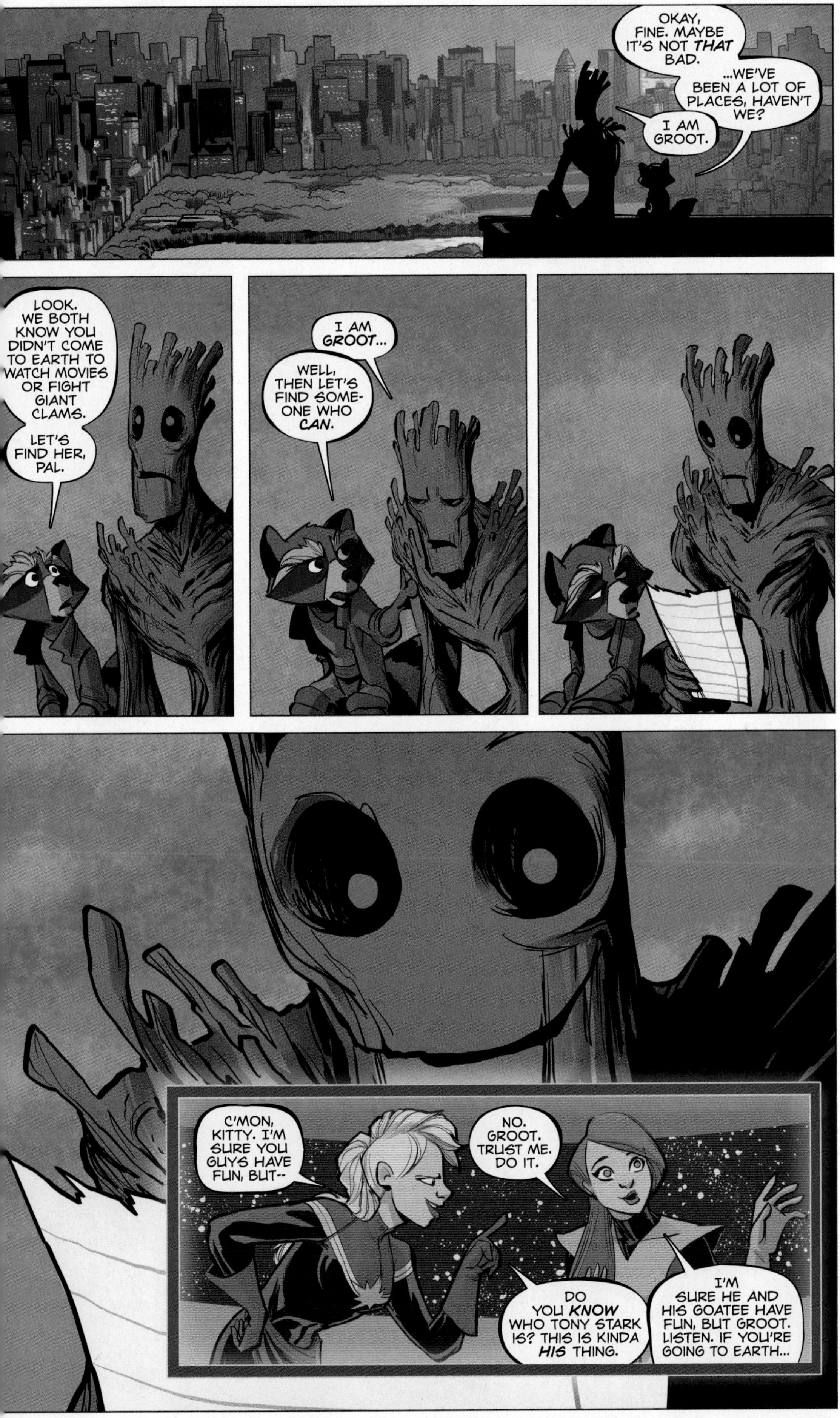
OKAY, FINE. MAYBE IT'S NOT *THAT* BAD.
...WE'VE BEEN A LOT OF PLACES, HAVEN'T WE?
I AM GROOT.
LOOK. WE BOTH KNOW YOU DIDN'T COME TO EARTH TO WATCH MOVIES OR FIGHT GIANT CLAMS.
LET'S FIND HER, PAL.
I AM *GROOT*...
WELL, THEN LET'S FIND SOME-ONE WHO *CAN*.
C'MON, KITTY. I'M SURE YOU GUYS HAVE FUN, BUT--
NO. GROOT. TRUST ME. DO IT.
DO YOU *KNOW* WHO TONY STARK IS? THIS IS KINDA *HIS* THING.
I'M SURE HE AND HIS GOATEE HAVE FUN, BUT GROOT. LISTEN. IF YOU'RE GOING TO EARTH...

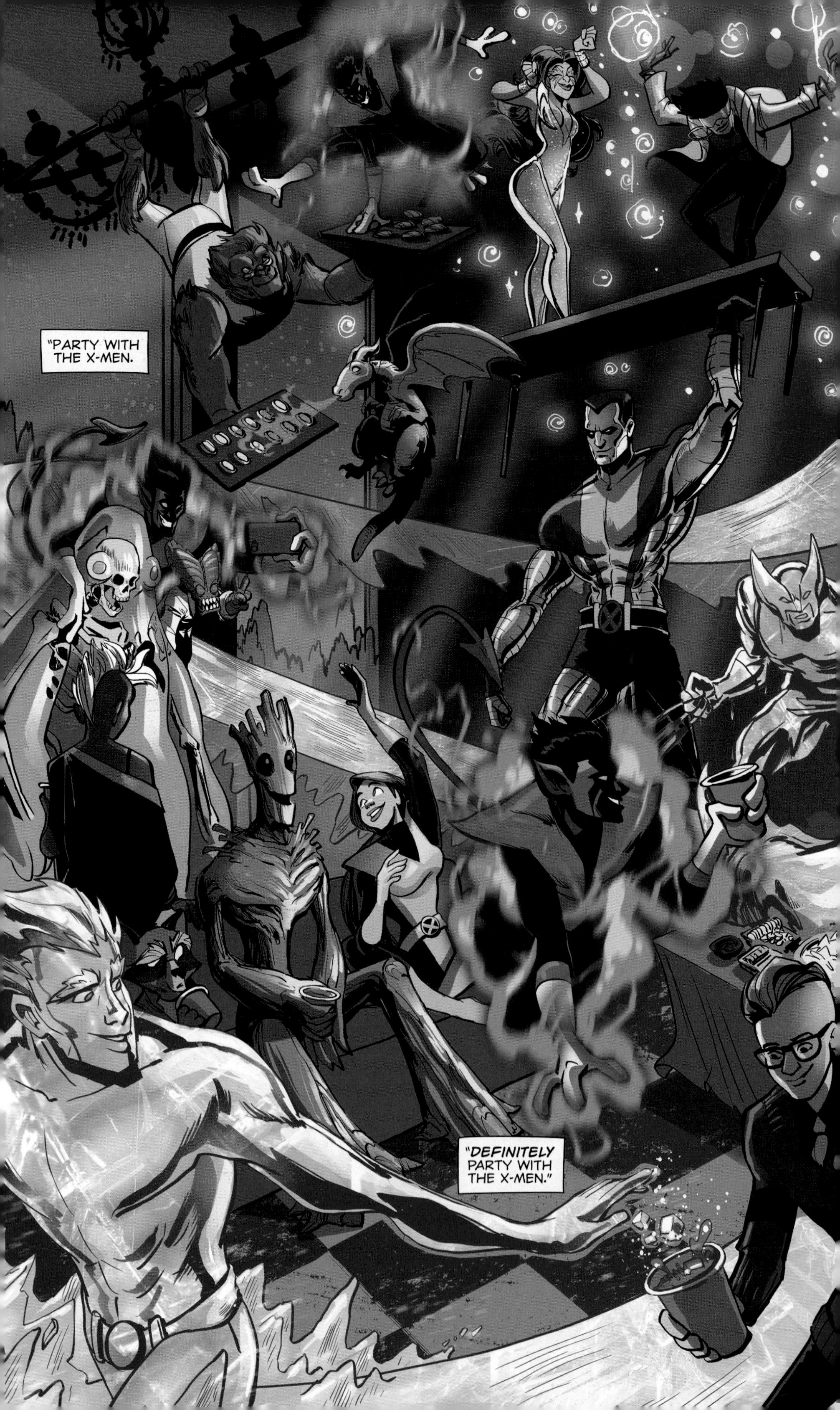
"PARTY WITH THE X-MEN.
"*DEFINITELY* PARTY WITH THE X-MEN."

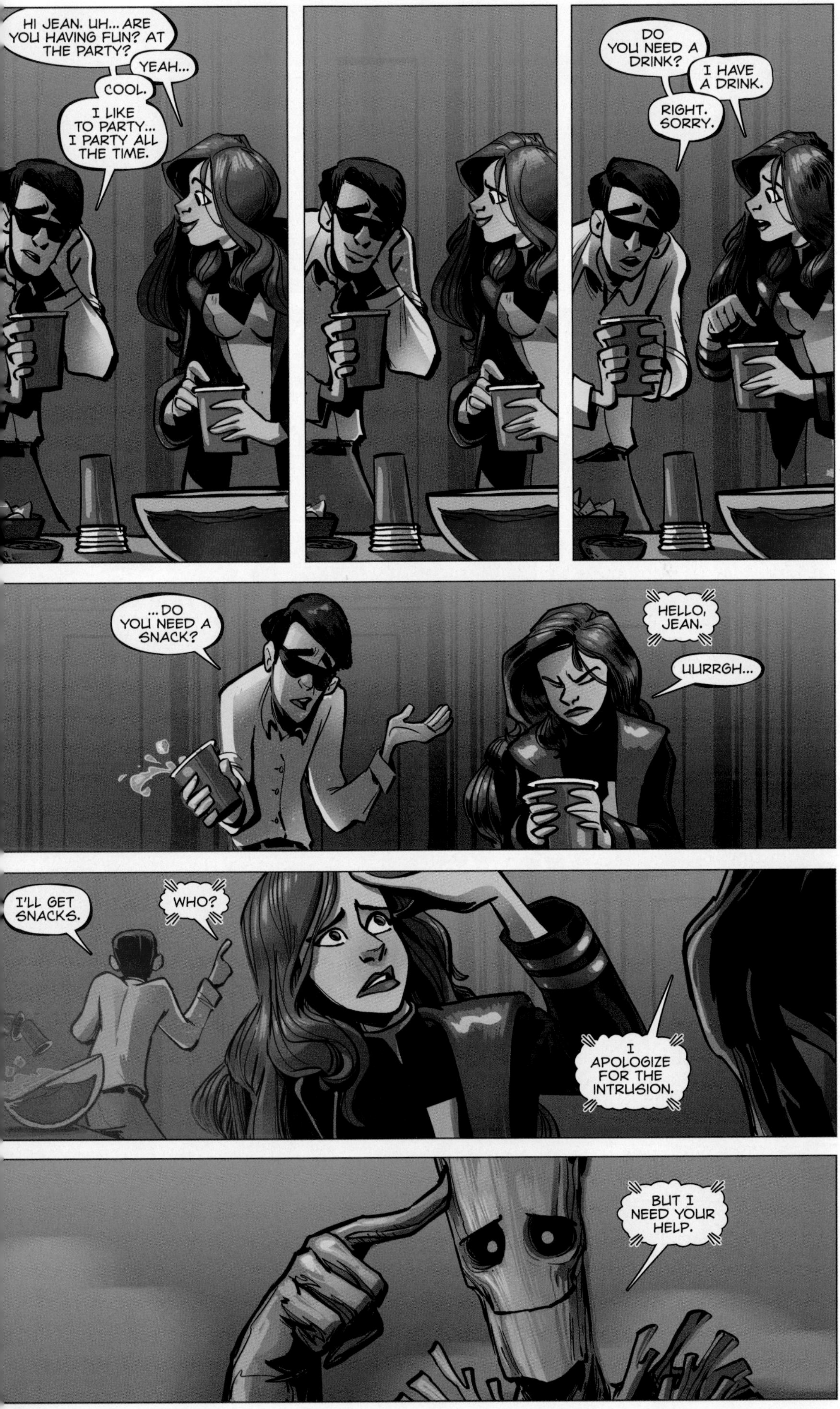
HI JEAN. UH... ARE YOU HAVING FUN? AT THE PARTY?
YEAH...
COOL.
I LIKE TO PARTY... I PARTY ALL THE TIME.
DO YOU NEED A DRINK?
I HAVE A DRINK.
RIGHT. SORRY.
...DO YOU NEED A SNACK?
HELLO, JEAN.
UURRGH...
I'LL GET SNACKS.
WHO?
I APOLOGIZE FOR THE INTRUSION.
BUT I NEED YOUR HELP.

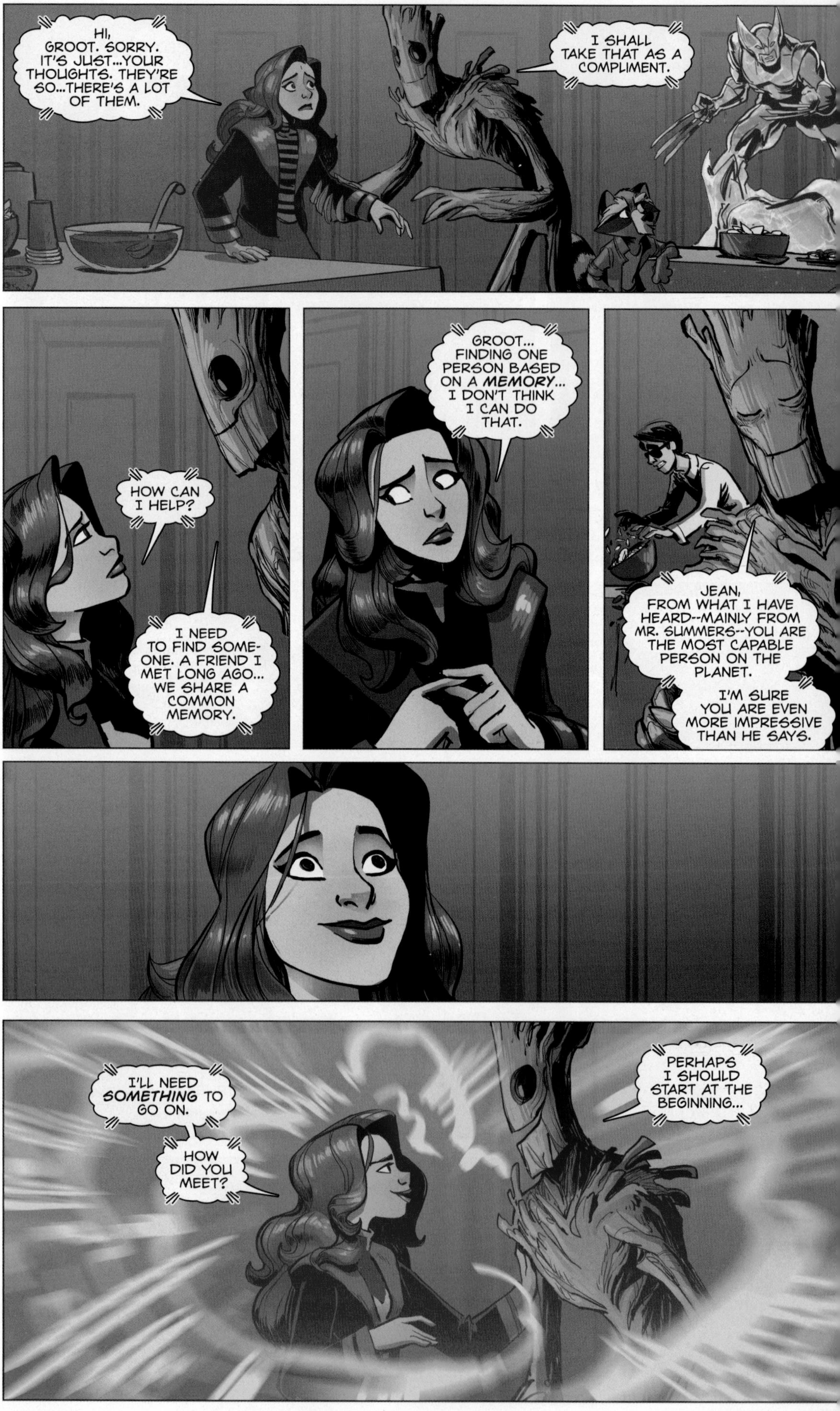
HI, GROOT. SORRY. IT'S JUST...YOUR THOUGHTS. THEY'RE SO...THERE'S A LOT OF THEM.
I SHALL TAKE THAT AS A COMPLIMENT.
HOW CAN I HELP?
I NEED TO FIND SOME-ONE. A FRIEND I MET LONG AGO... WE SHARE A COMMON MEMORY.
GROOT... FINDING ONE PERSON BASED ON A MEMORY... I DON'T THINK I CAN DO THAT.
JEAN, FROM WHAT I HAVE HEARD--MAINLY FROM MR. SUMMERS--YOU ARE THE MOST CAPABLE PERSON ON THE PLANET.
I'M SURE YOU ARE EVEN MORE IMPRESSIVE THAN HE SAYS.
I'LL NEED SOMETHING TO GO ON.
HOW DID YOU MEET?
PERHAPS I SHOULD START AT THE BEGINNING...

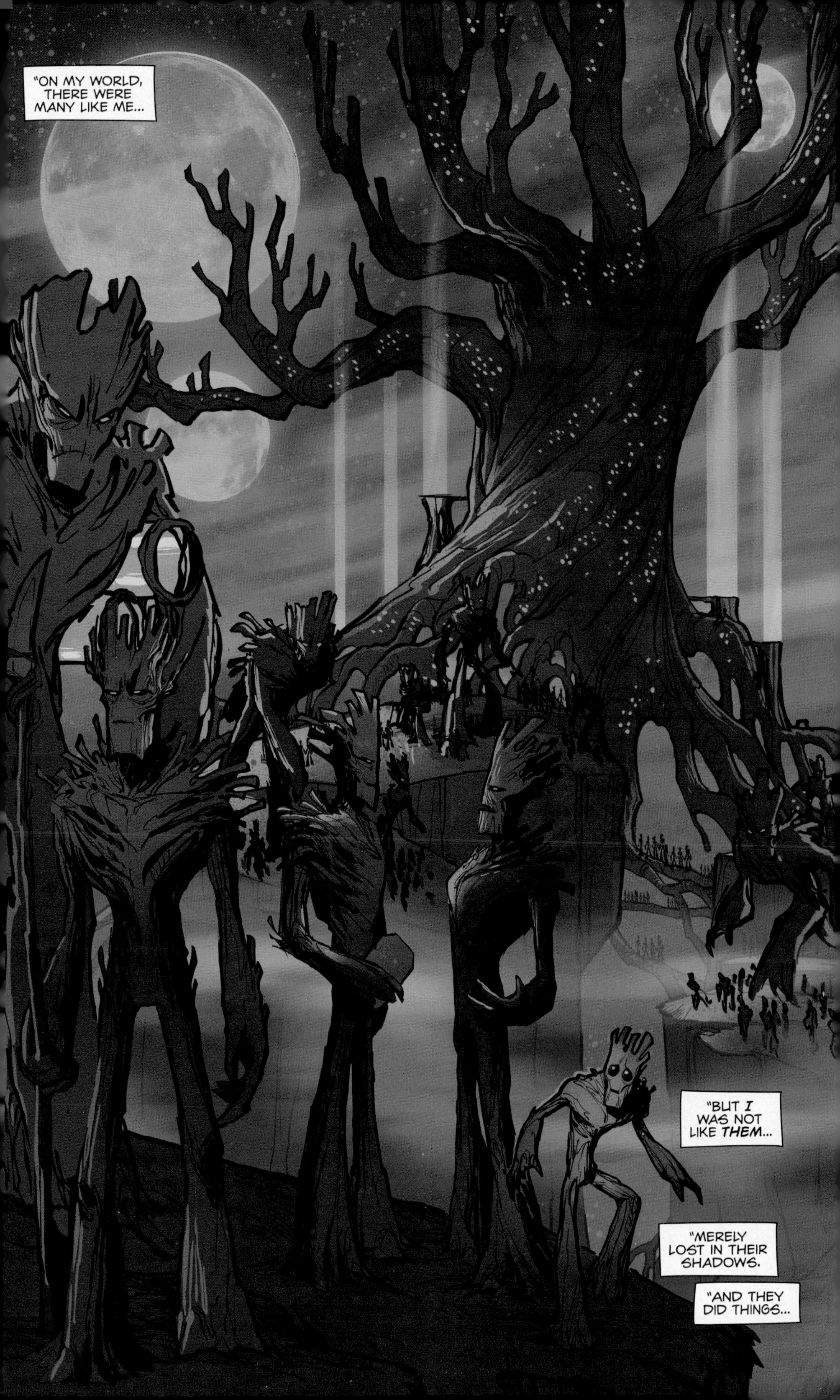
"ON MY WORLD, THERE WERE MANY LIKE ME...
"BUT *I* WAS NOT LIKE *THEM*...
"MERELY LOST IN THEIR SHADOWS.
"AND THEY DID THINGS...

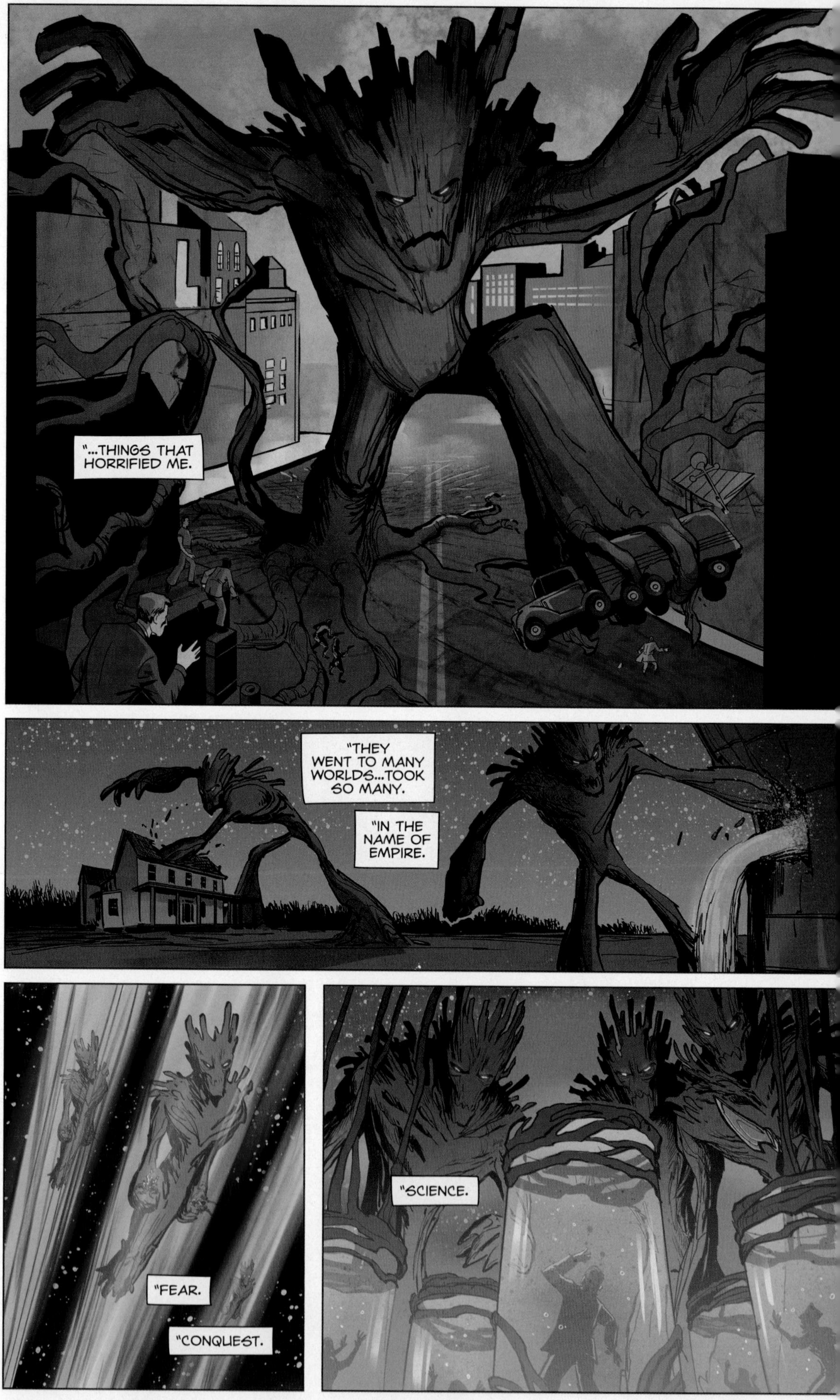
"...THINGS THAT HORRIFIED ME.
"THEY WENT TO MANY WORLDS...TOOK SO MANY.
"IN THE NAME OF EMPIRE.
"FEAR.
"CONQUEST.
"SCIENCE.

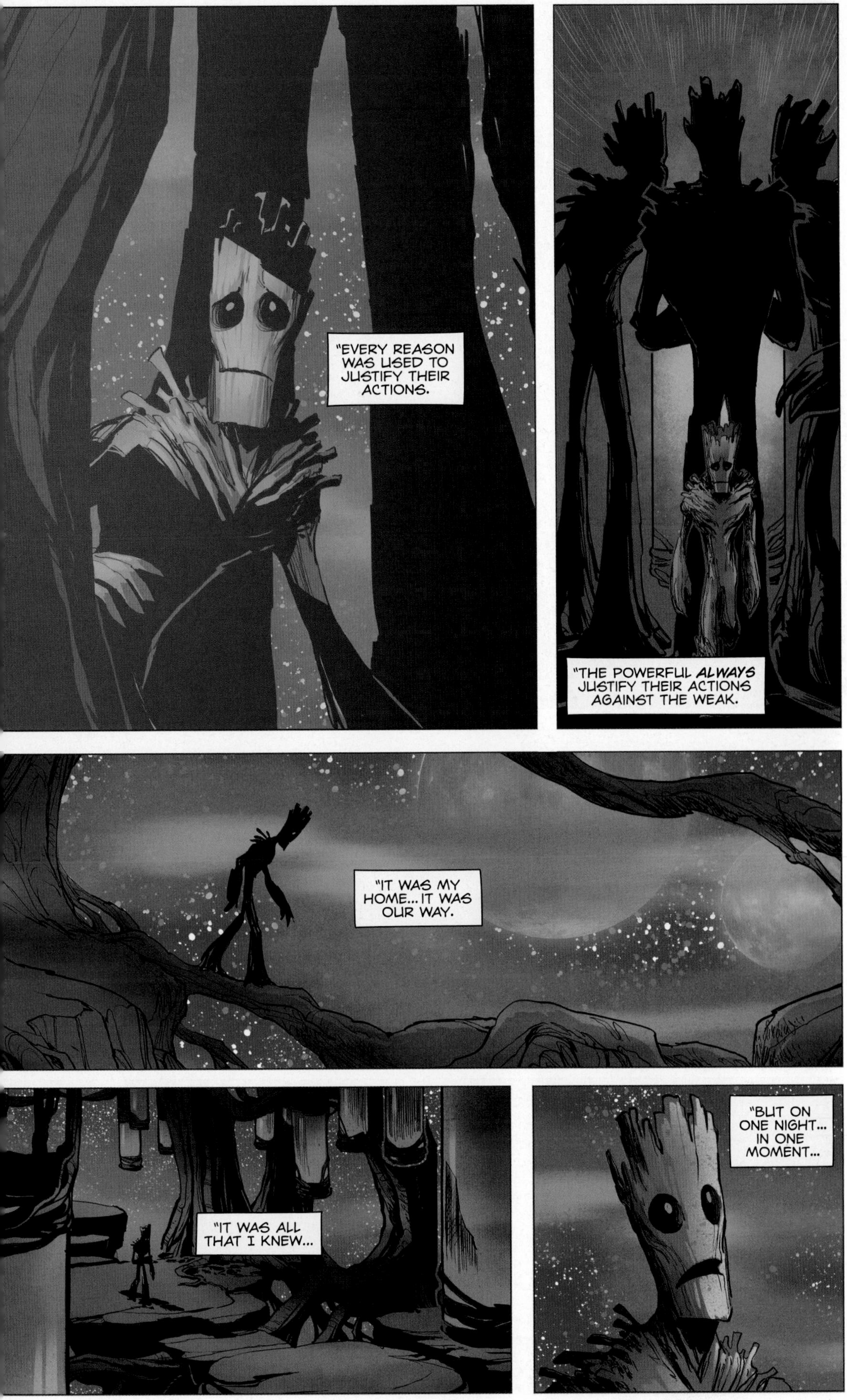
"EVERY REASON WAS USED TO JUSTIFY THEIR ACTIONS.
"THE POWERFUL ALWAYS JUSTIFY THEIR ACTIONS AGAINST THE WEAK.
"IT WAS MY HOME... IT WAS OUR WAY.
"IT WAS ALL THAT I KNEW...
"BUT ON ONE NIGHT... IN ONE MOMENT...

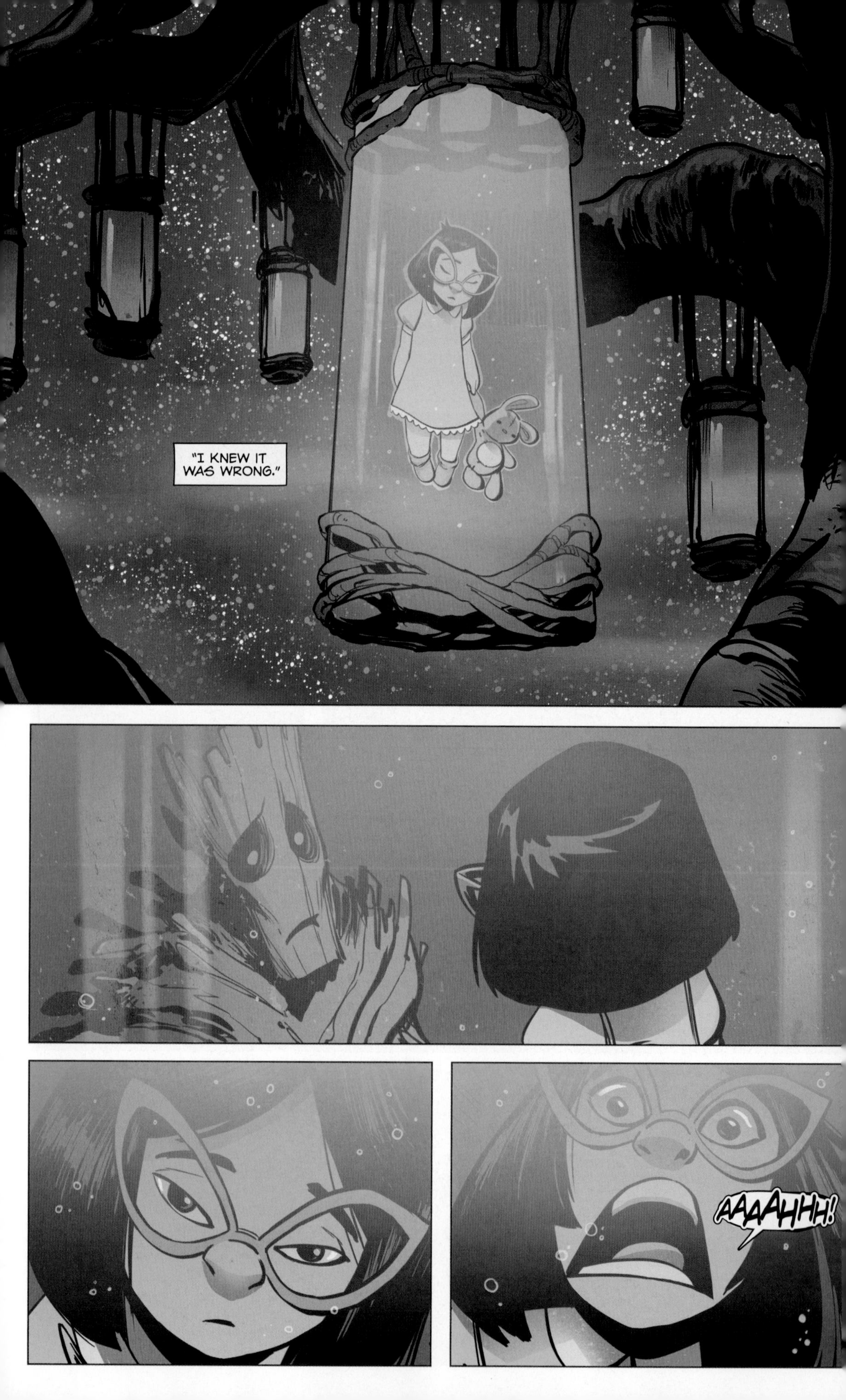
"I KNEW IT WAS WRONG."
AAAAHHH!

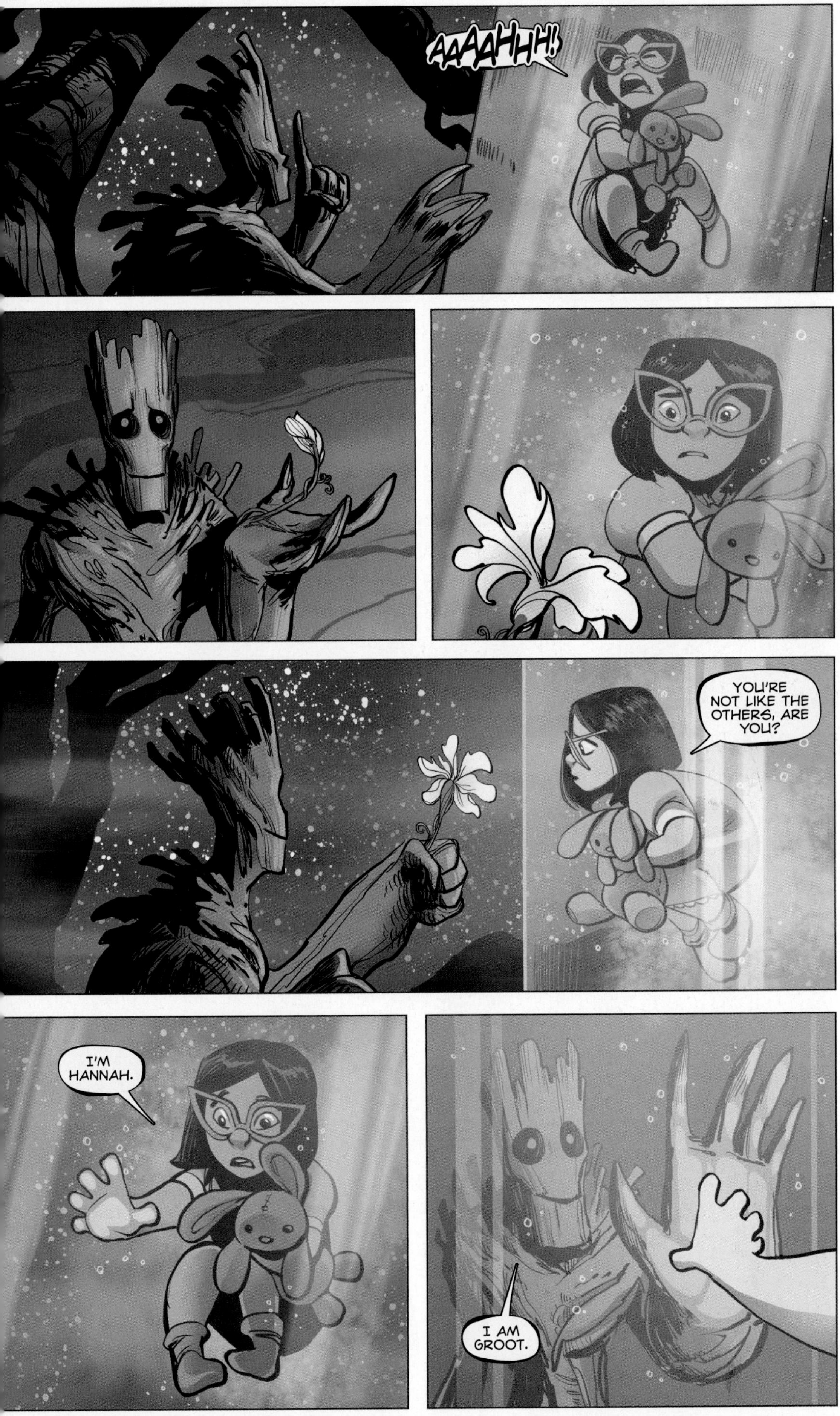
AAAAHHH!
YOU'RE NOT LIKE THE OTHERS, ARE YOU?
I'M HANNAH.
I AM GROOT.

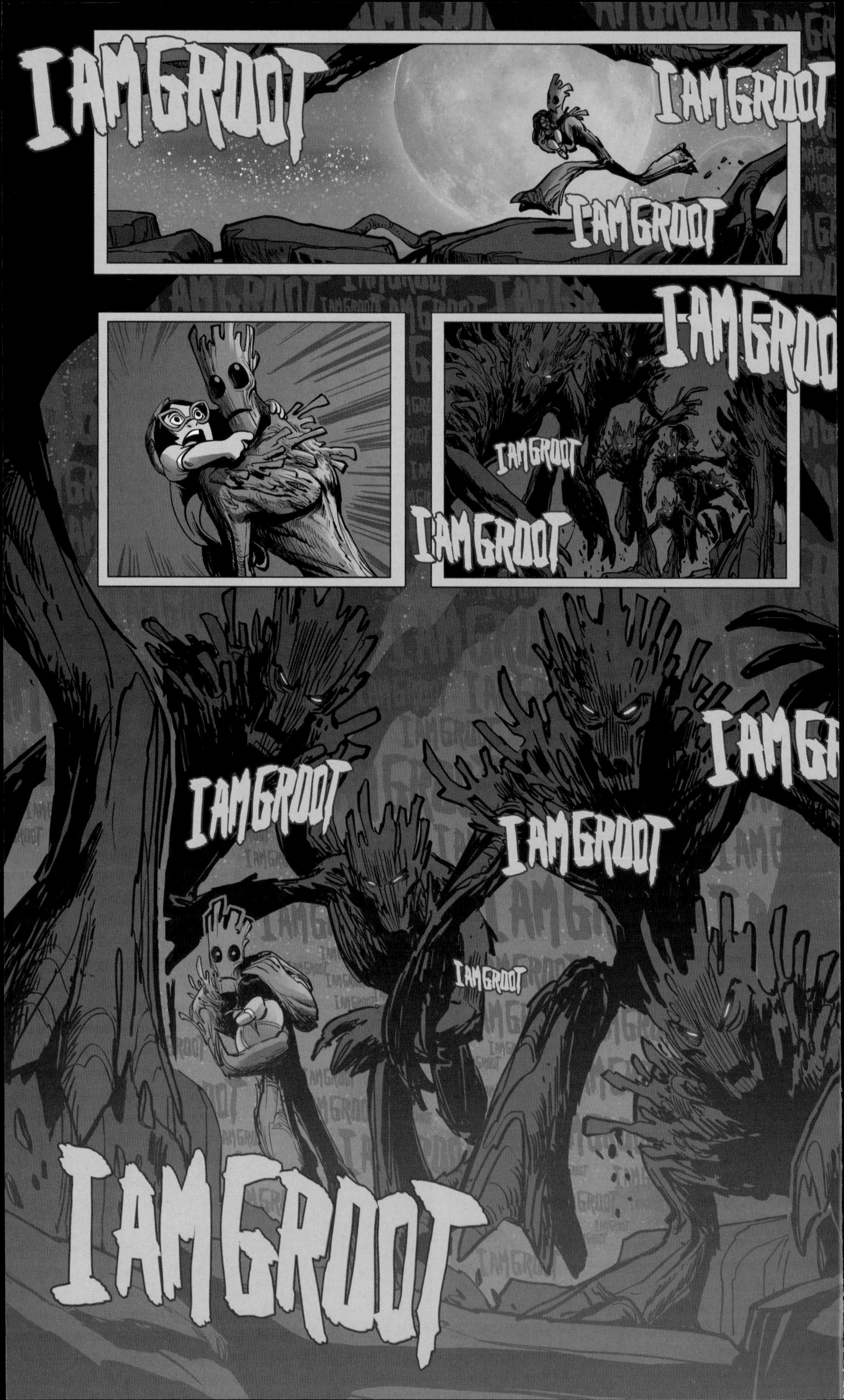
I AM GROOT
I AM GROOT
I AM GROOT
I AM GROO
I AM GROOT
I AM GROOT
I AM G
I AM GROOT
I AM GROOT
I AM GROOT
I AM GROOT

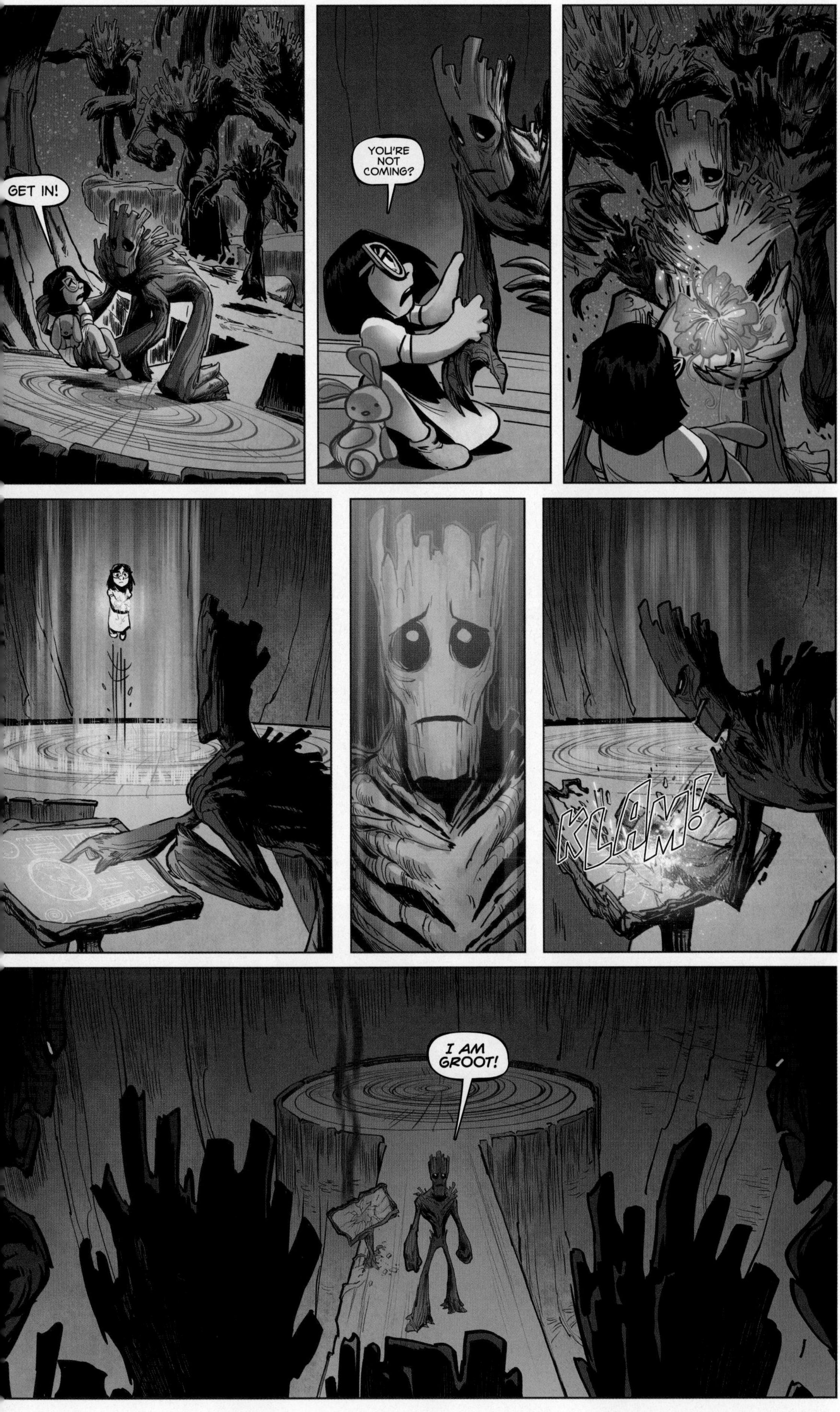
GET IN!
YOU'RE NOT COMING?
KLAM!
I AM GROOT!

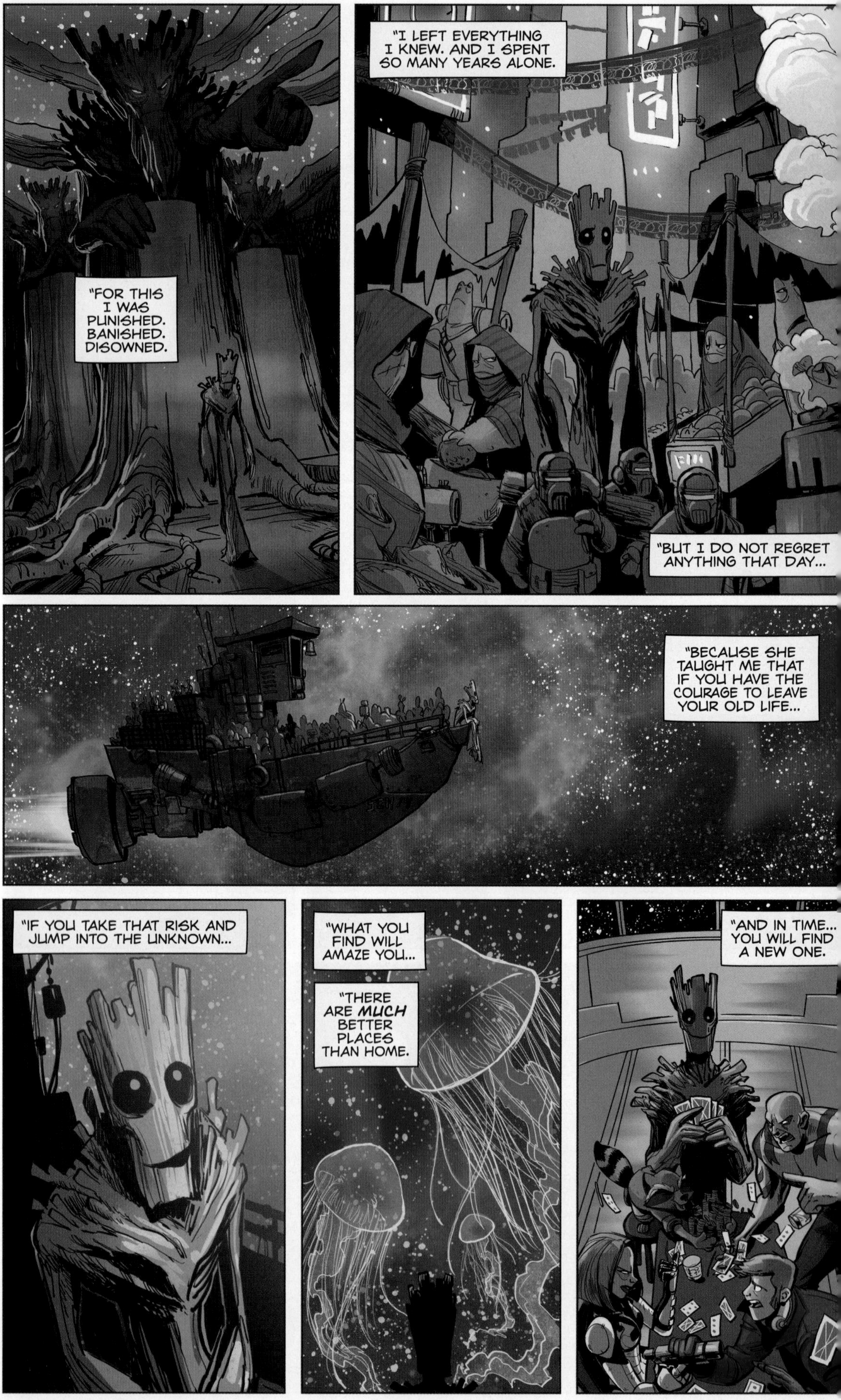
"FOR THIS I WAS PUNISHED. BANISHED. DISOWNED.
"I LEFT EVERYTHING I KNEW. AND I SPENT SO MANY YEARS ALONE.
"BUT I DO NOT REGRET ANYTHING THAT DAY...
"BECAUSE SHE TAUGHT ME THAT IF YOU HAVE THE COURAGE TO LEAVE YOUR OLD LIFE...
"IF YOU TAKE THAT RISK AND JUMP INTO THE UNKNOWN...
"WHAT YOU FIND WILL AMAZE YOU...
"THERE ARE *MUCH* BETTER PLACES THAN HOME.
"AND IN TIME... YOU WILL FIND A NEW ONE.

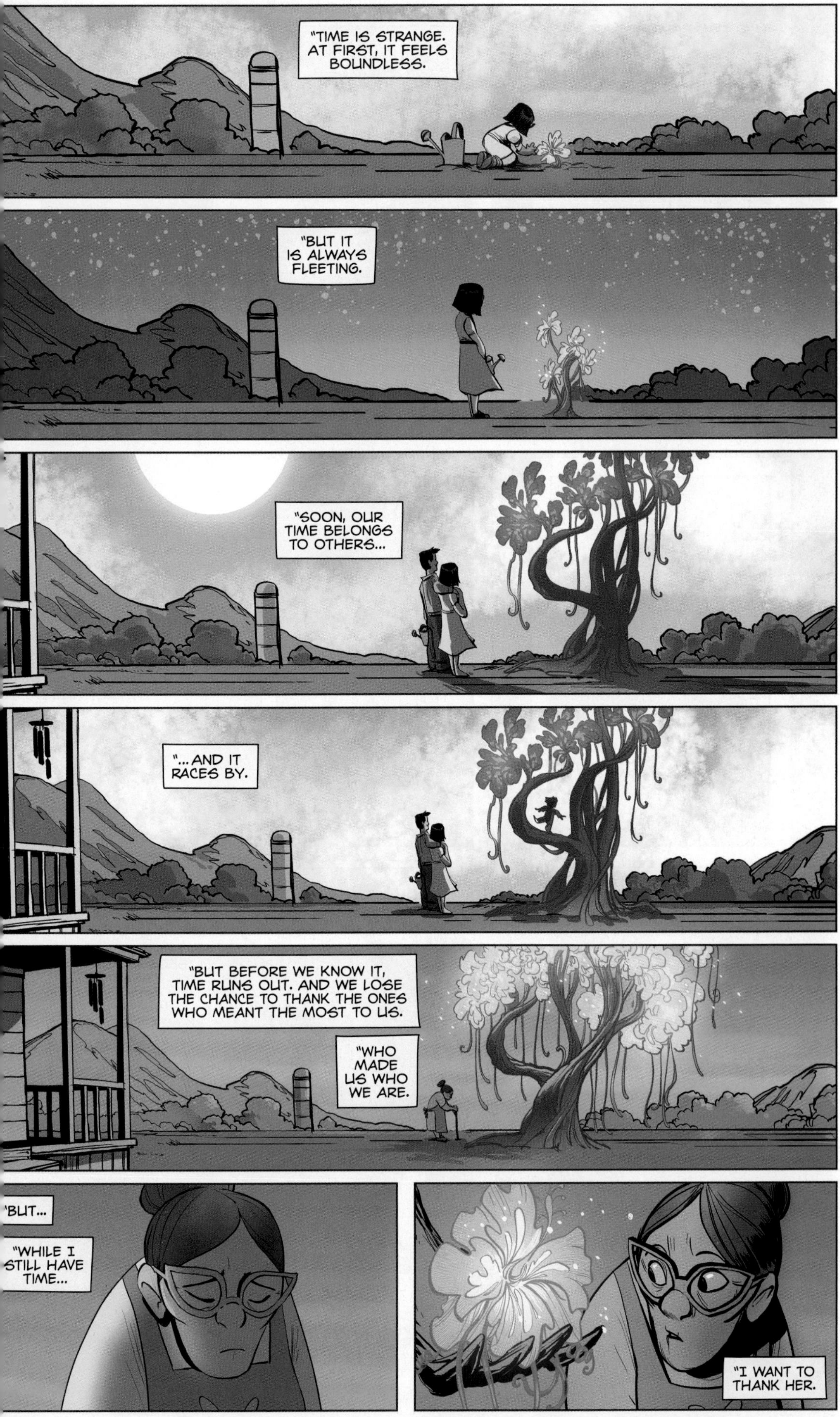
"TIME IS STRANGE. AT FIRST, IT FEELS BOUNDLESS.
"BUT IT IS ALWAYS FLEETING.
"SOON, OUR TIME BELONGS TO OTHERS...
"...AND IT RACES BY.
"BUT BEFORE WE KNOW IT, TIME RUNS OUT. AND WE LOSE THE CHANCE TO THANK THE ONES WHO MEANT THE MOST TO US.
"WHO MADE US WHO WE ARE.
"BUT...
"WHILE I STILL HAVE TIME...
"I WANT TO THANK HER.

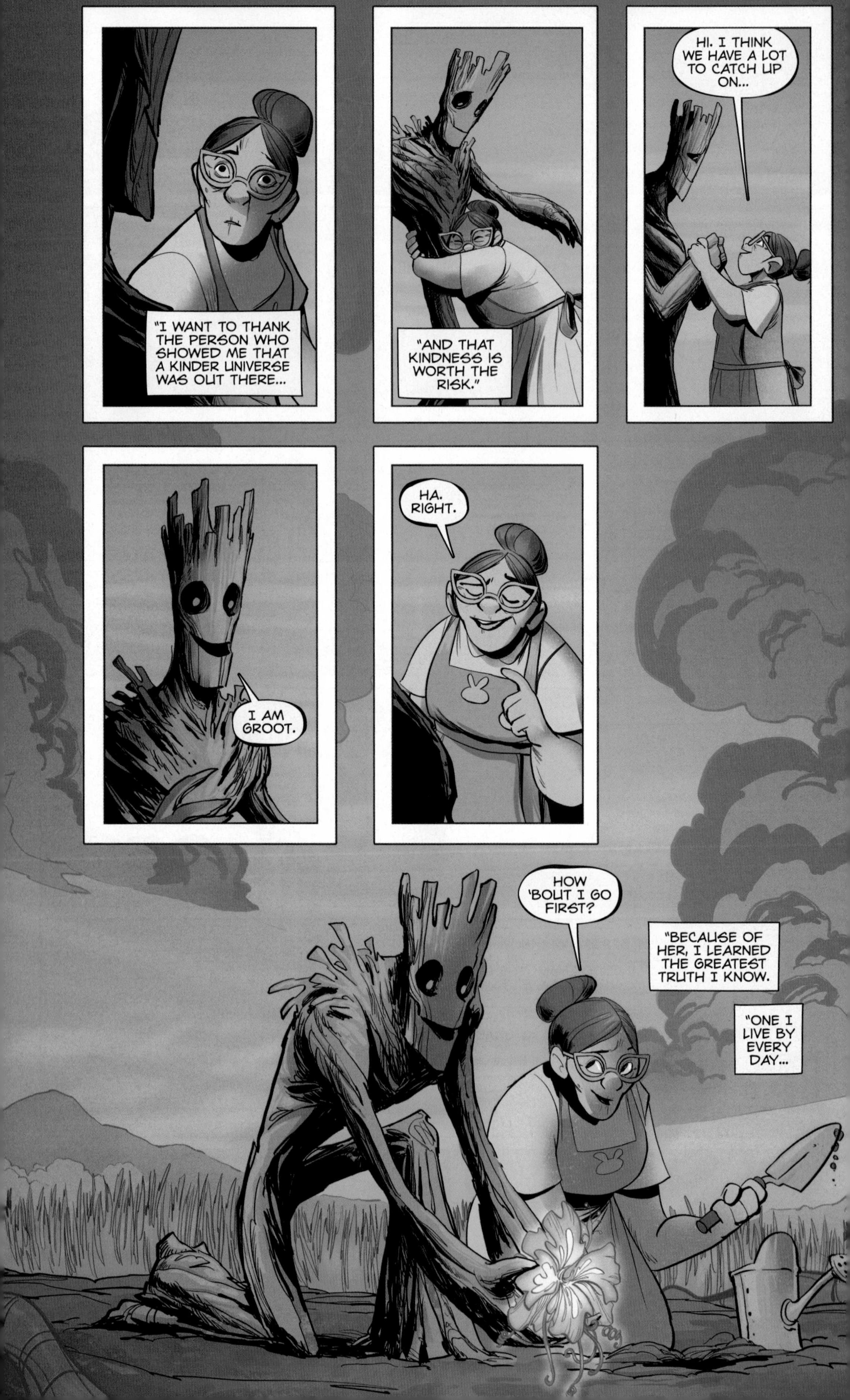
"I WANT TO THANK THE PERSON WHO SHOWED ME THAT A KINDER UNIVERSE WAS OUT THERE...
"AND THAT KINDNESS IS WORTH THE RISK."
HI. I THINK WE HAVE A LOT TO CATCH UP ON...
I AM GROOT.
HA. RIGHT.
HOW 'BOUT I GO FIRST?
"BECAUSE OF HER, I LEARNED THE GREATEST TRUTH I KNOW.
"ONE I LIVE BY EVERY DAY...

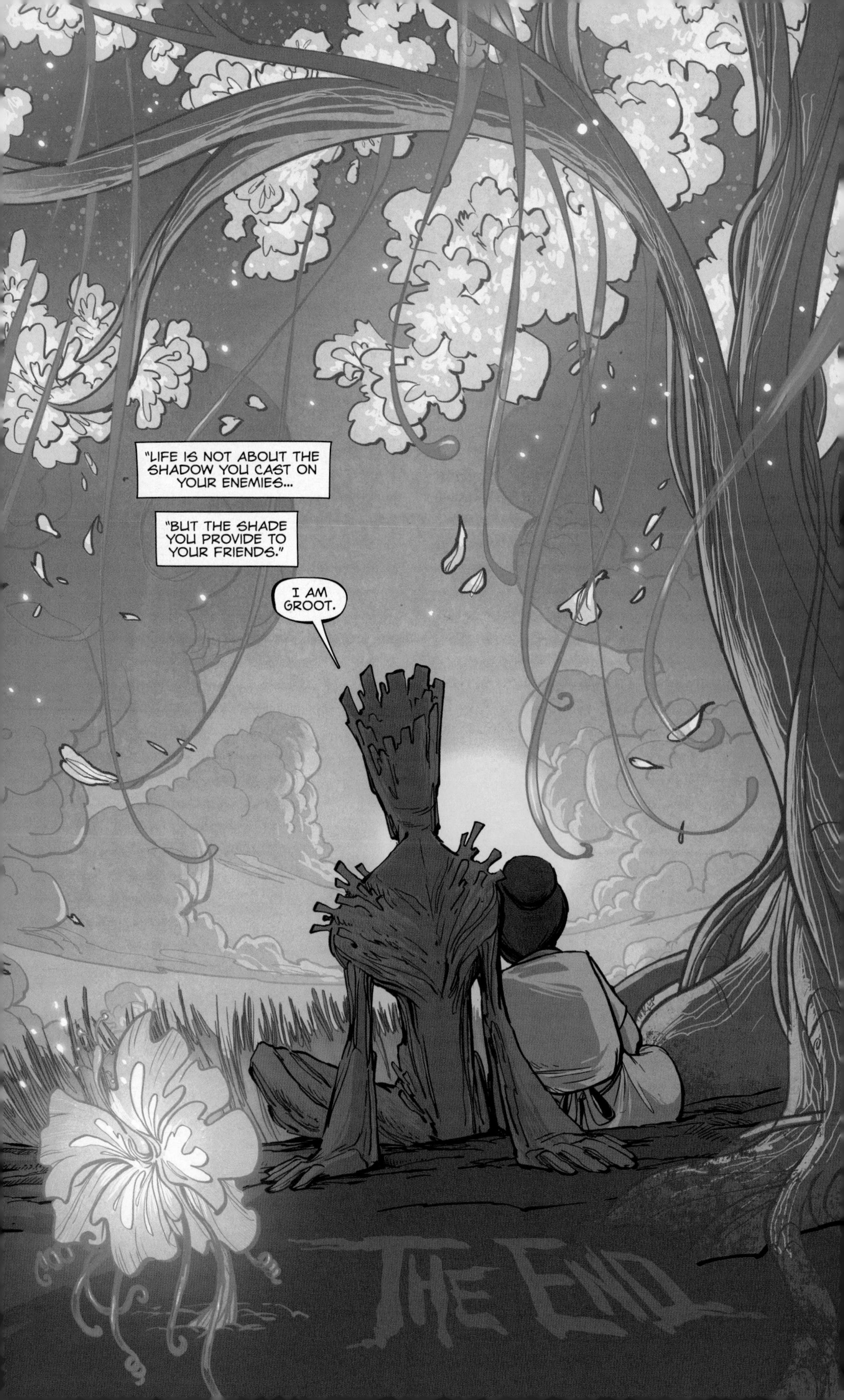
"LIFE IS NOT ABOUT THE SHADOW YOU CAST ON YOUR ENEMIES...
"BUT THE SHADE YOU PROVIDE TO YOUR FRIENDS."
I AM GROOT.
THE END

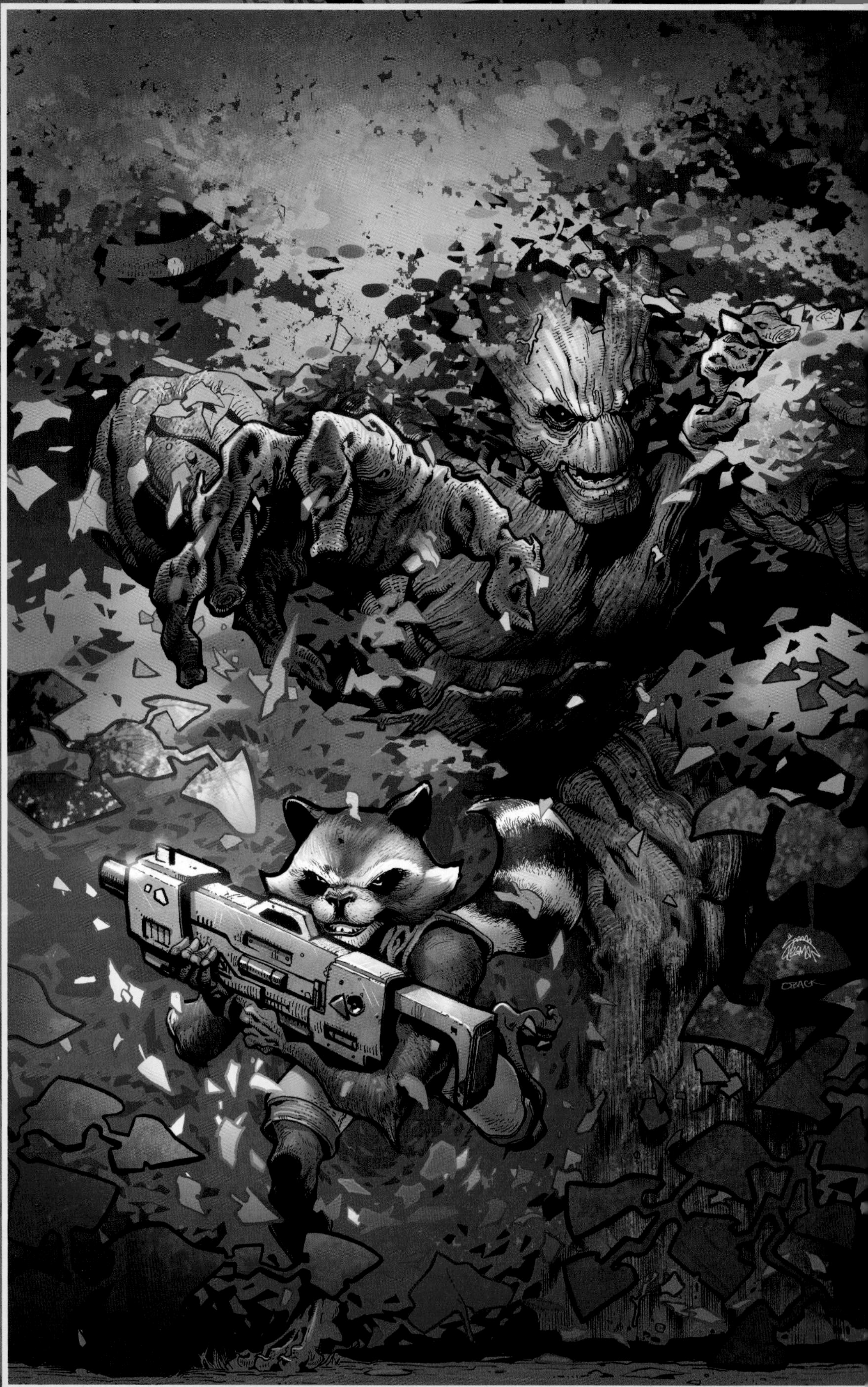

#1 Variant by RYAN STEGMAN & SONIA OBACK

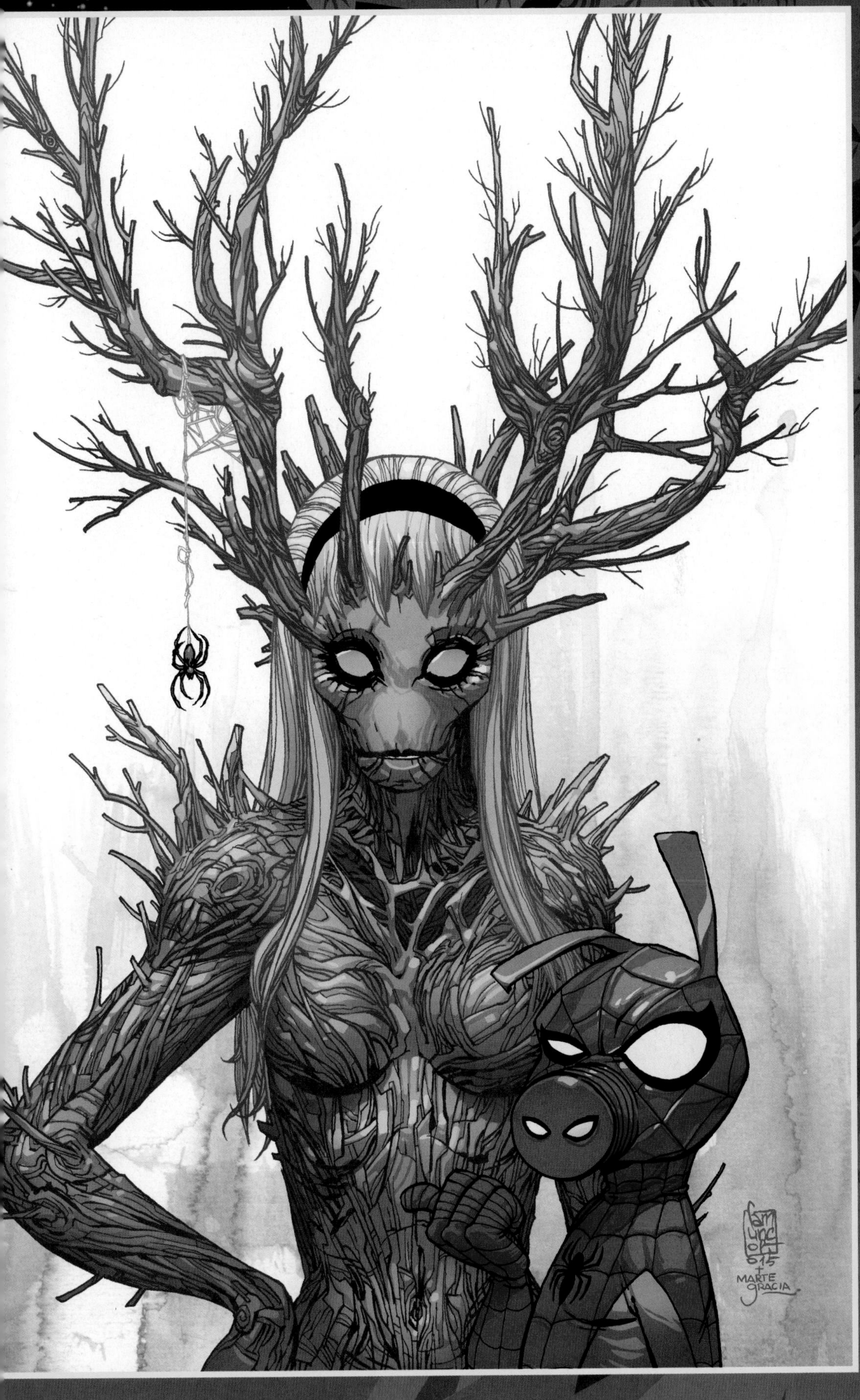
MARTE
GRACIA

#1 Gwoot Variant by **GIUSEPPE CAMUNCOLI & MARTE GRACIA**

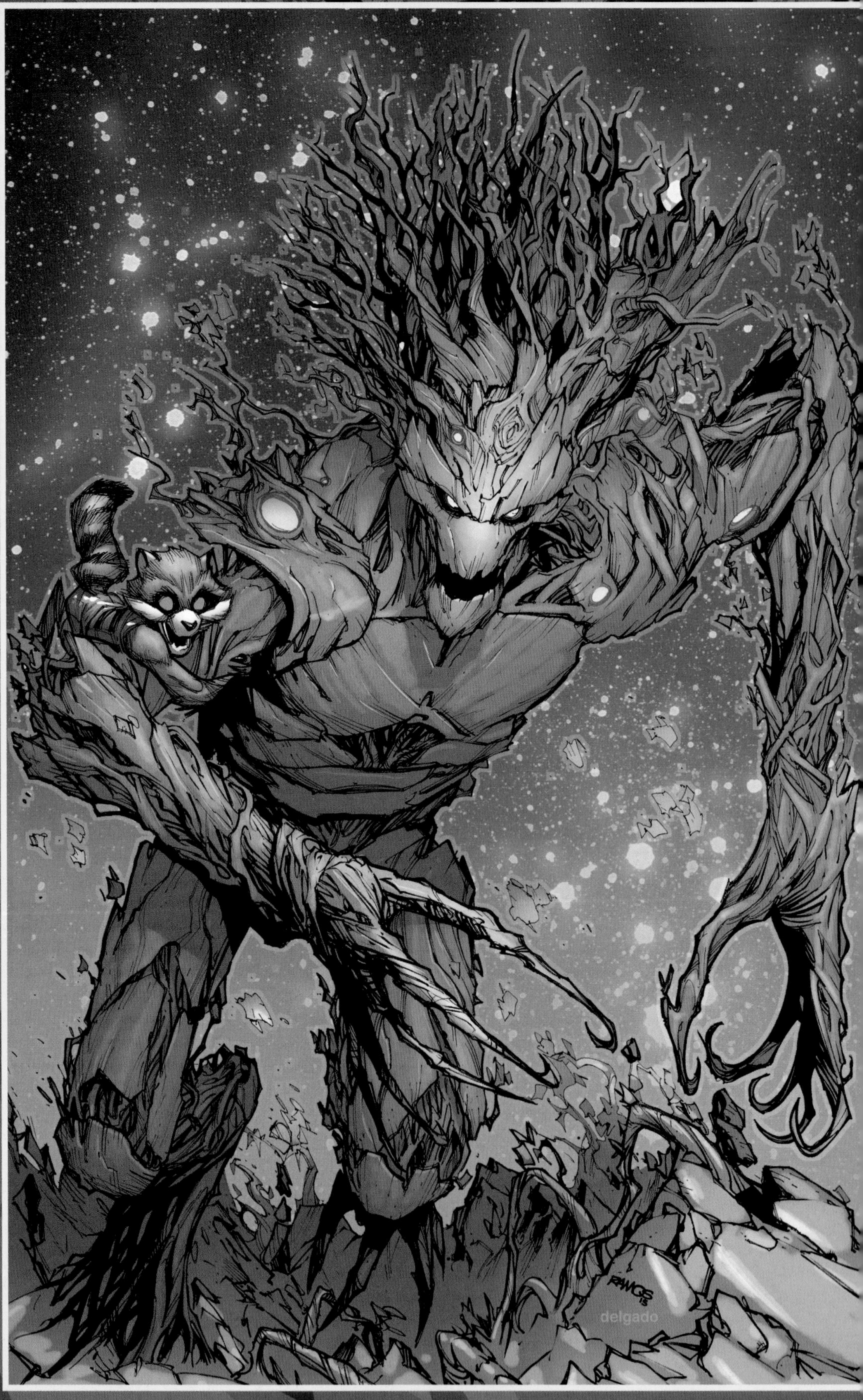
RAMOS 15
delgado

#1 Variant by **HUMBERTO RAMOS & EDGAR DELGADO**

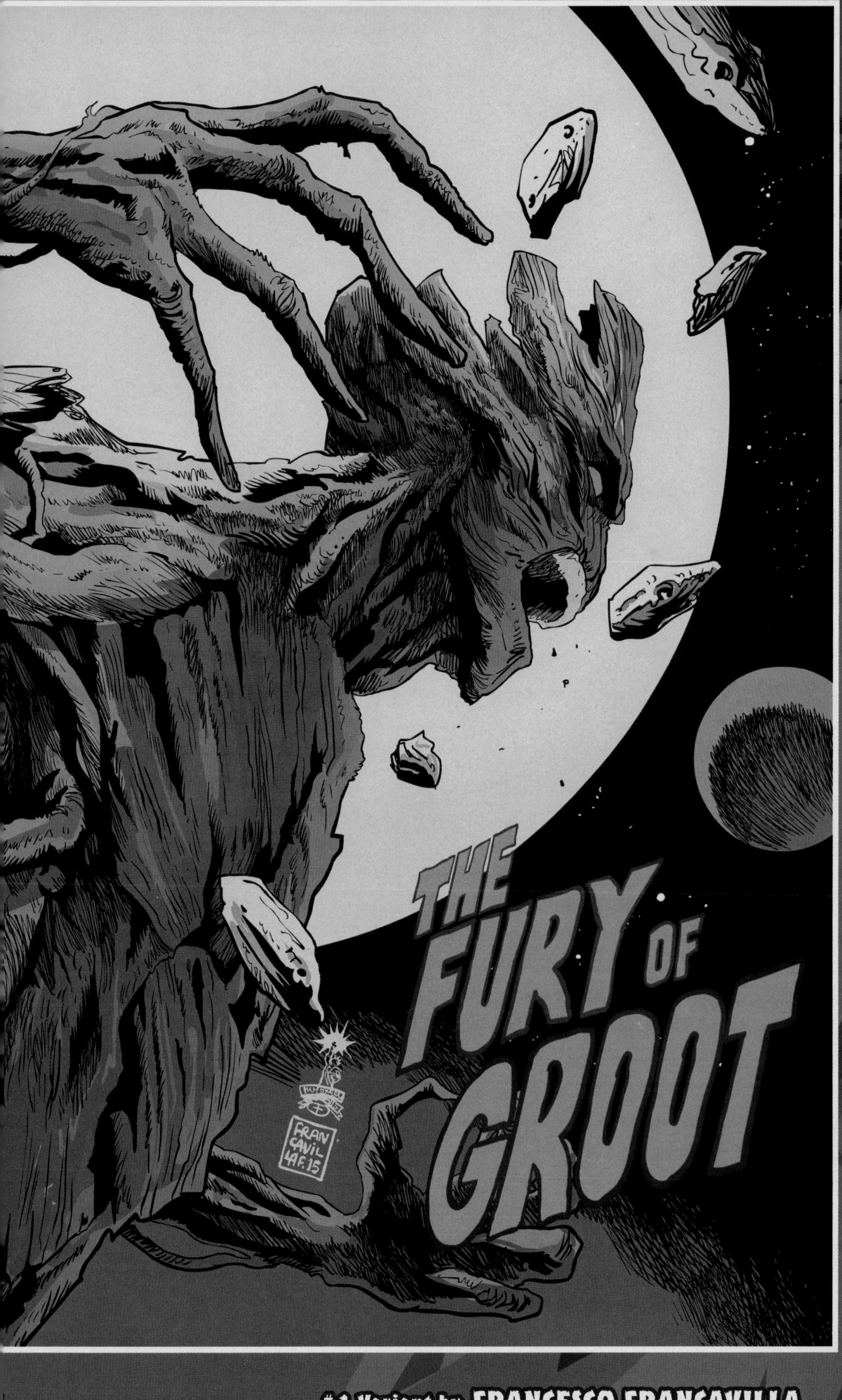
THE FURY OF GROOT
FRAN CAVIL LAF.15

#2 Variant by FRANCESCO FRANCAVILLA

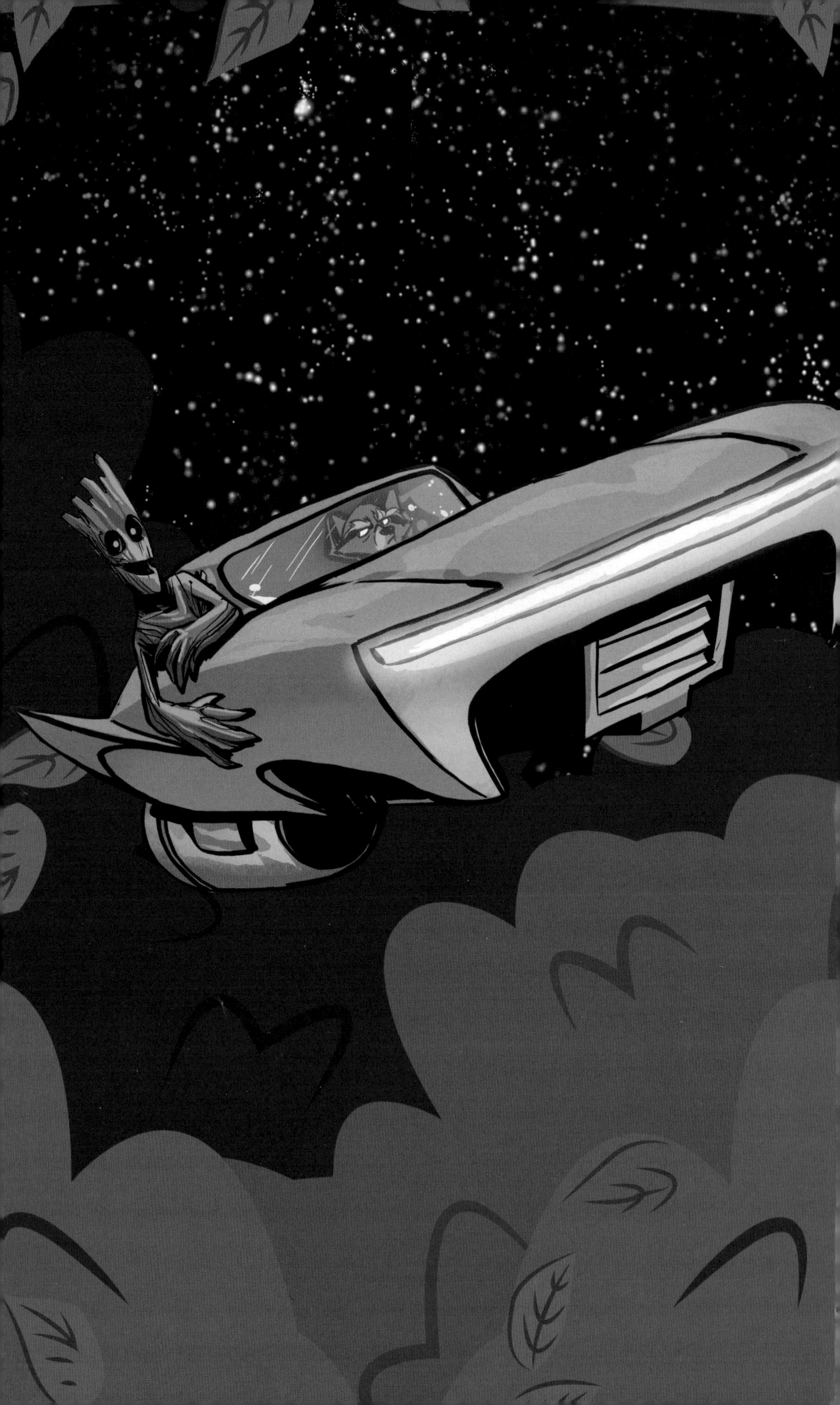